W9-DED-044

Rags and Riches

Keith E. Maskus, Peter M. Hooper, Edward E. Leamer, and J. David Richardson, Editors
Quiet Pioneering: Robert M. Stern and His International Economic Legacy

Bjarne S. Jensen and Kar-yiu Wong, Editors
Dynamics, Economic Growth, and International Trade

Kala Marathe Krishna and Ling Hui Tan
Rags and Riches: Implementing Apparel Quotas under the Multi-Fibre Arrangement

Rags and Riches

Implementing Apparel Quotas
under the Multi-Fibre Arrangement

Kala Marathe Krishna and Ling Hui Tan

Ann Arbor

THE UNIVERSITY OF MICHIGAN PRESS

Copyright © by the University of Michigan 1998
All rights reserved
Published in the United States of America by
The University of Michigan Press
Manufactured in the United States of America
⊖ Printed on acid-free paper

2001   2000   1999   1998   4   3   2   1

*A CIP catalog record for this book is available from
the British Library.*

Library of Congress Cataloging-in-Publication Data

Krishna, Kala.
    Rags and riches : implementing apparel quotas under
the Multi-fibre Arrangement / Kala Marathe Krishna and
Ling Hui Tan.
        p.   cm. — (Studies in international economics)
    Includes bibliographical references and index.
    ISBN 0-472-10934-0 (hardcover : alk. paper)
    1. Tariff on clothing.   2. Arrangement Regarding
International Trade in Textiles (1973)   3. Import
quotas.   4. Clothing trade.   I. Tan, Ling Hui.
II. Title.   III. Series.
HF2651.C635K75   1998
382'.456871—dc21   98-34301
                                                    CIP

Contents

Part IV.   Conclusion

Part V.   Appendices

Acknowledgments

The work reported here could not have been done without help and support from many sources.

We would like to express our gratitude to the World Bank, the National Science Foundation (Grant SBR-9320825), the Ford Foundation, and the Brookings Institution for research support.

At the World Bank, where the study was begun, Stan Fischer encouraged us to undertake our first big empirical project; Paul Mayo and Ron Duncan provided a first class research environment in the International Trade Division; Refik Erzan developed the initial project with us and was a valued coauthor; and Will Martin was a constant source of information and encouragement, as well as a highly regarded colleague and coauthor. Geoff Bannister contributed his independent work on Mexico to this volume.

We were very fortunate to have been assisted by many fine research assistants including: Monique Skruzny and Christopher Holmes at the World Bank; Jeff and Dave Chung at Harvard; Elaine McCormick Watt, Dan Gilligan and Kerstin Berglöf at the Fletcher School; Kishwar Ahmed at MIT; and Paul Jensen, Ataman Ozyildirim, and Cemile Yavas at Penn State. Stephanie Hubach edited the first draft of this book and vastly improved its readability.

We are also grateful to many people from various countries who generously provided us with information and shared their data with us, including James Anderson, Carl Hamilton, Paula Holmes, N. S. Kulkarni, S. S. Marathe, Peter Ngan, M. Pangestu, and Tom Prusa.

Kala Krishna would also like to thank her secretaries over the years: Ann Flack at Harvard; Mary Pyche at the Fletcher School; Teresa Benevento at MIT; and Sue Bryant at Penn State, all of whom were models of efficiency. Special thanks to Peter Angelos and Jennifer Wilkins for their superb desktop publishing skills.

Last, but not least, we are grateful to Vijay Krishna and Carlos Ramírez for their support throughout this project.

Kala Marathe Krishna
Ling Hui Tan

PART I
Introduction and Motivation

CHAPTER ONE

Overview

I. A Brief History of the MFA

The Multi–Fibre Arrangement (MFA) is among the most important non–tariff
trade barriers facing developing countries today. Established in order to achieve
the expansion of trade, the reduction of barriers to such trade, and the
progressive liberalization of world trade in textile products, while at the same
time ensuring the orderly and equitable development of this trade and avoidance
of disruptive effects in individual markets and on individual lines of production
in both importing and exporting countries,[1] it sanctions a structure of country–
and product–specific quotas on apparel and textiles exported by developing
countries to developed countries. These quotas are negotiated bilaterally
between the importing and exporting countries but are largely administered by
the exporting countries. Since the exporting countries control implementation
of the quotas, the presumption is that they also obtain the quota license rents
that ensue. However, it has been argued that, instead of furthering the economic
development of these developing countries, the MFA, by cutting off access to
their major export markets for textiles and apparel, effectively short–circuits
their industrialization process at a very early stage.

The MFA has its origins in the Voluntary Export Restraint (VER) on cotton
textile products that the United States negotiated with Japan in 1957. This VER
succeeded in curbing U.S. cotton good imports from Japan, but it led to a huge
increase in imports from new exporters, such as Hong Kong, Portugal, Egypt,
and India. In its quest for a more comprehensive solution to control cotton
imports, the United States initiated multilateral discussions, held under the
auspices of the General Agreement on Tariffs and Trade (GATT), which
eventually led to the Short Term Cotton Textile Arrangement (STA) in 1961.
The STA was in operation for one year; it was succeeded by the Long Term
Arrangement (LTA) on Cotton Textiles. The LTA was originally planned to be
effective for five years starting from 1962, but it was extended twice and lasted
until 1973. Although it worked well in restricting the supply of cotton textile
exports to the United States, the LTA indirectly contributed to an increase in
U.S. imports of textiles and apparel made of man–made fiber. As a result, the
United States sought to extend the LTA framework to cover wool and

---

1. GATT 1974, p. 6.

man–made fiber textile and apparel products; this led to the establishment of the MFA.

Despite being initially conceived as a temporary measure, the MFA has persisted for more than twenty years.[2] Since its inception in 1973, the MFA has been through five successive negotiations, with each round encompassing a wider range of products and countries. By the end of the second MFA round, the United States had succeeded in bringing more than 80 percent of its total imports of textile and apparel products under restraint by negotiating bilateral quotas with twenty supplying countries and agreements with consultative mechanisms with eleven other countries. Subsequent negotiations widened the country coverage to include many emerging suppliers such as Bangladesh and the Maldives. In the third MFA round, the United States also extended its fiber coverage to include silk blends and other vegetable fibers. The United States currently has over 140 individual textile and apparel categories under restraint, several of which are further divided into subcategories. There are presently some nine developed countries and 33 developing countries participating in the MFA.

The most recent round of trade talks—the Uruguay Round, concluded in 1994—included a plan for the eventual elimination of the MFA. The phaseout is based on 1990 import volumes and is to occur gradually in four stages over a ten year transitional period, with the adjustments heavily loaded toward the end of the period. Transitional safeguards will be permitted only on products not yet integrated into the GATT, and may include restricted and unrestricted products. The safeguards may be applied selectively on particular exporters, but only for a maximum of three years.

II. Purpose of This Book

The MFA has been widely studied and much attention has been devoted to its welfare consequences.[3] Yet in almost all this work, the tendency has been to take the simple static competitive model as the basis for empirical and policy analysis. Little effort has been made to look at whether this is the appropriate model to use in the given context, and what the implications of alternative assumptions might be. The assumption of competitive markets is usually defended on the grounds that there are a large number of producers in the textile and apparel market. However, several observers have noted that this assumption may not be accurate in many cases. For example, Goto 1989, p. 218 claims that

---

2. For a comprehensive account of the history and workings of the MFA, see Choi, Chung and Marian 1985, Keesing and Wolf 1980, and Hamilton 1990.

3. See, for example, Hamilton 1990 which analyzes the effects of the MFA and its proposed reforms from a variety of viewpoints.

"...[a]lthough governments of exporting countries under the MFA often allocate export licenses in a manner that helps exporters capture the quota rent, many of these exporters face large importing enterprises that can negotiate prices that capture some of the rent for themselves," and Khanna 1991, p.171 concludes from his survey of 35 textile and apparel exporting firms in India that "...for consignments where an exporter has to buy quotas, the importer bears about half the burden of the quota prices with the remainder being borne by the exporter whose profitability goes down." Such considerations are important for policy purposes as the welfare consequences of the MFA and its reform are affected by such variations in the underlying models.

Another largely neglected area concerns the actual implementation of the MFA quotas. Although each exporting country has a different set of rules governing the allocation and utilization of quota licenses, there are surprisingly few investigations into what these differences in quota administration policies imply for the size and distribution of quota rents. While descriptions exist of quota allocation schemes in different exporting countries,[4] theoretical analyses of these schemes and empirical studies of their outcomes are much harder to come by.

This book is an attempt—albeit preliminary—to fill this gap in the research. It has two broad objectives:

1. To look into the possibility that exporting countries may be receiving less quota rent than suggested by the standard competitive model by considering alternative theoretical setups, and undertaking some simple econometric tests.
2. To look more closely at the various quota implementation rules and their implications by describing how the details of quota implementation differ across countries, modeling some aspects of implementation, and attempting to relate some of the results to actual data.

Of course, there are considerable theoretical and empirical problems in meeting these objectives perfectly, but these questions are important enough to warrant a pragmatic approach. Before continuing, therefore, a few words of caution are in order regarding the data used in this book.

III. Data Issues

Data collection was one of the major challenges faced in this endeavor. Compatible cross–country data were extremely difficult to obtain as the exporting and importing countries employed different (and frequently changing)

---

4. See, for example, Morkre 1979 on Hong Kong, Hamilton 1984 on the ASEAN countries, and Trela and Whalley 1995 on seventeen countries including other Asian as well as Latin American and Caribbean countries.

methods of data classification, and even the MFA categories were not standardized for all the importing countries. For these reasons, the focus remained restricted to MFA exports to the United States, and a concordance for this trade was developed. A selected number of exporters—including Hong Kong, Korea, Indonesia, India, and Mexico—were chosen to serve as case studies.

The data from these exporting countries are classified according to MFA categories, but U.S. production data are indexed by Standard Index Classification (SIC) codes. In order to achieve some degree of comparability between the two sources, the data were aggregated into larger apparel groups. Ten such apparel groups were created:

1. dresses
2. skirts
3. playsuits
4. sweaters
5. trousers
6. men's coats
7. women's coats
8. knit shirts
9. woven shirts
10. underwear.

These groups are used throughout the book whenever reference is made to the data.

IV. Outline of the Book

Chapter Two provides further motivation for this book by presenting some suggestive evidence from several MFA-restricted exporting countries as well as Italy, a major non-restricted textile and clothing exporter. According to the predictions of the standard competitive model, the export price of clothing for these countries (inclusive of transport costs, duties, and the quota license price, if applicable) should be roughly correlated with the ex-factory price of comparable domestically-produced goods in the importing country. However, wide variations are found in price correlations between these exporting countries and the United States (the importing country). Several explanations are considered for this observation; they include differences in market structure which could affect the degree of rent sharing between the exporting countries and the U.S. importers, and differences in quota implementation rules which could have an impact on export prices as well as influencing market structure and rent sharing.

The first part of the book deals with rent sharing:

1. Chapter Three discusses the implications of imperfectly competitive market structures for the size and distribution of quota rent. It analyzes the consequences of market power on the sellers' side, and shows how this can lead to what is termed rent appropriation, that is, when the seller manipulates the product price in order to appropriate some or all of the potential quota rent. It also considers the effect of market power on the buyers' side, and how this can lead to what is termed rent sharing, that is, when the buyer is able to bargain a portion of the quota rent away from the seller.
2. Chapters Four through Six test for the existence of rent sharing using data from Hong Kong, Korea, and Mexico respectively.

The second part of the book turns its attention to quota implementation rules and their implications:

1. Chapter Seven provides further motivation for the importance of this issue. Descriptions of how MFA quotas are implemented in practice in six countries—Hong Kong, Korea, Indonesia, India, Pakistan, and Bangladesh—are put together in an appendix at the end of the book.
2. Chapters Eight through Twelve pick up on certain aspects of quota implementation adopted by these countries and analyze their implications on quota license prices and welfare in general. Some of these theoretical insights are then applied to actual license market data from Korea and Indonesia. Chapter Eight analyzes the difference between transferable and nontransferable quota licenses; Chapter Nine discusses the effect of introducing free quota (i.e., licenses that are allocated free of charge on a first-come-first-served basis); and Chapter Ten considers possible rationales for, and implications of, subdividing quota beyond that required by the MFA. Chapter Eleven contains some observations on how certain aspects of Korea's quota allocation system are reflected in patterns in quota holdings and transfers. Chapter Twelve does the same for Indonesia, using transactions-level data from license trading on the stock exchange to check for the existence of trading clubs which discriminate against new entrants.
3. Chapter Thirteen focuses on the idea that quota licenses have to be used within a certain period—usually twelve months—and develops a few simple models to trace the behavior of license prices over the course of this period. Chapter Fourteen complements this analysis by estimating a dynamic model of license price paths using monthly data from Hong Kong. Chapter Fifteen compares Indonesian license price data against

those imputed from Hong Kong license prices by means of a common procedure; the imputed prices are found to be overestimates, suggesting that there could be large differences in the efficiency of the quota allocation mechanisms used in the two countries.

4. The final chapter, Chapter Sixteen, concludes with a discussion of the lessons that can be drawn from the quota implementation experiences analyzed in this book and the very rich research possibilities that remain in this area.

V. Beyond the MFA

Is this book of interest for historians only, given that the MFA is in the stage of being phased out? Definitely not! The MFA is a rich source of natural experiments in policy implementation, with a wealth of issues to model and understand. The models developed in order to study aspects of the MFA have much wider appeal and links beyond the area of international trade. For example, the analysis in Chapter Nine of how free quota might be rationed is in some way analogous to the Harris-Todaro model of migration. The topic of Chapters Thirteen and Fourteen—dynamic license prices—is related to the literature on depletable or nonrenewable but perishable resources, as well as to the option pricing literature: the components of the price of such products and the implications of arbitrage are discussed, and an empirically testable model is devised and implemented.

Although this book seems to be rather narrow in its focus, its lessons are far more universal. A running theme of this book is that implementation practices matter a great deal. While the MFA outlined a set of country pair and product specific quota levels, the details of their implementation were left up to the individual exporter. As long as these quota levels were not exceeded, the importing country took no actions to restrict imports. Since the allocation of the quota licenses was also left in their hands, it was possible for exporting countries to retain any rents that might exist in domestic hands by simply allocating licenses to domestic agents. Of course, countries took many different routes in implementing their quotas. They also had very different experiences in exporting their products.

A good illustration of how implementation rules may lead to unexpected consequences is found in the practice, in some MFA-exporting countries, of allocating quota licenses free of charge to exporters who have proof of an order from an importing agent. The rationale for implementing this free quota is to put new exporting firms on a more equal footing with established firms who are usually allocated the lion's share of the quota on the basis of their historical performance. However, the introduction of this scheme has the little-recognized side effect of altering the balance of power between the exporting country and the importers: by tying the allocation of free quota to proofs of orders, the importer becomes critical to obtaining the quota, which gives him or her the opportunity to bargain for, and receive, part or all of the associated quota rent. Furthermore, as was the case in India, established firms were often able to obtain free quota for themselves by creating paper firms; the procedures established to plug this loophole resulted in extremely complicated procedures in India, with the consequent red tape, bureaucracy, and rent seeking which ended up hindering rather than helping Indian exports under the MFA.

Another illustration of an implementation scheme which backfired comes from Egypt, where attempts to raise the unit value of lint cotton exports by imposing a minimum export price led to a substantial loss of market share to competing exporting countries that were able to undercut the minimum price. When the minimum export price was replaced by an indicative price in 1997, Egypt's export orders rebounded.[5] Examples such as these illustrate the importance of analyzing the details of policy implementation and the dangers inherent in micromanagement of policy. Although the examples in this book are drawn from the MFA, they could easily apply to other attempts to regulate markets.

Consider, for example, efforts to control pollution through the issuance of pollution permits. One way is to control emissions on a firm-by-firm basis, with specific controls for each firm. Another alternative is to set a total level of emissions and to allocate or sell transferable pollution permits to the users; this would allow firms which find it costliest to adjust their emissions to buy permits from those who find it less costly to reduce pollution. The two implementation schemes clearly have different results with respect to the amount of revenue earned from the pollution permits, the incentives for entry and for investment in new capacity in the final goods market, and the choice of appropriate technology for pollution reduction.[6] The analysis of transferable versus nontransferable licenses in Chapter Eight provides a useful starting point for analyzing these issues; it shows that transferable permits are more efficient, but may raise less revenue than nontransferable permits under certain circumstances.

Another issue which is likely to become increasingly important in the future is the control of immigration by use of immigration permits. Such permits are currently being proposed by several oil-rich Gulf countries, where expatriate workers account for up to eighty percent of the labor force. At present, work permits in these countries are usually given out to foreigners on a case-by-case basis through a complex system of government rules and patronage that varies

---

5. See "Developments," Fall 1997, a quarterly newsletter of Development Alternatives Inc., Bethesda, MD.

6. See Stavins 1997 and Krishna and Ozyildirim 1998 for more on this issue.

by host country. The work permits are often employer- and/or job-specific; even when transfers occur, they are the result of bargains struck between employers and workers which are far from transparent and which need not be efficient. Many of the issues underlying the implementation of work permits and their allocation have parallels with those underlying the implementation of MFA quota licenses and their allocation discussed in this book. Much of the apparatus developed in this book will be useful in analyses of how to reform the work permit system by allowing permits to be traded, of the effect of selling such permits on the quality of the immigrants (when other countries do not sell their immigration permits and when they do), and of rent extraction from immigration.

Even the analysis of more mundane issues, such as how to maximize revenue from ticket sales for a concert, benefits from some of the models found in this book. For example, would one raise more revenue by prohibiting the re-selling of tickets or not? One might speculate that the tickets would be more valuable if they were less restrictive, that is, if they were transferable, but Chapter Eight shows that if buyers are ex ante similar enough, then it is better to make the tickets nontransferable.

Implementation is critical in almost every branch of policy making, not just in the design of permits or tickets. Market access requirements (MARs), such as those successfully lobbied for by the U.S. semiconductor industry in the 1980s to increase their market share in Japan, are now fast becoming a staple in the U.S. government's arsenal of trade policy instruments. Yet virtually no attention is being given to the mechanism by which such MARs should be carried out. In fact, there are a number of ways to implement an MAR: the importing country government could set minimum physical requirements on the use of imported intermediate goods, for example; in some cases, the importing country government could signal its commitment to the market share target by backing it with the promise of a subsidy or the threat of a tax while in other cases, the exporting country government could enforce the target by using the threat of sanctions in a linked market. With some implementation schemes the outcome is extremely anticompetitive, while under others it could actually be procompetitive. For example, if the market share target is made on an intermediate good (such as auto parts) and the exporting country government enforces it by threatening retaliation in a linked market, such as the final good market (cars) then such targets can be self-enforcing as well as procompetitive in certain cases.[7] On the other hand, if the market share target is enforced by means of a subsidy on the exporting firm or a tax on the importing firm, this could result in strategic behavior on the part of the firms involved, and create

---

7. See Krishna and Morgan 1996.

powerful incentives for anticompetitive behavior;[8] the strategic forces in this context are similar to those used in analyzing rent sharing in Chapter Three.

Another area in which market structure and particulars of implementation are of critical importance is in the definition of rules of origin within free trade agreements (FTAs). Under an FTA, tariffs are eliminated for trade between member countries but each member country is allowed to impose its own external tariffs on non-FTA imports. Rules of origin, which specify certain content requirements needed to treat a good as originating from the FTA, are thus an essential component of FTAs; their purpose is to prevent non-FTA goods from entering the FTA through the member country with the lowest external tariff. However, rules of origin can be defined in a variety of different ways, such as requirements in terms of domestic content or requirements that the product has been substantially transformed. This area of implementation is very poorly understood, yet different ways of specifying rules of origin can lead to different trade patterns and investment flows.[9]

Thus, it is easy to make the case that implementation of rules is crucial in practically every policy area. Although this book documents only examples under the MFA, the models presented here point to several significant implementation issues that have a wider applicability beyond the MFA, and serve as useful references for the analysis of many important aspects of policy implementation in international trade as well as in other areas of economics.

---

8. See Krishna, Roy and Thursby 1997.
9. See Krishna and Krueger 1995.

CHAPTER TWO

Validity of the Standard Competitive Model: Suggestive Evidence from Eight Countries[1]

I. Introduction

This chapter presents correlations between the prices of U.S.–produced apparel and imported apparel from several countries as a first step toward assessing the validity of the standard competitive model for the MFA market.

The basic model is one with competition in all the relevant markets. Both the demand and supply sides of the product market are assumed to be competitive. In addition, license holders act competitively and are willing and able to sell licenses at the price that clears the license market. This model is illustrated diagramatically in Figure 2.1, which is the standard textbook depiction. In Figure 2.1, RD represents residual demand from the importing country (call this the United States)—RD is given by subtracting U.S. supply and supply from sources other

Figure 2.1. License Price Determination in a Competitive Model

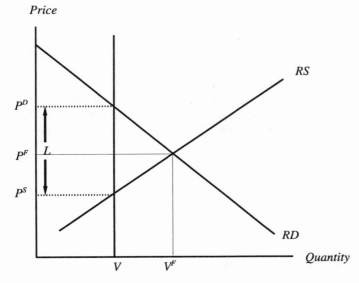

1. This chapter is based on Krishna and Tan 1997b.

than the exporting country of concern from total demand in the United States. RS depicts the residual supply from the exporting country—this is supply from that country less demand from all sources other than the United States. The intersection of the two gives the world price in the absence of quotas, P^F, and the level of imports from the exporting country to the United States, V^F.

If a quota is set allowing only V units to be imported, the home price at which this level of imports is demanded, P^D, exceeds the world price at which it is supplied, P^S. If the license market is competitive, then the license price, L, should equal the difference between P^D and P^S. Thus, if the quota licenses are allocated to agents in the exporting country, then all the quota rents will be retained in the exporting country if P^S+L (the adjusted export price) equals P^D. On the other hand, if the actual license price does not reflect the potential license price because, say, some part of the quota rent is shared with the importers (who are often large players in the market), then the above equality need not hold.

II. The Data

The quantity and value of apparel produced in the United States were obtained from Current Industrial Reports published by the U.S. Department of Commerce, Bureau of the Census. The statistics in these publication are based on surveys of all known manufacturers and jobbers (except the very small firms excluded from the scope of the survey) and represent total U.S. production of most major garments.[2] All domestic production is assumed to be consumed domestically—domestic production is assumed to be equal to sales to the home market. This is not unreasonable since the proportion of domestic apparel production exported overseas is relatively small (less than 10 percent in general).

The quantity of MFA apparel exports to the United States originating from selected countries, as well as their quota utilization ratios, was obtained from *Expired Performance Reports* issued by the U.S. Department of Commerce, Office of Textiles and Apparel. The MFA exporters used in this chapter were:

1. Hong Kong
2. Korea
3. Indonesia
4. India

---

2. In 1988, a number of new establishments were added to the survey. Most of these establishments began operating after the 1982 Census. The Bureau made no attempt to determine when they began operating or to obtain prior years' data. Therefore the 1988 data may not be strictly comparable to previous years.

5. Pakistan
6. Bangladesh

The c.i.f. value of U.S. apparel imports from these countries was obtained from U.S. IA–245 Import Trade tapes kindly provided by Tom Prusa. For comparison purposes, the value of U.S. imports from Italy, an unrestricted country, was also collected. The c.i.f. value of U.S. imports from these countries represents the adjusted price of MFA exports to the United States from these countries, inclusive of the license price, transport costs, and U.S. import duty.

Data on U.S. apparel production is classified according to Standard Industrial Classification (SIC) codes. Imports of restrained textiles and apparel, however, are classified according to the MFA categories of the United States, which in turn are groupings of seven–digit Tariff Schedule of the United States (TSUSA) categories. Concordance tables are available which link the SIC codes with the TSUSA classification but there is no straightforward mapping between the SIC and MFA classification systems. The MFA categories classify the different types of apparel by fabric type e.g., cotton, wool and man–made fiber. The SIC categories, on the other hand, classify apparel as men's, boys', women's/misses'/juniors' and girls'/children's/infants, with further subdivisions according to fabric type. Quantity figures are sometimes printed for certain fabric–type subdivisions, but value figures are not available. Moreover, the coverage of the individual SIC categories has changed many times over the years considered (1981–1988).

Due to these complications, the data had to be rearranged into new (larger) groups comprising several SIC and MFA categories, such that there was minimal overlap between the categories across groups. Ten such groups were defined:

1. dresses
2. skirts
3. playsuits
4. sweaters
5. trousers
6. men's coats
7. women's coats
8. woven shirts
9. knit shirts
10. underwear

As an intermediate step to keep the U.S. production data consistent over the eight years, SIC categories of similar items were assembled by:

1. men's/boys' outerwear
2. women's/girls'/infants' outerwear

3. men's/boys' nightwear and underwear
4. women's/girls'/infants' nightwear and underwear

The domestic price of each of the ten apparel groups was computed as a quantity–weighted average of the unit values of the production groupings which make up the group.[3] Similarly, the adjusted export price of each apparel group was taken to be a quantity–weighted average of the unit values of the MFA categories which make up the group. The quota utilization ratio for each apparel group was calculated as a quota–weighted average of the utilization ratios of the component MFA categories.[4]

The trade data used in this study exclude the MFA 800 series (silk blends or non–cotton vegetable fibers), which was first introduced in 1986. This may introduce some inconsistency in the data set since the U.S. production data are classified according to type of apparel rather than material. For example, for Group 1 (dresses), the U.S. price and U.S. sales figures may partly reflect prices and sales of silk dresses but the import prices and quantities will not. However, a quick glance at U.S. production figures for which some information is available on fabric breakdown indicates that this should not pose a serious problem.[5] Also, note that MFA category 440 was not under quota for any of the eight years considered. In the earlier years, there were also several other categories that were not under quota. Such categories were not used in computing the apparel group license utilization ratios.

---

3. The reason for quantity weights is as follows. Each apparel group i consists of one or more production grouping g, g=1,...,n. Let P_i denote the unit price of apparel group i, P_{ig} the unit price of production grouping g of apparel group i and Q_{ig} the quantity produced of production grouping g of apparel group i. Then: P_i = (Value of Imports)$_i$/(Quantity of Imports)$_i$ = $\Sigma_g [P_{ig} Q_{ig}/\Sigma_g Q_{ig}]$ = $\Sigma_g [P_{ig}(Q_{ig}/\Sigma_g Q_{ig})]$.

4. Each apparel group i consists of a few MFA categories, j. Quantity weights were used to compute the adjusted export price for an apparel group from the adjusted export prices of its component MFA categories for the same reason explained in the previous footnote. Similarly, if we let $UTIL_i$ be the utilization ratio for apparel group i, $\Sigma_j QUOTA_{ij}$ be the total quota on apparel group i, $UTIL_{ij}$ be the utilization ratio for MFA category j of apparel group i and $QUOTA_{ij}$ be the quota on MFA category j of apparel group i, then quota weights are used to compute $UTIL_i$ because:

$$UTIL_i = (Quantity\ of\ Imports)_i/(Total\ Quota)_i = \Sigma_j [UTIL_{ij} QUOTA_{ij}/\Sigma_j QUOTA_{ij}]$$
$$= \Sigma_j [UTIL_{ij}(QUOTA_{ij}/\Sigma_j QUOTA_{ij})].$$

5. Consider, for example, two items most likely to be made of silk: women's dresses and slips. In 1985 and 1986, dresses made of material other than cotton, wool or man–made fibers accounted for only about 4 percent of the total quantity of women's, misses' and juniors' dresses produced. The fraction of women's full–length and half–length slips produced in the US, made of material other than cotton, wool, or man–made fibers was negligible.

III. Price Correlations

Figures 2.2–2.8 plot the adjusted export price—inclusive of the license price, transport costs, and U.S. import duty—for the seven supplying countries against the U.S. price, across ten apparel groups and eight years. The adjusted export price is a measure of (P^S+L) and the U.S. price is a measure of P^D in Figure 2.1.

Observe the large differences in patterns. For Hong Kong and Korea, two of the world's most established apparel exporters, the points lie roughly on the forty-five degree line. In the case of Italy, the points lie above the diagonal, an observation which is consistent with the country's reputation as a high fashion exporter. For the remaining countries, there is a rough upward slope, but the points lie generally below the diagonal.

Table 2.1 is the matrix of correlation coefficients. All of these are positive, implying that all the prices tend to move in the same direction. However, the correlation of the adjusted export price with the U.S. price is very different across countries: it is highest for Italy, the unrestrained country, followed by Korea and Hong Kong; in between is Indonesia, with Pakistan, India, and Bangladesh at the bottom.

What could be behind these large differences in price correlations? Possible explanations for this statistical result include the following:

FIGURE 2.2. U.S. Prices and Adjusted Hong Kong Export Prices

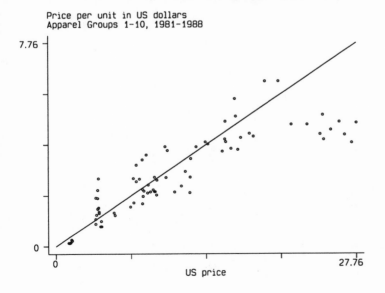

TABLE 2.1. Correlation Coefficients

	U.S. Price	Adjusted Hong Kong Price	Adjusted Korean Price	Adjusted Indian Price	Adjusted Indonesian Price	Adjusted Pakistan Price	Adjusted Bangladesh Price	Adjusted Italian Price
U. S. Price	1.0000							
Adjusted Hong Kong Price	0.8657	1.0000						
Adjusted Korean Price	0.8795	0.9359	1.0000					
Adjusted Indian Price	0.5454	0.6554	0.6017	1.0000				
Adjusted Indonesian Price	0.7911	0.7173	0.7014	0.5966	1.0000			
Adjusted Pakistan Price	0.6403	0.7137	0.6313	0.6940	0.6751	1.0000		
Adjusted Bangladesh Price	0.4118	0.3746	0.3107	0.2515	0.6026	0.3944	1.0000	
Adjusted Italian Price	0.9102	0.7107	0.7614	0.4371	0.8253	0.5695	0.4629	1.0000

1. *These apparel exports are not close substitutes for domestically produced apparel.* This would be consistent with the usual perception that countries in the Indian subcontinent (the prices of whose apparel exports appear to be more insulated from the prices of U.S.–made apparel, as evidenced by the low correlation coefficients) produce poorer quality goods which do not compete with those made in the United States. If this explanation is correct, then one should observe the adjusted export prices of these three countries moving together. In other words, their price correlations should be high. Furthermore, one would expect the correlation between their proces to be higher than the correlation with the U.S. price. Table 2.1 shows that the correlation between the adjusted prices of Indian exports and Pakistani exports is only 0.6940, although it is slightly higher than the correlation that either of these prices have with the U.S. price. The correlation between the adjusted prices of Bangladesh exports and Indian exports is lower than the correlation of either of these export prices with the U.S. price. The same is true for the adjusted prices of Bangladesh exports and Pakistani exports. Therefore, quality differences cannot fully explain the patterns observed in the data.

FIGURE 2.3. U.S. Prices and Adjusted Korean Export Prices

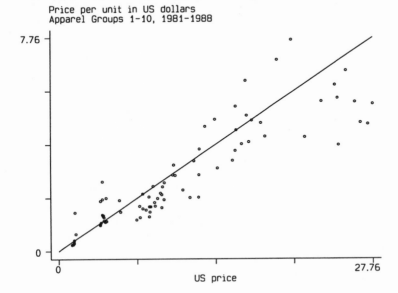

Price per unit in US dollars
Apparel Groups 1-10, 1981-1988

US price

2. *These countries have a large bureaucracy which creates many hidden costs for exporters.* This is particularly true in the case of India, Pakistan and Bangladesh. However, such costs should simply reduce the license price, leaving the adjusted export price unaffected. Thus, this explanation does not seem entirely satisfactory either.

3. *Uncertainty in exporting arising from the bureaucratic jungle, together with other obstacles associated with production in developing countries, make products from these countries relatively uncompetitive.* For example, one can think of these uncertainties as imposing costs on the importers, such as the inconvenience of not always being guaranteed delivery dates and quantities in advance, as a result of which, they may be willing to pay less for exports from these countries. However, note that both a low and high correlation coefficient are perfectly consistent with differences in price which are fixed in nature, so this is not an entirely satisfactory reason either, for the failure of prices to move together.

4. *MFA quota rents are not being captured by the exporters.* If the quota rents were in fact entirely appropriated by the importers, then the adjusted export price could actually track cost conditions in the exporting country rather than the U.S. price. The problem with testing this hypothesis is the difficulty in disentangling cost effects from quality effects: to the extent that higher costs are likely to make countries move

FIGURE 2.4. U.S. Prices and Adjusted Indonesian Export Prices

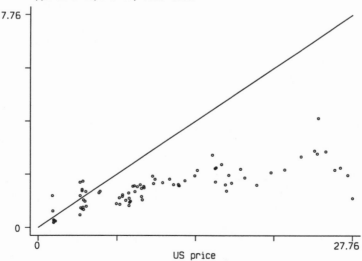

Price per unit in US dollars
Apparel Groups 1-10, 1981-1988

into the higher quality end of the product market—an empirical regularity few will dispute—export prices will tend to rise with costs. In the absence of more disaggregated data, quality decompositions are not possible using the standard index procedures.

5. *Quota allocation rules in these countries could be responsible for their adjusted export prices falling short of the U.S. price.* This could erode the bargaining power of these firms vis-à-vis their U.S. buyers. During price negotiations between the importers and exporters, it is common practice for the buyer to ask whether the supplier had to pay for his or her quota—if not, the offered price usually would not include the license price. As a result, the quota rents could end up in the pockets of the importers. This is particularly likely to be true since markets for quota licenses are not well established—and sometimes illegal—in these countries, and property rights are weak. Furthermore, many countries impose penalties for non-utilization of licenses, in the form of reductions in future allocations. This could reduce the price at which exporters are willing to sell their apparel, particularly toward the end of the quota year. Several countries also place restrictions on the transferability of the quota licenses. Given the maze of regulations for different types of quotas in each country, it is difficult to make any predictions in this regard.

FIGURE 2.5. U.S. Prices and Adjusted Indian Export Prices

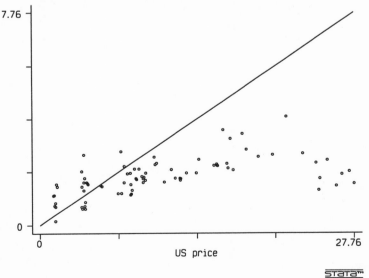

Price per unit in US dollars
Apparel Groups 1-10, 1981-1988

In summary, whether the cause be rent sharing, or costs to importers which make the exported product less competitive, the idea that these exporting countries are somehow receiving less rents out of the MFA than the static model might suggest cannot be dismissed.

IV. Patterns of Quota Utilization

The pattern of quota utilization in the exporting countries may be examined to see if it can assist in interpreting the price correlations that have been observed. Table 2.2 shows changes in the degree of quota utilization and the number of categories under quota over time.

A. Hong Kong, Korea, and Indonesia

Hong Kong and Korea were early exporters to the United States and exhibit high quota utilization rates throughout the sample period of 1981-88. Also, the number of apparel categories subject to quota in these countries increased over the period, from around twenty in 1981-82, to around 30 in the latter half of the decade. The same pattern is also apparent for Indonesia, which consistently recorded utilizations rates of more than 90 percent (with the exception of 1985),

Figure 2.6. U.S. Prices and Adjusted Pakistan Export Prices

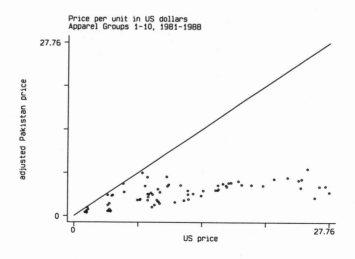

and which experienced a substantial increase in the number of products brought under restraint. Table 2.3A shows the correlations between the adjusted export prices and the U.S. price for 1981-82, and Table 2.3B shows the price correlations for 1983-88. In the case of Hong Kong, Korea, and Indonesia, the correlation between their adjusted export price and the U.S. price was higher in 1981-82 when there were fewer categories under quota. This is difficult to explain in standard terms, as quality upgrading over time (toward the U.S. quality level) would suggest the opposite. Note also that these countries generally have higher price correlations with other countries in the later years, which is consistent with quality upgrading by the other countries.

B. India, Pakistan, and Bangladesh

India and Pakistan, on the other hand, had a large number of categories under restraint in the early years, but the quotas were underutilized. In India, the quotas for these underutilized categories were eventually dropped and replaced with a less restrictive consultative arrangement.[6] This is why the quota utilization rate may be seen to jump up in 1983 for India. Over time, as the utilization rate rose, additional categories were brought under quota. There were no MFA quotas imposed on Bangladesh until it reached a threshhold presence in 1986. After that, the number of categories brought under restraint increased as its exports rose. For India, Pakistan, and Bangladesh, the correlation of their adjusted export prices with U.S. and world prices was lower in the first four years, 1981–84, than in the last four years, 1985–88 (Tables 2.4A and 2.4B). This could be due to a greater degree of economic development and integration with world markets, or quality improvements (making their goods closer substitutes for U.S. goods), or growth in the level of rent retention by exporters, or even learning on the part of importers of how to deal with the regulated environment.

C. Italy

In contrast, Italy's price correlation with the United States remained consistently high over the sample period. Its price correlation with Hong Kong and Korea fell slightly over the 1980s, but its price correlation with India, Pakistan, Bangladesh, and Indonesia rose, an observation which may be consistent with quality upgrading on the part of these developing countries.

---

6. There is usually no quantitative restriction imposed on a category under the consultative provision. Instead, the export volume is constantly monitored for sudden surges in growth, in which event quotas will be reinstated.

TABLE 2.2. Quota Utilization Rates for Six Countries, 1981-89*

Year	Hong Kong	Korea	Indonesia	India	Pakistan	Bangladesh
1981	0.9610 (21)	0.9458 (19)		0.6966 (31)	0.6311 (13)	
1982	0.9449 (20)	0.9668 (20)	1.0000 (2)	0.6592 (30)	0.6137 (5)	
1983	0.9923 (28)	0.9737 (28)	0.9919 (4)	0.9834 (6)	0.5510 (4)	
1984	0.9532 (30)	0.8018 (29)	0.9695 (9)	0.9978 (8)	0.8257 (8)	
1985	0.9238 (30)	0.9582 (31)	0.7936 (18)	0.9564 (8)	0.8569 (7)	
1986	0.9845 (30)	0.9737 (30)	0.9819 (22)	0.9840 (7)	0.8688 (7)	0.9658 (8)
1987	0.9899 (30)	0.9612 (30)	0.9444 (20)	0.9821 (10)	0.9516 (21)	0.9612 (13)
1988	0.9892 (30)	0.9009 (30)	0.9676 (20)	0.9707 (10)	0.8754 (22)	0.9196 (13)
1989	0.9608 (29)	0.9480 (31)	0.9869 (20)	0.9571 (10)	0.9005 (20)	0.9353 (13)

*Figures in parentheses are number of categories used to compute annual average utilization.

TABLE 2.3A. Price Correlations, 1981–82

	United States	Italy	Hong Kong	Korea	Indonesia	India	Pakistan	Bangladesh
United States	1.0000							
Italy	0.9710	1.0000						
Hong Kong	0.9677	0.9396	1.0000					
Korea	0.9491	0.9327	0.9867	1.0000				
Indonesia	0.9428	0.8751	0.8936	0.8425	1.0000			
India	0.4265	0.2512	0.5215	0.4931	0.5061	1.0000		
Pakistan	0.9048	0.8049	0.8869	0.8349	0.8822	0.5927	1.0000	
Bangladesh	0.5791	0.4970	0.4012	0.3361	0.7304	0.0768	0.5687	1.0000

TABLE 2.3B. Price Correlations, 1983–88

	United States	Italy	Hong Kong	Korea	Indonesia	India	Pakistan	Bangladesh
United States	1.0000							
Italy	0.9148	1.0000						
Hong Kong	0.8448	0.7085	1.0000					
Korea	0.8802	0.7869	0.9285	1.0000				
Indonesia	0.7926	0.8138	0.7592	0.7710	1.0000			
India	0.5850	0.5401	0.6870	0.6240	0.7108	1.0000		
Pakistan	0.6001	0.5752	0.6807	0.5886	0.7113	0.7125	1.0000	
Bangladesh	0.3891	0.4380	0.4467	0.3883	0.4913	0.4061	0.4338	1.0000

FIGURE 2.7. U.S. Prices and Adjusted Bangladesh Export Prices

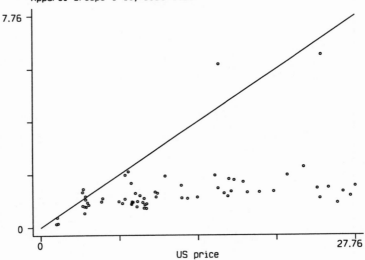

Price per unit in US dollars
Apparel Groups 1-10, 1981-1988

US price

FIGURE 2.8. U.S. Prices and Adjusted Italian Export Prices

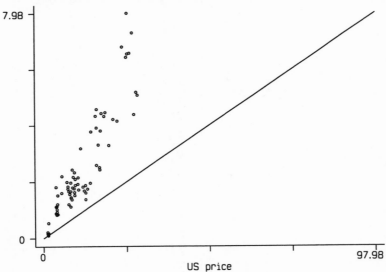

Price per unit in US dollars
Apparel Groups 1-10, 1981-1988

US price

TABLE 2.4A. Price Correlations, 1981–84

	United States	Italy	Hong Kong	Korea	Indonesia	India	Pakistan	Bangladesh
United States	1.0000							
Italy	0.9197	1.0000						
Hong Kong	0.9071	0.8111	1.0000					
Korea	0.9200	0.8334	0.9655	1.0000				
Indonesia	0.7101	0.7656	0.6737	0.6329	1.0000			
India	0.3655	0.2414	0.5197	0.4675	0.4997	1.0000		
Pakistan	0.5834	0.4581	0.7587	0.6133	0.5873	0.6576	1.0000	
Bangladesh	0.3471	0.3795	0.3398	0.2896	0.6029	0.1805	0.4296	1.0000

TABLE 2.4B. Price Correlations, 1985–88

	United States	Italy	Hong Kong	Korea	Indonesia	India	Pakistan	Bangladesh
United States	1.0000							
Italy	0.9178	1.0000						
Hong Kong	0.8449	0.6988	1.0000					
Korea	0.8790	0.7804	0.9267	1.0000				
Indonesia	0.8647	0.8829	0.7857	0.7929	1.0000			
India	0.6986	0.6691	0.7477	0.6784	0.7320	1.0000		
Pakistan	0.7035	0.7224	0.7038	0.6362	0.7953	0.7056	1.0000	
Bangladesh	0.7716	0.7713	0.7861	0.7016	0.8385	0.7989	0.8027	1.0000

PART II
Rent Sharing: Theory and Evidence

CHAPTER THREE

Imperfect Competition, Rent Appropriation, and Rent Sharing

I. Introduction

This chapter presents the theoretical foundation for the analysis of rent sharing. The possibility of rent sharing has been largely ignored in the existing literature on the MFA, which usually assumes that there is perfect competition all around and that quota rents accrue entirely to the country responsible for implementing the quotas, in this case, the exporting country.

In the basic competitive model, there is perfect competition in the market for products (textiles and apparel) and the market for quota licenses. However, in reality, imperfect competition can arise on the side of the buyers (i.e., monopsony or oligopsony), and/or on the side of the sellers (i.e., monopoly or oligopoly) in either or both the product market and the license market. Clearly, many different combinations of imperfections can arise in the two markets and it is not the intention in this chapter to study them all. Instead, the approach taken here is to begin by setting out the implications of perfect competition in all markets, and then contrasting them against the effects of certain market imperfections, distinguishing between rent appropriation and rent sharing.

When there is market power on the seller's side, the seller(s) may appropriate the quota rent by raising the price of the product to the highest level which buyers in the quota-restricted market are willing to pay. This causes the license price—which is equal to the difference between the demand price in the restricted market and the supply price set by the seller—to shrink to zero. This phenomenon is termed rent appropriation. The theoretical literature on rent appropriation is quite extensive; in this chapter, a brief recapitulation of the main results is presented.

When there is market power on the buyer's side, a different result arises, one which may be termed rent sharing. Rent sharing denotes the sharing of potential rent between the license holders and other agents, given the price differential created by the quota. In other words, rent sharing is said to occur when the license price falls short of the price differential in the quota-restricted and world markets. In contrast with rent appropriation, the theoretical literature on rent sharing is practically nonexistent; this chapter begins to fill the gap with some very simple models.

II. The Basic Competitive Model

The basic model is one with competition in all the relevant markets. Both the demand and supply sides of the product market are assumed to be competitive. In addition, license holders act competitively and are willing and able to sell licenses at the price that clears the license market.

The basic competitive model outlined in Chapter Two may be recapitulated as follows, using the illustration in Figure 2.1. The downward sloping line RD represents residual demand from the importing country, the United States, that is, total demand in the United States less supply from all sources other than the exporting country of concern. The upward sloping line RS depicts the residual supply from the exporting country, that is, supply from that country less demand from all sources other than the United States. The intersection of the two gives the world price in the absence of quotas, P^F, and the level of imports from the exporting country to the United States, V^F.

If a quota is set allowing only V units to be imported, the home price at which this level of imports is demanded, P^D, exceeds the world price at which it is supplied, P^S. Their difference is the license price, L. As is well understood, tariffs and quotas are equivalent in the basic competitive model, so the license price may be interpreted as the implicit tariff, that is, the specific tariff that would induce the same amount of imports as the quota, V.

As mentioned in chapters one and two, most studies of the MFA use this basic competitive model as their underlying framework for analysis. In this model, the quota rent can be measured by the area, LV, in Figure 2.1. Under the usual assumption that the quota takes a form of a voluntary export restraint by the exporting country, with the quota licenses being held by exporting agents, this means that the quota rent accrues entirely to the exporting country. However, as the following two sections point out, these assumptions may not be appropriate in reality. For one thing, the final distribution of quota licenses among agents in the exporting country may affect the structure of the license and/or product market, so that these agents no longer behave in a competitive fashion. Also, the way in which the MFA quotas are implemented may have an impact on the balance of power between the exporting country and the importing agents, leading to rent sharing between the exporting and importing countries.

III. Rent Appropriation

Bhagwati 1965 analyzes three departures from the base model of competition, from the perspective of the quota-imposing (domestic) country. He looks at the effect of monopoly in domestic supply and in the license market, as well as some combinations of these. His conclusions are:

1. When there is monopoly only in domestic supply, a quota makes demand less elastic for price increases, thereby augmenting the domestic producer's monopoly power.
2. When there is competitive supply at home and abroad, but monopoly in license holdings the monopolist holder of licenses may affect their value by affecting the utilization of licenses. The utilization rate will be chosen to maximize total license value. This makes the effective quota endogenous.
3. When there is monopoly in domestic supply and license holding:
   a. If the license holder is not the domestic monopolist, the home market is a duopoly. Hence, the quota changes the market structure. The solution concept chosen by him is essentially a Cournot–Nash equilibrium.
   b. If the license holder is the domestic monopolist, the monopolist can even further augment his monopoly power by effectively choosing his utilization ratio to maximize the sum of profits and license revenues.

Bhagwati 1965 does not address the possibility of foreign market power. If the foreign sellers have market power, no supply curve exists, as the supply price is chosen to maximize profits. This makes the world price a choice variable and its determination the result of profit–maximizing decisions of the suppliers. If the sellers have no licenses, they will have an incentive to raise their price to obtain the rents from the quota.[1]

Consider the case where there is a single foreign supplier of the product and markets are segmented. It is clearly optimal for the monopolist to raise his price in response to a quota so as to appropriate the entire quota rent. By closing the gap between the demand price and the supply price, the monopolist effectively strips the licenses of any value. This model with segmented markets is developed diagrammatically in Takacs 1987 and is mentioned in Shibata 1968 as well, and most recently in Krugman and Helpman 1989.

Krishna 1990 further develops a model in which there is costless arbitrage between the markets so the foreign monopolist cannot practice price discrimination.[2] The monopolist's price is an endogenous variable—by charging a high price, he can appropriate rents and he chooses to do so if this is profitable. This price depends on the quota level and his allocation of licenses. Even here, as long as the license market is frictionless and competitive, it is still the case that the value of a license equals the difference between the domestic

---

1. On the other hand, if they own some licenses, then this incentive is tempered as they take into account the value of their license holdings. These issues are explored in Krishna 1990 and 1991.

2. There may be domestic competitive supply, in which case the monopolist's demand in what follows should be interpreted as the residual demand curve.

price and the world price. However, in this model, as well as in those of Bhagwati discussed previously, the license price is endogenous and depends on other parameters such as the allocation of licenses and the product market structure and behavior.

To summarize, when there is product market power on the seller's side, the license price becomes an endogenous variable used by the producer to effect rent appropriation. However, it will still be true that the license price is equal to the difference between the domestic (demand) price and the world (supply) price, so there is no rent sharing.

IV. Rent Sharing

This section focuses on a different phenomenon, namely that of rent sharing. The distinction between rent sharing and rent appropriation is crucial. In contrast to rent appropriation, which refers to how producers with market power in effect appropriate quota rents by raising their product prices, rent sharing denotes the sharing of potential rent between the license holders (i.e., the exporters) and the importing agents, given the price differential created by the quota.

A. Monopsony

The basic competitive scenario outlined in Section II is quite different if there is monopsony power, that is, if there is a single buyer. Assume that the license market is competitive, as is the supply side. In Figure 3.1, the monopsonist retailer has a marginal revenue curve, MR, which is derived from the market demand for apparel, DD, and he faces an upward sloping supply, SS. His marginal cost curve, MC, lies to the left of SS—this is because he has to pay a higher price for all the inframarginal units in order to purchase an additional unit of apparel.

Under free trade, the monopsonist will import V^F units of apparel, which is given by the intersection of MC and MR. The lowest price at which this quantity will be supplied is P^F, and the monopsonist is willing to pay up to P^*. Since he is the sole importer, however, he can choose his price and so he will offer the lowest price, P^F, and sell the goods in the home market at price P^*.

Now suppose a quota, V, is imposed on apparel imports. The monopsonist's supply curve then becomes the kinked line, SBE and his marginal cost curve becomes ACE. The lowest price at which the quota amount will be supplied is $P^S(V)$, and the monopsonist will not pay more than $P^D(V)$, which is the price for which he will sell the imports in the home market. If he pays P, where $P^S(V) \leq P \leq P^D(V)$, then the price of a quota license will be $P - P^S(V)$, (i.e., the difference between the price paid and the supply price charged). The monopsonist will never choose to pay more than the supply price charged so he will buy the V units at price $P^S(V)$ and the license price will be zero. Note that this occurs not because there is no price differential in the home and world markets, but because the monopsonist, as the only importer of the good, can prevent trade from equalizing these prices. The more restrictive the quota is, the lower will be the price paid by the monopsonist. In any case, the competitive exporters are paid exactly enough to induce them to sell and they receive no rent. (Similar results can be shown to go through for oligopsony. See Krishna and Tan 1990.)

It is important to emphasize that in this case, unlike those discussed in the previous chapter, the license price is not given by the deviation of the domestic price from the world price. The license to import only has value if the price offered by the monopsonist exceeds the supply price. Since the monopsonist has sole buying power, the license price is always zero. The difference between the home price and the world price, however, is given by $P^D(V)-P^S(V)$ in Figure 3.1, and it is not equal to zero. Thus, monopsony power causes the license price to diverge from the difference in the supply and demand price.

B. Bilateral Monopoly

Now suppose there is competitive supply but concentration in license holdings, as well as market power on the buyer's side. This seems like a more realistic

Figure 3.1. Rent Sharing

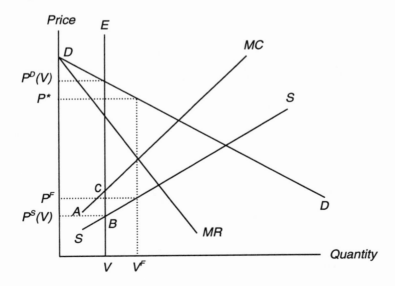

assumption since the existence of active trading in quota licenses in some MFA–exporting countries is evidence that the licenses have value. In this case, there is bilateral monopoly power, and the issue becomes one of sharing the potential license rents. The potential rent from a license equals the difference in the supply price in the exporting country and the demand price in the importing country. If a price between these two is the outcome of the bargaining process, then the license price is positive. However, the two prices are not separated by exactly the license price because of rent sharing.[3]

As a stark illustration of this argument, suppose that all the quota licenses are held by a single exporter (who may or may not be a producer), and that the license price is determined by a Nash bargaining process between the monopsonist and the license holder. The license holder's objective is to maximize his profit π_L, where:

$$\pi_L = VL \tag{1}$$

The monopsonist's objective is to maximize his profit π_M, where:

$$\pi_M = [P^D(V) - (L + P^S(V))]V. \tag{2}$$

$P^D(\cdot)$ is the inverse residual demand function and $P^S(\cdot)$ is the inverse residual import supply function, so $P^D(V)$ is the demand price and $P^S(V)$ is the supply price for the quota, V units. The license price is found by maximizing the weighted product of both parties' deviation from their fall–back payoff:

$$\Pi = (VL)^\beta [(P^D(V) - P^S(V) - L)V]^{1-\beta}. \tag{3}$$

For simplicity, assume both parties receive nothing in the absence of an agreement, so their fall–back payoffs are equal to zero.[4] The parameters β and $(1-\beta)$ represent the bargaining strengths of the license holder and the monopsonist respectively, where $0 \le \beta \le 1$.

The first order condition is:

$$VL^{-(1-\beta)}[P^D(V) - P^S(V) - L]^{-\beta}[\beta(P^D(V) - P^S(V)) - L] = 0 \tag{4}$$

---

3. The two prices may not be separated by exactly the license price for other reasons as well. These include factors such as unmeasured costs created by the quota and licensing system itself. For example, if it is difficult to manage the paperwork and bureaucracy imposed by the implementation system or to obtain licenses, then the difference between the demand and supply prices will exceed the license price.

4. This is not an unreasonable assumption for the license holder because quota licenses are product– and country–specific; in the absence of an agreement with the monopsonist, the exporter does not have the option of selling his licenses elsewhere.

which yields the solutions:

$$L = 0,$$

$$L = P^D(V) - P^S(V),$$ (5)

$$L = \beta[P^D(V) - P^S(V)],$$

of which only the third satisfies the second order condition for a maximum. Therefore the license price, which is the outcome of the Nash bargaining setup between the license holder and the monopsonist, is given by

$$L = \beta[P^D(V) - P^S(V)].$$ (6)

The more powerful the license holder is, the higher is the license price. In the extreme case when $\beta = 1$, the license holder has all the bargaining power and so he extracts the entire quota rent, VL, where the license price L is exactly equal to the difference between the demand and supply prices. At the opposite extreme when $\beta = 0$, the monopsonist controls the market: for each unit, he pays only the supply price P^s and reaps the rent given by the difference between the demand and supply prices. The license holder gets nothing, as the license price is equal to zero. For a value of β between 0 and 1, an intermediate result will obtain and the license price will not reflect the full difference between the demand and supply prices. The power of the license holders could be low for a number of reasons. In addition to facing monopsony power, institutional characteristics such as the distribution of free quota to exporters with an order in hand are likely to reduce the bargaining power of an exporter vis-à-vis a buyer.

V. Looking Ahead

Chapter Four examines the relationship between the U.S. (demand) price and the Hong Kong (supply) price, which includes the license price as well as tariffs and transport costs. In the absence of rent sharing, as argued above, these two should be equal. Moreover, their difference should not depend on factors such as concentration in quota holdings and the quota size and utilization ratio. In this way, the extent of rent sharing is estimated, along with the factors that seem to be influencing it. As far as possible, allowances are also made for price differences caused by compositional effects and certain types of product differentiation. The same is accomplished for Korea in Chapter Five. Making use of the fact that the Korean exchange rate is floating (in contrast to the Hong Kong exchange rate, which is pegged to the U.S. dollar) Chapter Five includes a test for a less restrictive form of rent sharing that allows for a broader definition of product differentiation. Chapter Six tests for rent sharing in Mexico.

CHAPTER FOUR

Testing for Rent Sharing in Hong Kong[1]

I. Introduction

The standard competitive model described in Chapter Two forms the basis for most empirical estimates of quota rents under the MFA. Under this model, a binding quota on imports will cause the price at which that level of imports is demanded to exceed the price at which it is supplied, with the difference being equal to the price of a quota license. Morkre 1984, for example, uses this result to estimate quota rents generated by U.S. MFA quotas on Hong Kong imports. Based on the assumption that "...the price of rights to export textiles from Hong Kong measures the gap between import price and unit cost in Hong Kong...[as] textile quotas are openly traded in Hong Kong so that the market price for transfers is expected to reflect the value of the price–cost difference,"[2] he finds that, in 1980, U.S. MFA quotas on Hong Kong generated quota rents equivalent to 23 percent of the total value of clothing imports from Hong Kong. Hamilton 1986 and Trela and Whalley 1990 also make use of Hong Kong quota license prices to measure rent income.

The assumption of competitive markets is usually defended on the grounds that the textile and apparel industry is characterized by a large number of producers. In the case of advanced exporters such as Hong Kong, further justification is provided by the fact that the quotas are efficiently implemented and are, to a large extent, transferable. However, it has also been claimed that "...[a]lthough governments of exporting countries under the MFA often allocate export licenses in a manner that helps exporters capture the quota rent, many of these exporters face large importing enterprises that can negotiate prices that capture some of the rent for themselves..."[3] In light of such observations, and the suggestive evidence presented in Chapter Two, this chapter seeks to question the a priori assumption of perfectly competitive markets. The approach adopted here is not to point to, and model, a particular form of market imperfection, but rather, to test if the implications of the perfectly competitive model are, in fact, borne out in the data. This is done by testing for evidence of rent sharing in the MFA market, using data from Hong Kong and the United States.

---

[1]This chapter is based on Krishna, Erzan and Tan 1994.
[2]Morkre 1984, p. 2.
[3]Goto 1989, p. 218.

As mentioned in Chapter Three, the difference between the demand price in the importing country (the United States) and the supply price in the exporting country (Hong Kong) may be referred to as the potential rent per unit. In the perfectly competitive model, the price of a quota license is exactly equal to this potential rent.[4] Rent sharing denotes the sharing of this potential rent between the license holders and other agents, given the price differential created by the quota. In other words, rent sharing is said to occur when the license price falls short of the potential rent. This could arise, for example, if U.S. importers have some degree of monopsony power which enables them to bargain for a share of the quota rent. In this case, for each unit of apparel exported from Hong Kong to the United States, the value of the license would accrue to the Hong Kong exporter and the remainder of the potential rent per unit would accrue to the U.S. importer.[5]

II. The Data

The data utilized in this study cover the time period 1981 to 1988 and pertain to three broad areas:

1. domestically (U.S.) produced apparel
2. imported apparel from Hong Kong
3. license holdings in Hong Kong

In order to maintain consistency between U.S. production data and import data, the units employed in this chapter are not MFA categories but the ten aggregated apparel groups described in Chapter Two:

1. dresses
2. skirts
3. playsuits
4. sweaters
5. trousers

---

[4] As explained in Chapter Three, this result also holds when there is rent appropriation in an imperfectly competitive product market. Rent appropriation occurs when a producer with market power raises his supply price in response to a binding quota, causing the license price and the gap between the demand price and the supply price (i.e., the potential rent per unit) to be reduced to zero. Given the large number of textile and apparel producers in most exporting countries, rent appropriation is less of a concern.

[5] The license price could also fall short of the potential rent in the presence of institutional rigidities in the quota administration system in Hong Kong. In this case, the value of the license will accrue to the Hong Kong producers, with the remainder of the potential rent being dissipated in dealing with the red tape and the bureaucracy associated with the quota.

6. men's coats
7. women's coats
8. woven shirts
9. knit shirts
10. underwear

Data were obtained for these groups for the following variables defined below, where the subscript i denotes the apparel group, and t denotes the year:

P_{it}^{US} = unit value of U.S. production, in U.S. dollars (i.e., the ex–factory price, not the retail price)

p_{it}^{HK} = f.o.b. Hong Kong price, in U.S. dollars, inclusive of the license price

$DUTY_{it}$ = U.S. ad valorem duty

$TRANSP_{it}^{HK}$ = per unit transport cost from Hong Kong to the United States, in U.S. dollars

P_{it}^{HK} = adjusted Hong Kong price, in U.S. dollars,[6] where

P_{it}^{HK} = $p_{it}^{HK} (1 + DUTY_{it}) + TRANSP_{it}^{HK}$

Q_{it}^{HK} = quantity of imports from Hong Kong, measured in pieces

$NEQUIV_{it}^{HK}$ = numbers equivalent of the Herfindahl index of concentration in license holding, defined as $1/(\Sigma x_k^2)$, where x_k equals the share of license holder k in total licenses

$QUOTA_{it}^{HK}$ = import quota, measured in pieces

$UTIL_{it}^{HK}$ = quota utilization ratio, where $UTIL_{it}^{HK} = Q_{it}^{HK} /QUOTA_{it}^{HK}$

$SALES_t$ = total retail sales in the United States, in billions of U.S. dollars

The data sources are the same as those described in Chapter Two. In addition, information on the concentration in license holdings in Hong Kong came from the Preliminary Allocation Quota Holders' List issued by the Textile Controls Registry in Hong Kong. This list was obtained for 1982 and 1986–1988.[7]

---

[6]The exchange rate between the Hong Kong dollar and the US dollar has been fixed at HK$7.80 to US$1 since 1983.

[7]Whereas there are frequent temporary transfers of licenses, permanent transfers occur much less often. According to Sung 1989, around 28 percent of the total quota is temporarily transferred, whereas only about 15 percent is permanently transferred. Hence, assuming that the license allocation does not alter much over the years, the 1982 allocation was applied to the years 1981 and 1983, and the 1986 allocation to the years 1984 and 1985. The concentration index for each group was calculated as a quantity–weighted average of the concentration indices of the MFA categories that make up the group.

III. Testing for Rent Sharing: Homogeneous Goods

In this and the following two sections, procedures are developed and implemented to test for the existence of rent sharing. If the apparel market is perfectly competitive, and U.S.- and Hong Kong-produced goods are homogeneous, then the price of a quota license should reflect the difference between the U.S. demand price and the Hong Kong supply price, if there is no rent sharing. The price of domestically–produced apparel (P_{it}^{US}) is used as a proxy for the U.S. demand price. Note that the data set for the ten apparel groups does not contain license prices explicitly; the license price is already included in the f.o.b. Hong Kong price (p_{it}^{HK}). Therefore, the test for rent sharing is accomplished by examining whether the f.o.b. price in Hong Kong, adjusted for tariffs and transport costs (P_{it}^{HK}), is equal to the U.S. price (P_{it}^{US}).

A. Equation Setup

The econometric test is set up in the following way. If there is perfect competition and no rent sharing, then:

$$[C_{it}^{HK} + L_{it}^{HK}(QUOTA_{it}^{HK}, NEQUIV_{it}^{HK}, ...)](1 + DUTY_{it})$$

$$+ TRANSP_{it}^{HK} \equiv P_{it}^{HK} = P_{it}^{US}$$

where:

C_{it}^{HK} = the marginal cost or supply price in Hong Kong, and
L_{it}^{HK} = the endogenously determined license price.

Information on C_{it}^{HK} was not available, but data were obtained on the adjusted Hong Kong price, P_{it}^{HK}. In the perfectly competitive model, $C_{it}^{HK} + L_{it}^{HK}(\cdot)$ is equal to p_{it}^{HK}, the f.o.b. Hong Kong price. The adjusted Hong Kong price, P_{it}^{HK}, defined as $p_{it}^{HK}(1+DUTY_{it})+TRANSP_{it}$, equal to the U.S. price P_{it}^{US}, which is determined by the intersection of the residual demand in the United States (RD) and the residual supply from Hong Kong (RS), which is, of course, restricted to be the quota level. In other words:

$$RD(P_{it}^{US}, DD_{it}, ...) = RS \equiv QUOTA_{it}^{HK}$$

$$\Rightarrow P_{it}^{US} = f(QUOTA_{it}^{HK}, DD_{it}, ...)$$

where DD_{it} represents factors which shift the residual demand curve in the United States. This forms the basis for the test.

Equation (1) regresses the adjusted Hong Kong price on the U.S. price, a constant, the quota utilization ratio, the quota level, the numbers equivalent of the Herfindahl index and the total retail sales in the United States:

$$P_{it}^{HK} = \alpha + \beta P_{it}^{US} + \gamma NEQUIV_{it}^{HK} + \delta UTIL_{it}^{HK}$$

$$+ \phi QUOTA_{it}^{HK} + \lambda SALES_t + \epsilon_{it}. \tag{1}$$

The right-hand side variables can be considered exogenous. If there is perfect competition, as noted above, P_{it}^{US} would be a function of $QUOTA_{it}^{HK}$ but it would not be a function of P_{it}^{HK}, hence the problem of simultaneous equation bias should not arise here. As quota license allocations are historically determined, $NEQUIV_{it}^{HK}$ can be also taken as given though it does vary over time with the composition of exports. The quota level, $QUOTA_{it}^{HK}$ is exogenously set through bilateral negotiations between Hong Kong and the United States. The utilization rate, $UTIL_{it}^{HK}$, should be one if the quota is binding; any departure from one is assumed to reflect exogenous difficulties in attaining full utilization due to frictions in the implementation system. The variable $SALES_t$ proxies for U.S. demand shifts; again, this should be exogenous as long as Hong Kong-produced apparel form an insignificant part of total retail sales in the United States.

The regression was run on pooled data across the ten apparel groups for the years 1981 through 1988. If there is no rent sharing and the goods are homogeneous, one should expect to observe $P_{it}^{HK} = P_{it}^{US}$. In other words, in equation (1), the constant should be zero and the coefficient on the U.S. price should be one. Furthermore, none of the other variables should be significant. The assumption that U.S. and Hong Kong apparel are perfect substitutes ensures that the license–inclusive Hong Kong price has to equal the domestic price in the United States. This means that the Hong Kong supply price (exclusive of the license price) has to vary one for one with the license price. For example, a reduction in the quota level or an outward shift in U.S. demand will tend to raise the U.S. price. However, the license price will go up as well, so that P_{it}^{HK} exactly matches P_{it}^{US}. A change in the license utilization rate may affect the license price but not P_{it}^{HK}, since the supply price will adjust to maintain the equality between P_{it}^{HK} and P_{it}^{US}. Similarly, the concentration of license holdings may affect the license price if there are substantial search costs, but it should not affect P_{it}^{HK} since the supply price will again adjust to ensure $P_{it}^{HK} = P_{it}^{US}$.

B. Regression Results

The results of equation (1) are reported in Table 4.1. Note that α is significantly different from zero at the 5 percent level, and that Hong Kong prices are lower than U.S. prices in general. This suggests that the license price embodied in P_{it}^{HK} falls short of the gap between the demand price (P_{it}^{US}) and the supply price. The null hypothesis of perfect competition everywhere is conclusively rejected (i.e., the hypothesis that $\beta = 1$ and $\alpha = \gamma = \delta = \phi = \lambda = 0$ jointly). The hypothesis that $\beta = 1$ can be rejected at the 1 percent level.

One can think of β as the marginal component of rent sharing. A one dollar increase in the U.S. price, therefore, is associated with a US$0.54 increase in

TABLE 4.1. Hong Kong: Regression Results for the Homogeneous Goods Model
Dependent variable = P_{it}^{HK}

Independent Variable	Coefficient	t–statistic
Constant	-12.8511	-3.1321[b]
	(4.1030)	
P_{it}^{US}	0.5426	9.6869[a]
	(0.0560)	
$NEQUIV_{it}^{HK}$	0.0642	2.8657[a]
	(0.0224)	
$UTIL_{it}^{HK}$	12.4319	3.4888[a]
	(3.5634)	
$QUOTA_{it}^{HK}$	-0.3519×10^{-7}	-3.6393[a]
	(0.9671×10^{-8})	
$SALES_t$	0.0356	1.7980[b]
	(0.0198)	

Number of observations = 64,
$R^2 = 0.8455$, Adjusted $R^2 = 0.8322$
Standard errors are in parentheses beneath the estimates of the parameters. (These standard errors do not differ appreciably from those obtained with the White 1984 correction, therefore the possibility of heteroscedasticity in the sample is discounted).
[a] Significant at the 1 percent level.
[b] Significant at the 10 percent level.

Results of hypothesis–testing:
F–statistic for the joint test of $\beta=1$ and $\alpha=\gamma=\delta=\phi=\lambda=0$:
$F = 26.2330$; reject the null hypothesis at the 1 percent level.
t–statistic for the test of $\beta=1$:
$t = -8.1654$; reject the null hypothesis at the 1 percent level (two–tailed test).

the Hong Kong price—this may indicate that US$0.46 of the price differential or rent is retained in the United States.[8]

In addition, note that, ceteris paribus, increasing the license market concentration lowers the Hong Kong price, as γ, the coefficient on NEQUIV $_{it}^{HK}$, is positive and statistically significant at the 1 percent level. The coefficients on UTIL$_{it}^{HK}$ and QUOTA$_{it}^{HK}$ are also significant at the 1 percent level. With everything else held constant, a higher quota utilization rate raises the Hong Kong price, and a higher quota reduces the Hong Kong price. Finally, λ, the coefficient on the demand shift parameter, SALES$_t$, is positive and significant at the 10 percent level, indicating that an increase in U.S. demand raises the Hong Kong price, all else constant. Recall that in the standard model, none of these variables should affect the equality of P_{it}^{US} and P_{it}^{HK}. The regression coefficient on each of these variables, NEQUIV $_{it}^{HK}$,UTIL$_{it}^{HK}$, QUOTA $_{it}^{HK}$, and SALES$_t$, is interpreted as the effect of that variable on P_{it}^{HK}, holding P_{it}^{US} and all the other regressors constant. However, in the absence of rent sharing, holding P_{it}^{US} constant at a given level implies that P_{it}^{HK} will also be fixed at that level and should not respond to changes in any of the other independent variables.

The results of equation (1) therefore seem inconsistent with the existence of perfect competition and perfect substitutability between U.S. apparel and imports from Hong Kong: the U.S. price is not tracked by the adjusted Hong Kong price, and other variables come in with significant coefficients.

IV. Allowing for a Composition Effect

There may be an alternative explanation for the pattern of coefficients found in equation (1), namely, that the Hong Kong product mix is not the same as that of the U.S. In other words, the null hypothesis described in the beginning of this section may be valid for the component MFA categories but not for the aggregate apparel groups. For example, the prices of cotton dresses, wool dresses and dresses made of synthetic fiber may be the same in both the United States and Hong Kong, but if the United States produces relatively more wool dresses, which are relatively more expensive, then the unit price of U.S. dresses on the whole will exceed the unit price of Hong Kong dresses on the whole. The composition of the U.S. and Hong Kong aggregate goods cannot be directly compared since the component categories are not the same. However, there is a way to circumvent this, as outlined below by testing the importance of this composition effect.

---

[8]It is possible that other cost factors associated with the quota system could account for part of this margin.

A. Equation Setup

Let i denote the apparel group (i=1,...,10), and let j denote the MFA categories that make up apparel group i (i=1,...,n).. For ease of exposition, the time subscript, t, is dropped. Then P_{it}^{US}, the U.S. unit price of apparel group i, may be written as:

$$P_i^{US} = \sum_j P_{ij}^{US}(Q_{ij}^{US}/Q_i^{US}) = \sum_j P_{ij}^{US} w_{ij}^{US} \tag{2}$$

where P_{ij}^{US} is the U.S. unit price of the jth MFA category belonging to apparel group i, Q_{ij}^{US} is the U.S. output of the jth MFA category of apparel group i, Q_i^{US} is the total U.S. output of apparel group i and w_{ij}^{US} is simply the quantity weight of category j in apparel group i, where:

$$\sum_j w_{ij}^{US} = 1.$$

Similarly, the Hong Kong unit price of apparel group i may be written as:

$$P_i^{HK} = \sum_j P_{ij}^{HK}(Q_{ij}^{HK}/Q_i^{HK}) = \sum_j P_{ij}^{HK} w_{ij}^{HK} \tag{3}$$

where:

$$\sum_j w_{ij}^{HK} = 1.$$

Note that there is only information on P_i^{US}, P_i^{HK}, P_{ij}^{HK} and w_{ij}^{HK}. Since the U.S. production data are not broken down into MFA categories, P_{it}^{US} and w_{ij}^{US} are not known. Suppose the following simplifying assumption is made:

$$P_{ij}^{US} = \alpha_i + P_{ij}^{HK}. \tag{4}$$

Then α_i captures the extent of rent sharing as it denotes the price difference between the United States and Hong Kong for apparel group i. Putting (4) in (2) and subtracting (3) gives us:

$$P_i^{US} - P_i^{HK} = \alpha_i + \sum_j \theta_{ij} P_{ij}^{HK} \tag{5}$$

where θ_{ij} denotes the difference between the U.S. and Hong Kong weighting of the jth category of apparel group i, and:

$$\sum_j \theta_{ij} = 0.$$

If there is no rent sharing, $\alpha_i = 0$.[9]

Now to determine whether the price difference between the United States and Hong Kong for each apparel group i is due to differences in the composition of the group or due to rent sharing, testing would focus on the significance of the θ_{ij}s and α_i. Specifically, if the null hypothesis states that there is no compositional difference between U.S. and Hong Kong apparel groups, and no rent sharing, then $\theta_{ij} = 0$ for all j, j=1,...,n and $\alpha_i = 0$.

Consider, for example, a typical apparel group equation with n=3 categories. Equation (5) is simply:

$$P_i^{US} - P_i^{HK} = \alpha_i + \theta_{i1}P_{i1}^{HK} + \theta_{i2}P_{i2}^{HK} + \theta_{i3}P_{i3}^{HK} + \epsilon_i. \tag{6}$$

If the restriction that $\theta_{i1}+\theta_{i2}+\theta_{i3} = 0$ is imposed, equation (6) becomes:

$$P_i^{US} - P_i^{HK} = \alpha_i + \theta_{i2}(P_{i2}^{HK}-P_{i1}^{HK})$$
$$+ \theta_{i3}(P_{i3}^{HK}-P_{i1}^{HK}) + \epsilon_{it}. \tag{7}$$

By running an equation like (7) for each apparel group i, i = 1,...,10, α_i, θ_{i2} and θ_{i3} were estimated. Table 4.2 lists the MFA categories, j, used for each apparel group, i. The composition effect was tested for each equation using an F–test of the hypothesis that $\theta_{ij} = 0$ for all component MFA categories j. The

---

[9]A more general formulation of (4) which allows for fixed and marginal components of rent sharing would have:

$$P_i^{US} = \alpha_i + \beta_i P_{ij}^{HK}$$

for all apparel groups i. Then (5) becomes:

$$P_i^{US} - P_i^{HK} = \alpha_i + \sum_j \theta_{ij}^* P_{ij}^{HK}$$

where:

$$\theta_{ij}^* = \beta_i w_{ij}^{US} - w_{ij}^{HK}.$$

For each of the ten apparel groups, the null hypothesis that $\beta_i = 1$ was tested by means of an F–test on the above model versus the restricted model, where $\sum_j \theta_{ij}^* = 0$. The null hypothesis could not be rejected for nine of the ten groups, indicating that the assumption of $\beta_i = 1$ in equation (4) is not too far off the mark.

TABLE 4.2. Hong Kong: Ten Apparel Groups and Component MFA Subcategories

Apparel Group (i)	$j = 1$	$j = 2$	$j = 3$	$j = 4$	$j = 5$
1. Dresses	336	436	636		
2. Skirts	342	442	642		
3. Playsuits	337	637			
4. Sweaters	345	445/6	645/6		
5. Trousers	347/8	447/8	647	648	
6. Men's Coats	334	434	634		
7. Women's Coats	335	435	635		
8. Woven Shirts	340	341	440	640	641
9. Knit Shirts	338/9	438	638/9		
10. Underwear	352	652			

TABLE 4.3. Hong Kong: Regression Results for the Composition Effect

Equation	α_i	θ_{i2}	θ_{i3}	θ_{i4}	θ_{i5}
$i = 1$	9.4702[a]	-3.2844[b]	-0.3486[a]		
	(5.6029)	(-3.8500)	(-6.0015)		
$i = 2$	10.1830[a]	-0.1224	0.4550[a]		
	(6.6417)	(-0.1400)	(-5.9327)		
$i = 3$	-0.6551	0.6143			
	(-0.3682)	(0.1795)			
$i = 4$	3.0509	0.3632	-0.4525[b]		
	(1.5353)	(0.4480)	(-3.2885)		
$i = 5$	9.5363[b]	-1.0542	-0.3245[c]	63.3601	
	(2.7706)	(-1.2591)	(-2.4188)	(2.0020)	
$i = 6$	-4.1817	-1.5632	0.2481[c]		
	(-1.1358)	(-1.3015)	(2.2307)		
$i = 7$	6.6749	2.4613	0.0932		
	(1.4917)	(0.9204)	(0.6546)		
$i = 8$	10.4073	-1.5547	-0.9868	-19.0655	1.5472
	(2.2719)	(-0.2659)	(-0.7952)	(0.2903)	(0.3730)
$i = 9$	2.9953	0.9389	-0.4433[b]		
	(1.9435)	(0.8932)	(-3.1434)		
$i = 10$	1.1877[a]	-0.7700[c]			
	(5.6368)	(-2.0135)			

The numbers in parentheses are t–statistics.
[a] Significant at the 1 percent level.
[b] Significant at the 5 percent level.
[c] Significant at the 10 percent level.

TABLE 4.4. Hong Kong: Results of F–tests for the Composition Effect

Equation	F statistics	Interpretation
i = 1	F(2,5) = 20.7474	Reject H_0: $\theta_{12}=\theta_{13}=0$[a]
	F(3,5) = 20.2810	Reject H_0: $\alpha_1=\theta_{12}=\theta_{13}=0$[a]
i = 2	F(2,5) = 17.9082	Reject H_0: $\theta_{22}=\theta_{23}=0$[a]
	F(3,5) = 26.3101	Reject H_0: $\alpha_2=\theta_{22}=\theta_{23}=0$[a]
i = 3	F(1,6) = 0.0322	Do not reject H_0: $\theta_{32}=0$[b]
	F(2,6) = 0.0912	Do not reject H_0: $\alpha_3=\theta_{32}=0$[b]
i = 4	F(2,5) = 6.8855	Reject H_0: $\theta_{42}=\theta_{43}=0$[a]
	F(3,5) = 55.6568	Reject H_0: $\alpha_4=\theta_{42}=\theta_{43}=0$[a]
i = 5	F(3,4) = 1.9510	Do not reject H_0:
	F(4,4) = 13.7561	$\theta_{52}=...=\theta_{54}=0$[b]
		Do not reject H_0:
		$\alpha_5=\theta_{52}=...=\theta_{54}=0$[b]
i = 6	F(2,5) = 4.3438	Do not reject H_0: $\theta_{62}=\theta_{63}=0$[b]
	F(3,5) = 31.3558	Reject H_0: $\alpha_6=\theta_{62}=\theta_{63}=0$[a]
i = 7	F(2,5) = 0.5669	Do not reject H_0: $\theta_{72}=\theta_{73}=0$[b]
	F(3,5) = 64.3784	Reject H_0: $\alpha_7=\theta_{72}=\theta_{73}=0$[a]
i = 8	F(4,3) = 1.4089	Do not reject H_0:
	F(5,3) = 1.9910	$\theta_{82}=...=\theta_{85}=0$[b]
		Do not reject H_0:
		$\alpha_8=\theta_{82}=...=\theta_{85}=0$[b]
i = 9	F(2,5) = 6.2320	Reject H_0: $\theta_{92}=\theta_{93}=0$[a]
	F(3,5) = 14.2639	Reject H_0: $\alpha_9=\theta_{92}=\theta_{93}=0$[a]
i = 10	F(1,6) = 4.0543	Do not reject H_0: $\theta_{10,2}=0$[b]
	F(2,6) = 219.5896	Reject H_0: $\alpha_{10}=\theta_{10,2}=0$[a]

[a] Significant at the 1 percent level.

[b] Significant at the 5 percent level.

price effect was tested using a simple t–test of the hypothesis that $\alpha_i = 0$. Both of these were also tested jointly using an F–test.

Evidence of compositional differences between the U.S.– and Hong Kong–produced apparel groups is therefore somewhat mixed. For three apparel groups (playsuits, trousers, and woven shirts) the joint hypothesis of no rent sharing and no composition effect cannot be rejected, meaning that the U.S.–Hong Kong price differential is mainly white noise. Of the seven remaining apparel groups, three exhibit a significant rent sharing effect at the 5 percent level.

V. Allowing for Differentiated Products

What if there exist real or perceived differences between U.S.–produced apparel and imports from Hong Kong? If U.S. and Hong Kong goods are not perfect substitutes, then the price of Hong Kong products (including the license price) need not equal the price of U.S.–produced clothing, even in the absence of rent sharing. In other words, if the assumption of homogeneous goods is dropped, then the price differential observed in the previous sections could simply be an indication of product differentiation instead of (or together with) rent sharing. While it is not possible to deal with product differentiation in general because of data limitations, certain aspects of it can be controlled, as explained below.[10]

A. Equation Setup

Suppose imports from Hong Kong are of a different quality than domestically–produced clothing. Following Swan 1970, the quality of a product may be thought of as the amount of services obtained from its consumption. These services are a homogeneous good with a uniform price, s_{it}. To the extent that two products embody unequal amounts of services, they will differ in quality and hence, in price. Let q_{it}^{US} denote the amount of services in one unit of U.S.–produced clothing i at time t, and q_{it}^{HK} the amount of services in one unit of Hong Kong–produced clothing i at time t.

Let u_{it} and v_{it} denote random error terms. Then $P_{it}^{US} = s_{it}q_{it}^{US} + u_{it}$, and $P_{it}^{HK} = s_{it}q_{it}^{HK} + v_{it}$, if the errors enter additively; and $P_{it}^{US} = s_{it}q_{it}^{US}u_{it}$, and $P_{it}^{HK} = s_{it}q_{it}^{HK}v_{it}$, if the errors enter multiplicatively.[11] Assuming random errors which enter additively into the formula, then:

$$P_{it}^{HK} - P_{it}^{US} = s_{it}(q_{it}^{HK} - q_{it}^{US}) + (v_{it} - u_{it}),$$

or:

$$P_{it}^{HK} = P_{it}^{US} + s_{it}(q_{it}^{HK} - q_{it}^{US}) + \epsilon_{it},$$

where $\epsilon_{it} = v_{it} - u_{it}$, and ϵ_{it} satisfies the usual assumptions for a random error term. Let Z_{it} denote the difference between the quality of Hong Kong clothing and U.S. clothing, that is, $Z_{it} = s_{it}(q_{it}^{HK} - q_{it}^{US})$.

---

[10]It would be ideal to be able to estimate a simultaneous equation system based on Armington's 1969 model.

[11]The case of multiplicative errors is considered in Krishna and Tan 1994; the results are similar to those presented here.

Equation (1), taking into account quality differences, should then be:

$$P_{it}^{HK} = \alpha + \beta P_{it}^{US} + \gamma NEQUIV_{it}^{HK} + \delta UTIL_{it}^{HK} + \phi QUOTA$$
$$+ \lambda SALES_t + \pi Z_{it} + \epsilon_{it}. \tag{8}$$

By assuming homogeneity and thereby excluding Z_{it}, equation (1) has regression coefficients which suffer from omitted variable bias. For example, if there is an improvement in the quality of Hong Kong goods, coupled with a deterioration in the quality of U.S. goods, then Z_{it} and P_{it}^{HK} will rise and P_{it}^{US} will fall. In this case, Z_{it} is negatively correlated with P_{it}^{US} and positively correlated with P_{it}^{HK}, and both effects work to bias the estimate of β downward in equation (1),[12] creating an impression of rent sharing. Furthermore, a negative correlation can be expected between Z_{it} and $QUOTA_{it}^{HK}$. It has been shown that more restrictive quotas tend to induce imports of a higher quality, since quotas are typically volume, rather than value restrictions.[13] Therefore, the omission of Z_{it} would cause the estimate of ϕ in regression (1) to be biased downward. There is no clear relation between quality differences and license concentration or quota utilization, so that there is no prior expectation as to the effect on the coefficients on $NEQUIV_{it}^{HK}$, $SALES_t$ and $UTIL_{it}^{HK}$ caused by the omission of Z_{it}.

Since there is no way of measuring s_{it}, q_{it}^{HK}, or q_{it}^{US}, quality differences cannot be held constant by including Z_{it} as an independent variable. However, Z_{it} can be captured to some extent through the use of apparel group dummies and a time trend. In other words, it is assumed that Z_{it} is a linear function of time, t: $Z_{it} = z_i + \mu t$ for i = 1,...,10, and t = 1,...,8. This entails the assumption that the quality difference changes by the same amount every year for each apparel group. In the absence of a direct measure of quality differences, this is the best possible approach.[14]

The new regression equation is:

$$P_{it}^{HK} = \alpha_{10} + \alpha_1 GRP_1 + ... + \alpha_9 GRP_9 + \mu t + \beta P_{it}^{US}$$
$$+ \gamma NEQUIV_{it}^{HK} + \delta UTIL_{it}^{HK} + \phi QUOTA_{it}^{HK} + \lambda SALES_t + \epsilon_{it}. \tag{9}$$

---

[12]This follows directly from the formula for omitted variable bias. See Johnston 1985, p.260 for example.

[13]See Rodriguez 1979 and Krishna 1987.

[14]Year dummies can be used instead of a time trend. This is a slightly more flexible specification as it will allow the year–to–year changes in quality differences to vary with time. However, the results are not very different from the simpler specification with a time trend.

If there is no rent sharing and there are no quality differences, then P_{it}^{HK} $=P_{it}^{US}$. (Recall that P_{it}^{HK} includes the license price). In other words, $\alpha_1, ..., \alpha_{10}$ and μ should be zero and β should be 1. Moreover, none of the other variables should enter significantly into the equation.

If there is no rent sharing but there are time–varying quality differences of an additive form, that is if an American product is worth a fixed number of dollars more (or less) than its counterpart imported from Hong Kong, then it should be observed, for the ith apparel group at time t: $P_{it}^{HK} = a_{it} + P_{it}^{US}$, where a_{it} is the intercept term for apparel group i at time t:

$$a_{it} = \begin{cases} \alpha_{10} + \alpha_i + \mu t & \text{for } i=1,...,9, \\ \alpha_{10} + \mu t & \text{for } i=10. \end{cases}$$

The intercept for each apparel group, a_{it}, would give an estimate of the quality difference in the products by country of origin at time t. The coefficient on P_{it}^{US} should still be one and γ, δ, ϕ and λ should still be zero. In other words, the null hypothesis is: $\beta = 1$ and $\gamma = \delta = \phi = \lambda = 0$. If the null hypothesis is proven false, then the evidence suggests the existence of rent sharing.

B. Regression Results

The results of regression (9) are shown in Table 4.5. The adjusted R^2 is quite high at 0.95, suggesting that the regression has captured most of the relevant factors. The estimate of β is 0.37, and it is significantly less than 1.[15] Furthermore, the null hypothesis that $\beta=1$ and $\gamma = \delta = \phi = \lambda = 0$ can be rejected at the 5 percent level. This seems to suggest that some form of rent sharing exists. As explained in Section III, β may be thought of as representing the marginal component of rent sharing. From the results of regression (9), a US\$1 increase in the U.S. price is associated with a US\$0.37 increase in the adjusted Hong Kong price; if the model is correct, US\$0.63 of the marginal price differential, or rent, is retained in the United States.

---

[15] Of course, it is always possible that this low β estimate could be the result of measurement error bias. This could arise if, as a result of concordance and aggregation, the P_{it}^{US} values are only noisy proxies for their true values.

TABLE 4.5. Hong Kong: Regression Results for the Differentiated Products Model

Dependent variable = P_{it}^{HK}

Independent Variable	Coefficient	t–statistic
Constant	-2.0111 (14.8309)	-0.1356
P_{it}^{US}	0.3702 (0.1641)	2.2560[a]
$NEQUIV_{it}^{HK}$	-0.0359 (0.0239)	-1.5037
$UTIL_{it}^{HK}$	0.6881 (2.5227)	0.2728
$QUOTA_{it}^{HK}$	-0.4021×10^{-7} (0.1036×10^{-6})	-0.3882
$SALES_t$	0.0547 (0.1203)	0.4543

Number of observations = 64

$R^2 = 0.9655$, Adjusted $R^2 = 0.9547$

Nine apparel group dummies and a time trend included.

Standard errors are in parentheses beneath the estimates of the parameters.

[a] Significant at the 5 percent level.

Results of hypothesis–testing:

F–statistic for the joint test of $\beta=1$ and $\gamma=\delta=\phi=\lambda=0$:

F = 3.2268; reject the null hypothesis at the 5 percent level.

t–statistic for the test of $\beta=1$:

t = -3.8384; reject the null hypothesis at the 1 percent level (two–tailed test).

CHAPTER FIVE

Testing for Rent Sharing in Korea

I. Introduction

The textile and apparel industry has played a significant role in Korea's export–driven industrialization. During the 1980s, according to Hamilton and Kim 1989, the volume of apparel exports from Korea grew by 155 percent, and textile and apparel exports accounted for some 25 percent of total exports. A sizeable portion of these exports were sent to the United States. The United States has always been Korea's largest export market for textiles and apparel, at times accounting for more than one–third of Korea's total exports of textiles and apparel.

Compared to the case of Hong Kong, much less has been written about the impact of the MFA restrictions on Korean textile and apparel exports. One study by Kim 1986 estimates the tariff equivalent of MFA quota rents in Korea to be approximately 17 percent in 1983, and that removal of MFA restrictions could increase Korean textile and apparel exports to the United States by an average of US$1,677 million. This estimate is based on the 1980 tariff equivalents of Hong Kong MFA exports to the United States calculated by Tarr and Morkre 1984: it is simply the weighted average of the Tarr and Morkre tariff equivalents for 23 MFA categories with Korean exports as weights. As will be demonstrated in Chapter Fifteen, however, there may be many problems with this procedure, as cost differences, institutional differences, and the possibility of rent sharing could make it inappropriate to estimate Korean license prices based on Hong Kong license prices.

This chapter follows the approach of Chapter Four to test for the existence of rent sharing between Korean apparel exporters and U.S. importers. The analysis is taken a step further by testing a model that allows for differentiated goods beyond the services model of quality differentiation. As explained later, this test is made possible because, unlike the Hong Kong dollar which has been fixed at HK$7.80 to US$1.00 since 1983, the Korean won is not pegged to the U.S. dollar.

II. The Data

The data set for this empirical analysis is very similar to that used in Chapter Four. It covers the time period 1981–88 and pertains to three broad areas:

1. Domestically (U.S.) produced apparel
2. Imported apparel from Korea
3. License holdings in Korea

Data were obtained for nine apparel groups. The apparel groups are defined as in Chapter Three. Not all MFA categories were subject to quota in the eight years considered, hence, in order to maintain consistency, unrestricted observations were dropped from the sample.[1]

Data were collected for the nine apparel groups (denoted by the subscript i) on the following variables between 1981 and 1988 (where the subscript t denotes the year):

P_{it}^{US} = unit value of U.S. production, in US dollars

p_{it}^{K} = f.o.b. Korean price, in U.S. dollars, inclusive of the license price

$DUTY_{it}$ = U.S. ad valorem duty

$TRANSP_{it}^{K}$ = per unit transport cost from Korea to the United States, in U.S. dollars

P_{it}^{K} = adjusted Korean price, in U.S. dollars, where

P_{it}^{K} = $p_{it}^{K} (1 + DUTY_{it}) + TRANSP_{it}^{K}$

Q_{it}^{K} = quantity of imports from Korea, measured in pieces

$NEQUIV_{it}^{K}$= numbers equivalent of the Herfindahl index of concentration in license holding, defined as $1/(\Sigma x_k^2)$, where x_k equals the share of license holder k in total licenses

$QUOTA_{it}^{K}$ = import quota, measured in pieces

$UTIL_{it}^{K}$ = quota utilization ratio, where $UTIL_{it}^{K} = Q_{it}^{K} / QUOTA_{it}^{K}$

EXC_t^{K} = exchange rate, expressed as won price of US$1

$SALES_t$ = retail sales in the United States, in billions of U.S. dollars

The data sources are the same as those in Chapter Four, except for the Korean license holding data which were obtained from the Korea Garment and Knitwear Export Association. The exchange rate information was taken from the *International Financial Statistics*. The rate used is the average annual market rate quoted in won per U.S. dollar. U.S. retail sales data were obtained from the OECD's *Main Economic Indicators*.

---

1. Several MFA categories, particularly in the earlier part of our sample, were designated Export Recommendation (or ER) products for which there are no explicit limits. Category 652 (man-made fibre underwear) was an ER product for the duration of the entire sample and this was the reason why we dropped Apparel Group 10 (underwear) from our sample.

III. Testing for Rent Sharing

A. Homogeneous Goods

Following the methodology developed in Chapter Four, the first step was to test for rent sharing under the assumption that Korean apparel exports and U.S.-produced apparel are homogeneous goods. The following equation was run:

$$P_{it}^K = \alpha + \beta P_{it}^{US} + \gamma NEQUIV_{it}^K + \delta UTIL_{it}^K$$

$$+ \phi QUOTA_{it}^K + \epsilon_{it}$$

$$(1)$$

where the variables are defined as in the previous section. In the absence of rent sharing, one should observe $P_{it}^K = P_{it}^{US}$; hence the null hypothesis is that $\alpha = \gamma = \delta = \phi = 0$ and $\beta = 1$.

The results of regression (1) are shown in Table 5.1. Note that whereas the estimates of α, γ and δ are not significantly different from zero, the β estimate is significantly less than one. In fact, the coefficient on P^{US} indicates that a

TABLE 5.1. Korea: Results of the Homogeneous Goods Model

Dependent variable = P_{it}^K

Independent Variable	Coefficient	t–statistic
Constant	0.9897	0.264
	(3.7488)	
P_{it}^{US}	0.6251	8.2403[a]
	(0.0759)	
NEQUIV$_{it}^K$	0.0382	0.2831
	(0.1350)	
QUOTA$_{it}^K$	-0.5419 x 10^{-7}	-3.1745[a]
	(0.1707 x 10^{-7})	
UTIL$_{it}^K$	4.3610	0.8786
	(4.9634)	

Number of observations = 55
$R^2 = 0.8139$, Adjusted $R^2 = 0.7990$
Standard errors are in parentheses beneath the parameter estimates.
[a] Significant at the 1 percent level.

Results of hypothesis testing:
F–statistic for joint test of $\beta = 1$ and $\alpha = \gamma = \phi = \delta = 0$:
F = 6.4887; reject the null hypothesis at the 1 percent level.
t–statistic for test of $\beta = 1$:
t=-4.9415; reject the null hypothesis at the 1 percent level.

US$1 increase in the U.S. price is associated with only a $0.63 increase in the price of a comparable Korean export, implying that the remaining $0.37 could be seized by the U.S. importers. Furthermore, although the ϕ estimate is very small, it is statistically significant and suggests that a larger quota is associated with a lower Korean export price. In the perfectly competitive model, this should not be the case since changes in the quota level would simply be reflected in the license price, which would adjust so as to equate P^K (which is inclusive of the license price) with P^{US}. The F–test of the null hypothesis is easily rejected at the 1 percent level.

B. The Services Model

Next, the assumption of homogeneous goods was relaxed to allow for differences in quality between Korean–produced apparel and U.S.–produced apparel. Following Chapter Four, the services model first put forward by Swan 1970 was used. This model accounts for basic vertical product differentiation by defining the quality of a product as the number of services obtained from its consumption, where services are a homogeneous good with a uniform price. To the extent that Korean and U.S. products embody unequal amounts of services, they will differ in quality and hence, in price. Of course, there are no data on the price and quantity of services. However, one can proxy for the value of quality differences using apparel group dummies and a time trend. (Note that this is subject to the constraint that the quality differences change by the same amount each year for every apparel group). Depending on the assumptions chosen regarding the error term, the appropriate specification may be in levels or in logs.

Table 5.2 presents the results of the regression:

$$P_{it}^K = \alpha_1 + \sum_{i=2}^{9} \alpha_i GRP_i + \mu t + \beta P_{it}^{US} + \gamma NEQUIV_{it}^K$$

$$+ \delta UTIL_{it}^K + \phi QUOTA_{it}^K + \epsilon_{it} \tag{2}$$

If there is no rent sharing and Korean apparel exports are of the same quality as apparel manufactured in the United States, then $P_{it}^K = P_{it}^{US}$ (i.e., $\alpha_1 = \alpha_2 = ... = \alpha_9 = \mu = \gamma = \delta = \phi = 0$ and $\beta = 1$) should be observed. If there is no rent sharing, but differences in quality between Korean–produced and U.S.–produced apparel, then the null hypothesis is $\gamma = \delta = \phi = 0$ and $\beta = 1$.

From Table 5.2, it seems clear that the homogeneous goods assumption is not a good assumption because the intercept, the coefficient on t, together with the coefficients on six of the eight apparel group dummies are statistically significant. The β estimate is significantly less than one; in fact, it is lower than the previous estimate, indicating that a US$1 increase in the U.S. price of an apparel item is accompanied by only a US$0.35 increase in the Korean price of a good of comparable quality. This means that 35 percent of the price of Korean apparel exports is retained as rents in the United States. This figure is strikingly similar to the one estimated for Hong Kong, which is approximately 38 percent.

The estimates of δ and ϕ are now statistically insignificant; however, the estimate of γ is marginally significant, suggesting that an increase in license holding concentration is accompanied by a reduction in the adjusted Korean price. A possible explanation for this may be found in Rottenberg's 1985 contention that "a very large fraction of all quota holdings is in the hands of the large trading companies." These trading companies own subsidiaries that manufacture part of the output they export under their allotted quotas. The

TABLE 5.2. Korea: Results of the Services Model

Dependent variable $= P_{it}^{K}$

Independent Variable	Coefficient	t–statistic
Constant	10.6838	1.9100[a]
	(5.5937)	
P_{it}^{US}	0.3531	1.6542
	(0.2135)	
NEQUIV$_{it}^{K}$	0.3497	1.5981
	(0.2188)	
QUOTA$_{it}^{K}$	-0.1531×10^{-6}	-0.7377
	(0.2075×10^{-6})	
UTIL$_{it}^{K}$	-2.3454	-0.6505
	(3.6055)	

Number of observations = 55
$R^2 = 0.9525$, Adjusted $R^2 = 0.9374$
Nine apparel group dummies and a time trend included.
Standard errors are in parentheses beneath the parameter estimates.
[a] Significant at the 10 percent level.

Results of hypothesis testing:
F–statistic for joint test of $\beta=1$ and $\alpha=\gamma=\phi=\delta=0$:
F = 3.6831; reject the null hypothesis at the 5 percent level (but not at the 1 percent level).
t–statistic for test of $\beta=1$:
t = -3.0302; reject the null hypothesis at the 1 percent level.

subsidiaries are in turn also allowed to subcontract their manufacturing to other firms.[2] Theoretically, therefore, this arrangement allows the quota–holding trading companies to seek out the lowest cost firms to which they can sub–contract their manufacturing for export.[3] The F–test of the joint null hypothesis that $\gamma = \delta = \phi = 0$ and $\beta = 1$ can be rejected at the 5 percent level but not at the 1 percent level.

Table 5.3 presents the results of the log specification:

$$\log P_{it}^{K} = \alpha_1 + \sum_{i=2}^{9} \alpha_i GRP_i + \mu t + \beta \log P_{it}^{US}$$

$$+ \gamma NEQUIV_{it}^{K} + \delta UTIL_{it}^{K} + \phi QUOTA_{it}^{K} + \epsilon_{it}. \tag{3}$$

The results are very similar to those in Table 5.2 except that the coefficient on the utilization rate is now significantly negative. The F–test of the joint null hypothesis that $\gamma = \delta = \phi = 0$ and $\beta = 1$ can now be rejected at the 1 percent level. However, the disadvantage of the log specification is that it cannot be used to draw any direct implications about rent sharing, since the coefficient on P^{US} should be equal to one even in the presence of marginal rent sharing.

IV. A Differentiated Goods Model

The drawback of the services model used in the previous section is that it only accounts for homogeneous vertical product differentiation, in the sense that a product embodying a greater number of services is better (i.e., of a higher quality) than one consisting of fewer services, but that the services provided by the different products are perfect substitutes. In reality, however, products could be fundamentally different, despite being substitutes, at some level, for one another. One designer dress, for example, is not the same as n dresses from a mass producer, although some substitution may well exist between the two. If Korean–produced apparel is of a different variety (not necessarily of a worse or better quality) than U.S.–produced apparel then the restrictions imposed by the

---

2. Rottenberg 1985 estimates that "about one–fifth of trading company exports of apparel are produced by firms that they own and the residuum is produced by other firms with which they contract."

3. However, in practice, according to Rottenberg 1985 p.31, trading companies "form long–term associations with a fixed set of manufacturing firms. Subcontractors for a given trading firm are a stable, continuous and firm set as a matter of 'ethics'. The trading companies give technical assistance to the manufacturing firms with which they are associated but they sever relationships, once established, only with great reluctance. Indeed, in times of slack demand when production must be reduced by the trading companies, the reduction is said to be made in the output of the trading companies' own plants rather than in those of the contracted manufacturers."

models studied until now need not apply. In particular, the restrictions on the coefficient of the U.S. price and on the quota level need not apply.

In this section, a simple version of this general model is set up and estimated. The model makes strong predictions about the relationship between the dollar price of Korean goods in the United States and changes in the dollar–won exchange rate in the presence of a binding quota, and under free trade. This prediction can be tested using Korean data due to the fact that unlike Hong Kong, Korea was not on a fixed exchange rate with the United States during the period under study. In testing the predictions of the model in the absence of a quota, data on imports from Italy to the United States were used. As will be made clearer in the following paragraphs, the exchange rate variable plays a key role in helping to determine if the data conform to the basic assumptions of the competitive model.

A. Equation Setup

Consider the following model of differentiated goods. The U.S. demand for Korean exports of good i at time t can be written:

$$D(\overset{(-)}{P_{it}^K}, \overset{(+)}{P_{it}^{US}}, \overset{(+)}{q_{it}^K}, \overset{(-)}{q_{it}^{US}}, \overset{(+)}{SALES_t}) \tag{4}$$

where q denotes quality and the variable $SALES_t$ stands for the amount of retail sales in the United States and serves as a demand shift parameter. The expected signs of the partial derivatives are indicated above the variables:

1. U.S. demand for Korean exports varies negatively with their dollar price and positively with their quality.
2. U.S. demand for Korean exports varies positively with the dollar price of the comparable U.S. product and negatively with the quality of the U.S. product, since U.S.-produced and Korean-produced goods are (imperfect) substitutes.

In the absence of a quota, the supply of Korean exports would be a function of their won price (which depends on their dollar price and the exchange rate) and on the quality of the Korean goods. At a given dollar price, an increase in the exchange rate, or appreciation of the dollar, shifts out the supply function of Korean exports. An increase in the quality of Korean exports is associated with an increase in the cost of production which shifts the supply curve in at any given dollar price and exchange rate. An increase in the dollar price increases supply, other things equal. This allows the supply of Korean exports to be given by the following equation, where the signs of the partial derivatives are summarized above the relevant variables for ease of reference:

$$\overset{(+)\quad(+)\quad(-)}{S(EXC_t^{K},\ P_{it}^{US},\ q_{it}^{K})} \tag{5}$$

where EXC_t^{K} is the exchange rate (in won per U.S. dollar).

These demand and supply curves are depicted in Figure 5.1 as a function of the dollar price of exports. Their intersection gives the equilibrium price of Korean exports. Note that:

1. An increase in the U.S. price of the substitute good would shift out the demand for Korean exports, raising their price in equilibrium.
2. An increase in the quality of Korean goods would shift out their demand and shift in their supply. Both effects would lead to an increase in their price.
3. An increase in the quality of the U.S. good, for a given price of the U.S. good, would shift in the demand for the Korean export and reduce its price.
4. An improvement in the state of demand, proxied for by the retail sales index $SALES_t$, would shift out the demand for Korean exports, raising their equilibrium price.

Hence, under free trade, the price of Korean exports would be given by:

$$\overset{(+)\ (+)\quad(-)\quad(-)\quad(+)}{P_{it}^{K}(P_{it}^{US},\ q_{it}^{K},\ q_{it}^{US},\ EXC_t^{K},\ SALES_t,\ldots).} \tag{6}$$

Note that an appreciation of the dollar, other thing constant, is predicted to result in a reduction in the dollar price of exports.

Now, consider the effect of imposing a binding quota. In this case, the supply curve for Korean exports is restricted by the quota level, as depicted in Figure 5.1. The difference between the supply price and the demand price, at this given quota level, equals the implicit license price denoted by L in Figure 5.1. Now, any factor that affects the supply curve, without affecting the demand curve, will not affect the equilibrium price in the standard competitive model. Thus, an appreciation of the dollar, which shifts the supply curve to RS', should have no effect on the equilibrium dollar price of Korean exports, if this model is correct. The only effect would be to raise license prices. The effect of an appreciation of the dollar is depicted in Figure 5.1. Moreover, note that with a binding quantitative restraint in place, an increase in the quota level will reduce the equilibrium price of Korean exports. Hence the equilibrium price of quota–constrained Korean exports would be:

$$\overset{(+)\ (+)\ (-)\quad\ (-)\qquad(+)}{P_{it}^{K}(P_{it}^{US},\ q_{it}^{K},\ q_{it}^{US},\ QUOTA_{it}^{K},\ SALES_t).} \tag{7}$$

B. Regression Results

In order to test if the data conform to this model, the following regression was run:

$$P_{it}^{K} = \alpha_1 + \sum_{i=2}^{9} \alpha_i GRP_i + \mu t + \beta P_{it}^{US} + \gamma NEQUIV_{it}^{K} + \delta UTIL$$

$$+ \phi QUOTA_{it}^{K} + \theta SALES_t + \lambda EXC_t^{K} + \epsilon_{it} \tag{8}$$

This regression is clearly motivated by the competitive model above. One might be concerned about using the U.S. price as an exogenous variable. However, to the extent that the U.S. market is large compared to Korean exports, the U.S. price will be exogenous in relation to Korean prices—thus, the endogeneity issue may be ignored. It would, of course, be best to specify and estimate an integrated world market system of equations for all exporters and importers but the huge data requirements involved prevent us from doing so.

Note that the competitive model with differentiated products does predict a negative sign for the coefficient on QUOTA$_{it}^{K}$ and does not predict a unit coefficient for the U.S. price in the regressions run in the previous section. Thus, the results in Table 5.1 may be consistent with the competitive model with differentiated products: the coefficient on the quota variable is negative and strongly significant while the coefficient on utilization is not significantly

FIGURE 5.1. Korea: The Effect of a Supply Shift

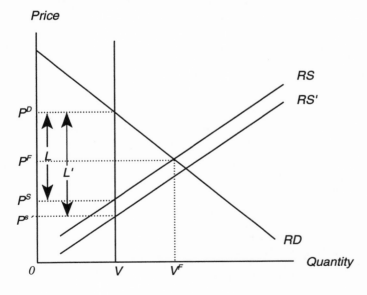

different from zero in Table 5.1. However, that regression omits a variable, the exchange rate, and does not allow for quality differences. Allowing for quality differences makes the coefficient on $NEQUIV_{it}^K$, the numbers equivalent, significant in Tables 5.2 and 5.3, and the coefficient on $UTIL_{it}^K$, the utilization ratio, significant in Table 5.3. This is in contradiction to the predictions of the general competitive model.

Since no direct measure of the quality of Korean and U.S. goods was available, apparel group dummies and a time trend were used to proxy for q^K and q^{US}. Under the null hypothesis of the competitive model with differentiated products, one should observe $\gamma = \delta = \lambda = 0$. However, the results in Table 5.4 show that whereas the estimates of γ and δ are now not significantly different from zero, that of λ is significantly negative so that an appreciation of the U.S. dollar (i.e., an increase in EXC_t^K) is accompanied by a fall in the adjusted

TABLE 5.3. Korea: Results of the Services Model (in logs)

Dependent variable = $\log P_{it}^K$

Independent Variable	Coefficient	t–statistic
Constant	2.1979	3.3258[a]
	(0.6608)	
$\log P_{it}^{US}$	0.1904	0.9122
	(0.2088)	
$NEQUIV_{it}^K$	0.0348	2.5942[a]
	(0.0134)	
$QUOTA_{it}^K$	0.5254×10^{-8}	0.4095
	(0.1283×10^{-7})	
$UTIL_{it}^K$	-0.4634	-2.0408[b]
	(0.2271)	

Number of observations = 55
$R^2 = 0.9786$, Adjusted $R^2 = 0.9719$
Nine apparel group dummies and a time trend included.
Standard errors are in parentheses beneath the parameter estimates.
[a] Significant at the 1 percent level.
[b] Significant at the 5 percent level.

Results of hypothesis testing:
F–statistic for joint test of $\beta=1$ and $\alpha=\gamma=\phi=\delta=0$:
$F = 7.1236$; reject the null hypothesis at the 1 percent level.
t–statistic for test of $\beta=1$:
$t = -3.8782$; reject the null hypothesis at the 1 percent level.

model and does not rely on the special assumptions on differentiation, namely the services model, made earlier.

C. Comparison with an Unrestricted Exporter

As a final check, an analogous regression was run for Italy, an unconstrained exporter under the MFA:

$$P_{it}^{IT} = \alpha_1 + \sum_{i=2}^{9} \alpha_i GRP_i + \mu t + \beta P_{it}^{US}$$

$$+ \theta SALES_t + \lambda EXC_t^{IT} + \epsilon_{it}.$$

(9)

Under the competitive model, the coefficients on P_{it}^{US} and $SALES_{it}$ are expected to be positive, and the coefficient on EXC_{it}^{IT} is expected to be negative. The results are reported in Table 5.5. Note that the predictions of the competitive model are well borne out for Italy, although the coefficient on the U.S. price is not significant. This could just be a reflection of the fact that the Italian exports serve a very different niche from domestic U.S. production. However, an appreciation of the dollar relative to the Italian lira, other things constant, results in a reduction in the dollar price of Italian exports.

All of this leads to the conclusion that the predictions of the simple competitive models are not validated by the data. Rent sharing between importers and exporters is, however, consistent with this evidence.

TABLE 5.4. Korea: Results of the Differentiated Goods Model

Dependent variable $= P_{it}^K$

Independent Variable	Coefficient	t–statistic
Constant	11.4144	0.6658
	(17.1449)	
P_{it}^{US}	0.1759	0.8142
	(0.2160)	
NEQUIV $_{it}^K$	0.0671	0.2808
	(0.2389)	
QUOTA $_{it}^K$	-0.2123×10^{-6}	-1.0194
	(0.2083×10^{-6})	
UTIL $_{it}^K$	1.0876	0.2825
	(3.8497)	
EXC $_t^K$	-0.9879×10^{-2}	-2.3094[a]
	(0.4278×10^{-2})	
SALES$_t$	0.1183	0.6329
	(0.1869)	

Number of observations = 55
$R^2 = 0.9589$, Adjusted $R^2 = 0.9431$
Nine apparel group dummies and a time trend included.
Standard errors are in parentheses beneath the parameter estimates.
[a] Significant at the 5 percent level.

Results of hypothesis testing:
F–statistic for joint test of $\gamma=\delta=\lambda=0$:
$F = 2.6147$; do not reject the null hypothesis.

TABLE 5.5. Italy: Results of the Differentiated Goods Model

Dependent variable $= P_{it}^{IT}$

Independent Variable	Coefficient	t–statistic
Constant	4.425	0.1107
	(40.1191)	
P_{it}^{US}	1.1275	1.3846
	(0.8143)	
EXC $_{it}^{IT}$	-0.0142	-4.3376[a]
	(0.0034)	
SALES$_t$	0.2361	0.4553
	(0.5184)	

Number of observations = 80
$R^2 = 0.9182$, Adjusted $R^2 = 0.9021$
Nine apparel group dummies and a time trend included.
Standard errors are in parentheses beneath the parameter estimates.
[a] Significant at the 1 percent level.

CHAPTER SIX

Testing for Rent Sharing in Mexico[1]

I. Introduction

This chapter investigates the case of Mexico's exports of apparel to the United States under the MFA. As the fifth most important exporter of apparel into the U.S. market, Mexico should be part of any study that measures the distribution of rents accruing from the MFA. Because of the institutional arrangements that govern trade between the United States and Mexico, however, Mexico presents a particular challenge.

First, there is no organized market for export licenses in Mexico, and hence no explicit export license price.[2] Quota constrained exports are allocated to potential exporters on a historical basis. The implication of this arrangement is that there may be a high degree of concentration in the quota allocation for those products in which the quota is binding.

Second, Mexican exports of apparel to the United States are influenced by market sharing arrangements that allow assembly of apparel in Mexico using U.S. inputs for re–export to the United States. This trade may be within the same firm with operations in both the United States and Mexico, or may be the result of subcontracting arrangements between U.S. firms and Mexican assembly operations. Either of these arrangements has implications for export pricing strategies and market power relationships that may affect rent sharing.

Third, even the quotas negotiated under the MFA have liberal provisions under an arrangement which essentially eliminates the restrictiveness of the MFA for Mexican exports produced with U.S. inputs. This arrangement, known as the Special Regime, went into effect in 1989, and clearly has some influence on whether quotas are binding and whether rents exist.

Finally, it should also be noted that very few of the quotas imposed on Mexican exports are actually binding, so that even excluding the effects of the institutional arrangements described above, the potential rents accruing from MFA export restraints are probably very small. Thus, the welfare effects of quota restrictions on Mexican exports, and of market imperfections that might lead to rent sharing, are probably not large. Nevertheless, this case provides a suitable test for the existence of perfect markets and rent sharing, with some bearing for a more sober assessment of the effects of MFA restrictions on developing countries.

---

1. This chapter is based on Bannister 1994.
2. The transfer of export rights is illegal, and there is no evidence of informal markets for these.

II. Institutional Arrangements

A. Export Licensing

Textiles and apparel exported from Mexico to the United States under the MFA are restricted by visas which allow Mexican exports to pass through U.S. customs. They are not restricted at the point of exit by Mexican customs officials. The export visas are distributed by Mexican officials according to the amount of quota negotiated under the MFA. First priority to fill the quota is given to firms that exported in the previous year. Any leftover quota is distributed to new entrants in the market. After the initial allocation, firms can increase their share of quota when there is unused quota quantity available, and when the firm can show that it has already exported 70 percent of its initial allocation. Visas are specific to a particular consignment, and are valid from the date of issuance until December 31 of the same year.

What are the implications of this arrangement? The initial allocation of export permits (visas) does not take place through an auction mechanism. This means that any rent created by the export restrictions benefits the exporter rather than the government. Further, since visas are distributed on a historical basis it is probable that significant concentration exists in the distribution of these rents. Although there is no market for export permits, there is an unobservable implicit valuation the exporter confers on the export visa, which is equal to the amount he would be willing to pay for the right to export. To the extent that quotas are binding, this shadow price is positive, although it will vary from firm to firm. If quotas are not binding, the implicit price is zero. For a binding quota, this implicit price will be equal to the quota premium or the unit rent created by the quantity restrictions, and will be included in the f.o.b. price of Mexican exports to the United States that are restricted under the MFA.

B. Trade Regimes

Two different institutional arrangements operate to diminish the trade barriers to Mexican apparel exports entering the United States. The first of these is the provision under chapter 9802.00 of the harmonized tariff schedule (HTS 9802.00) that allows for special treatment of goods assembled in Mexico from U.S. components. This provision allows American apparel firms to export cut cloth for assembly in Mexico's in–bond industry (the *maquiladora* industry) and reimport the final goods, paying tariffs only on the value added in Mexico. In most cases, the facilities in Mexico used for assembly are owned by U.S. firms, so that Mexican apparel exports entering the United States under HTS 9802.00 constitute movements of goods within the same firm, even though they are registered as imports into the United States under the MFA (USITC, 1991).

HTS 9802.00 is essentially a tariff provision, but it has implications for rent sharing. If rents exist, then U.S. firms with assembly operations in Mexico owning a large share of the quota will be the principal beneficiaries of the quota restrictions.[3] The evidence in Table 6.1 shows that, for Mexican apparel exports to the United States, this is probably the case. From 1988 to 1991, 85–90 percent of all Mexican apparel exports under the MFA entered the United States under HTS 9802.00 provisions, with 60–70 percent of their value added in the United States.

The second institutional arrangement affecting Mexican exports of apparel into the United States is a special provision of the MFA known as the Special Regime. It effectively eliminates quotas under the MFA for apparel assembled in Mexico from fabric cut and formed in the United States. The test for eligibility for the Special Regime quota treatment is more stringent than that for HTS 9802.00 tariff provisions since the former requires that fabric be formed and cut in the United States while the latter only requires the cutting to take place in the United States. Although Special Regime quotas are often filled, they are administered in such a way that utilization rates have been allowed to exceed 100 percent. Thus it may appear that rents exist for those exports that enter the United States under the Special regime when, in fact, no rents are being generated. The Special Regime was instituted in 1988, although it only became effective in 1989. In 1990, 43.5 percent of apparel exports from Mexico into the United States under the MFA entered under the Special Regime.[4]

C. Quota Arrangements

In addition to the Special Regime and HTS 9802.00, there are different quota arrangements within the MFA that affect the restrictiveness of the quotas. There are three types of quotas:

1. Specific Limit: A specific limit quota is a quantity constraint which increases at a fixed rate per year (in most cases 6 percent, with the exception of cotton fiber which increases at 2 percent per year). If the quantity restriction is met, then a specific limit quota is binding.
2. Designated Level: A designated level is an informal barrier whose restrictiveness depend on the discretion of the administrators of the quota in the United States. Mexican officials can request an increase in

---

3. This is not a case particular to Mexico. Large U.S. importers that also manufacture and assemble apparel overseas, such as Liz Claiborne, often have claims to large fractions of available quota in developing countries.

4. For a more detailed description of these arrangements and their implications for textile trade under the North American Free Trade Agreement, see Bannister and Low 1992.

the quota for a specific year which may or may not be granted depending on the U.S. administrator's judgment as to what effect this will have on the U.S. market.[5]

3. Consultation Mechanisms: Consultation mechanisms impose no quantitative limit, but establish a mechanism by which the United States can consult with Mexico when exports are perceived to be affecting the U.S. market adversely. In practice, these consultation mechanisms have not been binding.

The arrangements described above affect a very large proportion of Mexican exports of apparel to the United States. Table 6.2 shows how they affect the groups of apparel that have been most bound by quota arrangements between 1981 and 1990. The first column shows the average rate of quota utilization (quantity of exports/quota). In general, a consistent quota utilization rate of 90 percent or above may be considered to indicate that the quota is binding. The groups in Table 6.2 are aggregations of MFA categories, some of which were quota bound and some of which were not. In addition, not all groups were bound in all years. The most consistently bound groups were trousers, woven shirts and underwear. Of the groups presented, only sweaters did not have a significant component of exports entering the United States under HTS 9802.00. Between 80–90 percent of the exports of all other groups entered under HTS 9802.00, with an average value added in Mexico between 43 percent for shirts and 22 percent for underwear. This suggests that some of the rents accruing from the MFA in these products are captured by U.S. firms assembling apparel in Mexico. Under this type of quota, all were subject to either designated consultation levels or specific limits, except for sweaters, which were only subject to consultation mechanisms.

Trousers, woven shirts, and underwear, being the most tightly constrained groups of exports, are probably where the rents, if any, are being generated.[6] Yet, as shown in the last column of Table 6.2, a high proportion of these exports in these groups entered the United States under the Special Regime and thus are effectively not bound, at least from 1989 on. Table 6.2 thus reinforces the contention that available rents from MFA quota restrictions are small, and under the most optimistic assumption that exporters receive all the rent, Mexican producers still capture only a portion.

---

5. According to officials from the Department of Commerce, there are some MFA categories in which petitions for increase of the designated levels have been denied, so that there is reason to believe that at least in some cases these quotas are binding also.

6. In the analysis that follows, these are considered to be the quota-bound groups.

TABLE 6.1. Mexico: Percentage of MFA Exports from Mexico to the United States Entering Under HTS 9802.00

	1988		1989		1990		1991	
	9802.00	U.S.Value Added	9802.00	U.S. Value Added	9802.00	U.S. Value Added	9802.00	U.S. Value Added
All MFA	72.20	69.30	76.87	61.50	73.20	65.70	75.50	66.20
Apparel	84.90	69.40	90.68	61.50	88.32	66.30	89.52	66.30
Other	28.30	68.90	30.08	61.50	28.01	63.50	29.27	66.01

Source: U.S. Department of Commerce, Office of Textiles.

TABLE 6.2. Mexico: Summary Data for Apparel Exports

Group	Average Quota Utilization 1981–90	Average Percent of MFA under 9802.00 1987–90	Average Percent Value Added in U.S.	Type of Quota	Average Percent Special Regime 1988-90
1. Sweaters	38.10	1.20	33.00	cm	0.00
2. Trousers	70.70	83.10	67.30	dl/sl	83.70
3. Men's Coats	42.90	88.20	65.50	dl	4.60
4. Women's Coats	51.80	80.10	70.10	dl/sl	29.20
5. Woven Shirts	63.40	89.70	57.70	sl	74.20
6. Underwear	59.30	82.30	78.30	dl/sl	59.70

Source: World Bank data tapes and U.S. Department of Commerce data.
cm = consultation mechanism, dl = designated level, sl = specific limit

III. The Data

The apparel groups used in this study are similar to those defined in Chapter Two. Six apparel groups were examined:

1. sweaters
2. trousers
3. men's coats
4. women's coats
5. woven shirts
6. underwear

The data include observations for the following variables from 1981 to 1990, where i indicates the apparel group, and t indicates the year:

P_{it}^{US} = unit value of U.S. production, in U.S. dollars

p_{it}^{M} = f.o.b. price of apparel imports from Mexico, in U.S. dollars

$DUTY_{it}$ = ad valorem tariff in the United States

$TRANSP_{it}^{M}$ = unit transport cost from Mexico to the United States

P_{it}^{M} = adjusted Mexico price, where

P_{it}^{M} = $p_{it}^{M}(1+DUTY_{it}^{M}) + TRANSP_{it}^{M}$

Q_{it}^{US} = U.S. sales of U.S. production

Q_{it}^{M} = Mexican exports to the U.S. market

$NEQUIV_{it}^{M}$ = numbers equivalent of the Herfindahl index of concentration among Mexican exporters

$QUOTA_{it}^{M}$ = quota level for Mexican exports to the United States

$UTIL_{it}^{M}$ = quota utilization rate defined as $UTIL_{it}^{M} = Q_{it}^{M} / QUOTA_{it}^{M}$

The sources and composition of these data may be found in a data appendix available from the author.

IV. Testing for Rent Sharing

As mentioned above, the implicit valuation of the quota rents is included in the Mexican f.o.b. price of exports to the United States. Thus, one can test for rent sharing by comparing the unit value of U.S. production with the Mexican f.o.b. price, appropriately adjusted for tariffs, transport costs, and HTS 9802.00 tariff concessions. Arbitrage in the U.S. market will cause these two prices to equalize if markets are competitive and all goods are homogeneous within each group. It is reasonable to assume that Mexican exporters are small, and therefore price–takers, in the U.S. market. However, if U.S. importers have monopsony power, this can lead to rent sharing if they can maintain a lower price for their imports than they pay for U.S. production.

Figure 6.1 plots the adjusted Mexican f.o.b. price on the vertical axis against the U.S. price on the horizontal axis for all six groups of products examined in this study. The arrow represents the forty–five degree line. The chart clearly shows that there is a significant difference between the two prices. The U.S. price is above the Mexican price in almost every instance, indicating that either sustained quality or composition differences or rent sharing may exist.

A. Equation Specification

To test the significance of this difference, the following regression was run using time series data from 1981 to 1990, pooled over the six apparel groups:

$$P_{it}^{M} = \alpha + \beta P_{it}^{US} + \gamma NEQUIV_{it} \\ + \delta UTIL_{it}^{M} + \phi QUOTA_{it}^{M} + \epsilon_{it} . \tag{1}$$

At this point, the variation over groups of apparel is not considered, and so α is maintained constant. As pointed out in Chapter Four, in this equation, the right-hand side variables can be considered exogenous to the Mexican exporter. If there is no rent sharing, and markets are perfectly competitive, and if all goods are assumed homogeneous within groups, then $P_{it}^{M} = P_{it}^{US}$. In this case the

FIGURE 6.1 Mexico: U.S. Price and Mexican Adjusted Price

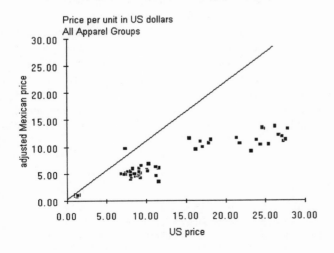

coefficient on the U.S. price is not expected to be significantly different from one, and all other parameters not to be significantly different from zero. If, however, rent sharing exists, or if the assumption of homogeneous goods is violated (by differences in quality or composition, for example), then the coefficient on P_{it}^{US} may be different from unity, and the coefficients on the other variables may be significant.

To test the robustness of the results of this regression (found in Table 6.3), an alternative specification of the model in the logarithms of the variables was used. Under this specification, the coefficient on the log of the U.S. price can be interpreted as an elasticity of price transmission, while the other coefficients can be interpreted as elasticities reflecting the effects of the different characteristics of the quota–license market on the Mexican f.o.b. price. The constant term can be interpreted as a proportional shift parameter. A Box–Cox test for model specification shows that the log–linear specification fits the data better.[7]

B. Regression Results

Table 6.3 presents the results of running regression (1) on:

1. all groups,
2. the quota bound groups,
3. non–bound groups.[8]

The first significant result is that for all three regressions, the hypothesis of perfect competition ($\beta = 1$ and $\alpha = \gamma = \delta = \phi = 0$) and the hypothesis that the coefficient on the U.S. price, β, is equal to one, are both rejected. While this does not confirm the existence of rent sharing, it is consistent with the rejection of the hypothesis of perfect competition in the market for Mexican exports to the United States in these groups of apparel. The intercept and the coefficient on the U.S. price are significant in all three regressions. In this context, the intercept can be interpreted as reflecting the effects of any fixed difference between the two prices common to all groups of apparel (the fixed component), and the coefficient on the U.S. price reflects the change in the Mexican price for

---

7. For a description of the Box–Cox test see Maddala 1992, p.220 or Fomby et al. 1984, p.423. The test consists of comparing the sum of squared residuals of the two models after performing a simple transformation of the data. The sum of squared residuals for the linear specification was 4.163. For the log–linear specification, it was 2.289.

8. The definition of the groups is based on the data in Table 6.2.

TABLE 6.3. Mexico: Regression Results for Equation 1, Linear Specification

Dependent variable = P_{it}^M

Independent	All Groups	Bound Groups	Unbound
Constant	2.4515[a]	0.6050[b]	4.6597[a]
	(0.5964)	(0.3146)	(0.9263)
P_{it}^{US}	0.4094[a]	0.4676[a]	0.4474[a]
	(0.0257)	(0.0310)	(0.0478)
$UTIL_{it}^M$	-0.8343	-0.2752	-2.483[c]
	(0.9247)	(0.4502)	(1.4850)
$QUOTA_{it}^M$	-2.29×10^{-8}	-6.79×10^{-9}	6.21×10^{-7}
	(2×10^{-8})	(1×10^{-8})	(7×10^{-7})
$NEQUIV_{it}^M$	-0.0012	0.0029[a]	-0.0153[b]
	(0.0022)	(0.0011)	(0.0075)
Adjusted R^2	0.872	0.942	0.775
Number of observations	60	30	30
t–test of $\beta=1$	-22.89; reject[a]	-17.16; reject[a]	-11.5; reject[a]
F-test of $\beta=1$ and $\alpha=\gamma=\delta=\phi=0$	338.71; reject[a]	292.09; reject[a]	268.81; reject[a]

Standard errors in parentheses.

[a] Significant at the 1 percent level.

[b] Significant at the 5 percent level.

[c] Significant at the 10 percent level.

unit change in the U.S. price, all other things held equal (the marginal component).[9]

The results of the regression in logs are presented in Table 6.4. As before, the hypothesis of perfect competition ($\beta = 1$ and $\alpha = \gamma = \delta = \phi = 0$) is rejected for all three regressions. However, it is interesting to note that the hypothesis of $\beta = 1$ cannot be rejected for the unbound groups. In contrast with the linear specification, the intercept terms cease to be significantly different from zero. However, the coefficient on the log of the U.S. price is significant at the 1

---

9. Later in the chapter the intercept is allowed to vary across groups so as to explore the possibility that the fixed component can be explained by group–specific fixed differences in quality between U.S. production and imports from Mexico.

TABLE 6.4. Mexico: Regression Results for Equation 1, Log–linear Specification
Dependent variable = log P_{it}^M

Independent		Bound Groups	Unbound Groups
Variables	All Groups	(2,5,6)	(1,3,4)
Constant	0.2639	0.3082	0.9294
	(0.4178)	(1.1384)	(0.9968)
log P_{it}^{US}	0.8090[a]	0.8027[a]	0.8752[a]
	(0.0491)	(0.0450)	(0.1209)
log $UTIL_{it}^M$	-0.0995[c]	-0.1003[c]	-0.1776[b]
	(0.0660)	(0.0735)	(0.1012)
log $QUOTA_{it}^M$	-0.0244	-0.0525	-0.0166
	(0.0248)	(0.0552)	(0.0857)
log $NEQUIV_{it}^M$	-0.0211	0.0759	-0.2501[b]
	(0.0583)	(0.0674)	(0.1293)
Adjusted R^2	0.939	0.976	0.735
Number of Observations	60	30	30
t–test, $\beta=1$	-3.889 reject[a]	-4.377 reject[a]	-1.031 cannot reject[a]
F–test, $\beta=1$ and $\alpha=\gamma=\delta=\phi=0$	97.093 reject[a]	97.096 reject[a]	49.113 reject[a]

Standard errors in parentheses.
[a] Significant at the 1 percent level.
[b] Significant at the 5 percent level.
[c] Significant at the 10 percent level.

percent level for all groups, and the coefficient on the log of the utilization rate is significant at the 5 percent and 10 percent level. The log of the numbers equivalent is significant and negative at the 5 percent level for the unbound groups. Although it is difficult to interpret the negative coefficients on $UTIL_{it}^M$ and $NEQUIV_{it}^M$, these results are not inconsistent with those of the linear specification, or with the hypothesis of rent sharing for the bound groups of apparel.

V. Allowing for Compositional Differences

Although the results in the previous section seem to indicate the possible existence of rent sharing, there are other possible explanations for the difference between the Mexican export price and the U.S. price. One possible explanation is a difference in the composition of the groups of apparel, with Mexican exports concentrating on the lower–value MFA categories that make up the groups, and U.S. products concentrating on the higher–value end. Each of the groups examined is an aggregation of categories in the MFA export data and different categories of U.S. production data. The problem faced when attempting to compare the unit value of U.S. production to the unit value of Mexican exports under the MFA is that at the most disaggregated levels, the two category groupings are not compatible. In aggregating them to the more comparable group levels, some compositional bias is inevitable, and this may show up in the marginal rent sharing parameter β, the coefficient on P_{it}^{US}, or in the intercept term. This section tests whether the price differences detected earlier can be explained entirely by this compositional bias. If composition bias cannot be ruled out, then the assumption of homogeneous product groups cannot be maintained and some accounting for product differences must be made.

A. Equation Setup

The procedure for testing compositional differences follows that of Chapter Four. The aggregate prices can be decomposed into their production-weighted components as follows:

$$P_i^{US} = \sum_j P_{ij}^{US}(\frac{Q_{ij}^{US}}{Q_i^{US}}) = \sum_j P_{ij}^{US} w_{ij}^{US}, \quad i=1,...,6, \quad j=1,...,n \tag{2}$$

where the subscript j refers to the MFA category belonging to apparel group i. Q_{ij}^{US} is the quantity of U.S. output in category j of group i, and Q_i^{US} is total output in group i. Hence w_{ij}^{US} is the quantity weight of category j in group i of U.S. production. Similarly, for Mexico:

$$P_i^{M} = \sum_j P_{ij}^{M}(\frac{Q_{ij}^{M}}{Q_i^{M}}) = \sum_j P_{ij}^{M} w_{ij}^{M}, \quad i=1,...,6, \quad j=1,...,n. \tag{3}$$

The difference between the adjusted Mexican export f.o.b. price and the U.S. unit value of production at the group level can then be expressed:

$$P_i^{M} - P_i^{US} = \sum_j P_{ij}^{M} w_{ij}^{M} - \sum_j P_{ij}^{US} w_{ij}^{US}. \tag{4}$$

Data exist for P_i^{M}, P_i^{US}, P_{ij}^{M}, and w_j^{M} only. To circumvent this problem it is assumed that the following relationship holds for each subgroup (MFA category) j within each group :

$$P_{ij}^{M} = \alpha_i + \beta_{1i} P_{ij}^{US} + \beta_{2i} X_{ij} + \epsilon_{ij} \tag{5}$$

where X_{ij} is a general term for the independent variables included in equation (1):

1. the level of the quota,
2. the utilization rate, and
3. the numbers equivalent of the Herfindahl index of concentration in export supply.

Note that α, β_1, and β_2 are assumed to be constant over all the members of each group i. Solving for P_i^{US} and substituting into (4) yields:

$$P_i^M - P_i^{US} = \gamma_i + \sum_j (w_{ij}^M - \delta_{1i} w_{ij}^{US}) P_{ij}^M$$
$$+ \delta_{2i} \sum_j w_{ij}^{US} X_{ij} + \delta_{1i} \sum_j w_{ij}^{US} e_{ij}. \tag{6}$$

where $\gamma_i = \alpha_i / \beta_{1i}$, $\delta_{1i} = 1 / \beta_{1i}$, and $\delta_{2i} = \beta_{2i} / \beta_i$. With one key assumption, equation (6) can be estimated and the coefficient on P_{ij}^M tested to determine if the composition effect is statistically significant: the assumption is that $\delta_{2i} = 0$ for all ij, that is, that the change in the Mexican export price is entirely determined by the change in the U.S. price, and variables such as quota levels, quota utilization, and concentration have no systematic effect. This seems to be a strong assumption, but it is borne out in the aggregate by the results of estimating equation (1) for all groups. Introducing this assumption, the regression equation then becomes:

$$P_i^M - P_i^{US} = \gamma_i + \sum_j \theta_{ij} P_{ij}^M + u_i, \tag{7}$$

where $\theta_{ij} = (w_{ij}^M - \delta_{1i} w_{ij}^{US})$, and $u_i = \delta_{1i} \sum_j w_{ij}^{US} e_{ij}$. In order for $E(u_i)$ to be equal to zero and for the regression to be well specified, the additional assumption that $E(w_{ij} e_{ij}) = 0$ must be made.

To test for significant differences in the U.S. and Mexican category weights, w_{ij}^{US} and w_{ij}^M—a compositional bias—it is necessary to impose the additional restriction that δ_{1i}, the reciprocal of the marginal component of the price relationship in each group, is equal to one. When this is the case, the sum of the coefficients on the P_{ij}^M terms in equation (7) is equal to zero, since $\sum_j w_{ij}^M = \sum_j w_{ij}^{US} = 1$. The validity of this restriction can be tested using a joint F–test on the coefficients of the P_{ij}^M terms in (7). If the test cannot reject the hypothesis that $\sum_j \theta_{ij} = 0$, then it is considered sufficient evidence that $\delta_{1i} = 1$. At this point, the significance of the individual θ_{ij} coefficients can be examined for evidence of a composition effect, that is, a difference between w_{ij}^M and w_{ij}^{US}. In addition, the joint hypothesis that all the θ_{ij} coefficients are equal to zero can be tested for further evidence of a composition effect.

If the hypothesis that $\Sigma_j \theta_{ij} = 0$ is rejected, then more information could be brought to the problem. In particular, the known w_{ij}^M can be used to test for the difference directly. First, note that an estimate of δ_{1i} can be obtained from the estimates of the coefficients θ_{ij}:

$$\delta_{1i} = 1 - \sum_j \theta_{ij}, \tag{8}$$

so that for each individual category, the U.S. share can be estimated as:

$$w_{ij}^{US} = \frac{w_{ij}^M - \theta_{ij}}{1 - \sum_j \theta_{ij}}. \tag{9}$$

Whether w_{ij}^{US} is significantly different from w_{ij}^M must be tested, that is, whether:

$$w_{ij}^M = \frac{\theta_{ij}}{\sum_j \theta_{ij}}. \tag{10}$$

If the hypothesis in (10) is rejected, then significant compositional differences exist. Unfortunately, (10) is a nonlinear hypothesis that depends on the distribution of w_{ij}^M, and is very difficult to implement. However, even without testing (10), estimates of δ_{1i} can be obtained and examined for their significance.

The regressions in (7) were run together in a seemingly unrelated regression framework to correct for contemporaneous correlation of the error terms due to exogenous shocks that might affect them in a similar manner. It seems likely that in the case of Mexico during the 1980s, such correlation exists.[10] If contemporaneous correlation does exist, then the seemingly unrelated regression framework will yield more efficient estimates of the coefficients.[11]

B. Regression Results

Table 6.5 presents the results of regression (7). Differences in composition are indicated by significant θ coefficients in:

---

10. Economy–wide events such as the debt crisis in 1982 and the subsequent imposition of exchange controls are typical events that might lead to contemporaneous correlation of the error terms.

11. For a discussion of the relative efficiency of seemingly unrelated regression estimates versus OLS estimates see Fomby, Hill and Johnson 1984, pp.155-166.

1. Group 1 at the 1 percent and 5 percent significance levels,
2. Groups 2 and 3 at the 10 percent level,
3. Group 4 at the 5 percent level.

However, without testing whether $\delta_{1i} = 1$ in each group, little confidence can be maintained in these coefficients as indicators that a composition effect is at work.

Table 6.6 presents the results of F–tests. The first column tests for the existence of a marginal effect, that is, if δ_{1i} is different from one, which is implied when the sum of the θ_{ij} coefficients is not equal to zero. The second column tests for the composition effect, that is, if each θ coefficient is different from zero. The third column tests for the existence of rent sharing against the joint null hypothesis that both the intercept, γ_i (the fixed rent sharing effect), and all the θ coefficients (which include δ_{1i}, and thereby β_{1i} , the marginal component) are equal to zero. If the hypothesis in column one is not rejected, the results of the tests in columns (2) and (3) can be interpreted. If it is rejected, the analysis cannot continue since δ_{1i} not equal to one could cause an erroneous rejection of the hypothesis that no composition effect exists.

The hypothesis of no marginal effect ($\delta_{1i} = 1$) can be rejected for Groups 2 and 4. Of the remaining Groups 1, 3, 5, and 6, only in Group 1 was the hypothesis that no composition effect was at work rejected. For Groups 1,

TABLE 6.5. Mexico: Testing for the Composition Effect

	γ_i	θ_{1i}	θ_{2i}	θ_{3i}	θ_{4i}	θ_{5i}
Group 1	-4.412	1.178[a]	0.638[a]	-0.537[a]	0.579[a]	0.409
	(4.0361)	(0.3018)	(0.1602)	(0.1536)	(0.3496)	(1.0833)
Group 2	1.131	-0.428	-0.011	0.053	0.888[b]	
	(1.8777)	(0.4093)	(0.0201)	(0.0355)	(0.4239)	
Group 3	23.059[b]	-1.554[b]	0.010			
	(8.3124)	(0.8387)	(0.0484)			
Group 4	22.570[a]	-0.572[b]	-0.129			
	(4.1507)	(0.2117)	(0.1340)			
Group 5	5.896[c]	0.076	-0.498	-0.039	0.011	-0.065
	(3.4188)	(0.2967)	(0.3835)	(0.0299)	(0.0483)	(0.4308)
Group 6	0.173	0.274	-0.082			
	(0.1608)	(0.2363)	(0.1146)			

System weighted R^2 = 0.8142.
Standard errors in parentheses.
[a] Significant at the 1 percent level.
[b] Significant at the 5 percent level.
[c] Significant at the 10 percent level.

3, 5, and 6, the hypothesis that no rent sharing was in effect could be rejected. Under the most conservative assumptions, then, testing for rent sharing can take place only in Groups 3, 5, and 6 with the assurance that no composition effect will bias the results.

VI. Testing for Fixed Differences in Quality

Another factor that might explain the difference between the price of U.S. production and the Mexican adjusted f.o.b. import price is a difference in the quality of the apparel. If Mexican imports are perceived to be of lower quality, they will receive a lower price. Mexican exports will then be imperfect substitutes for their U.S. counterparts, and the assumption of homogeneous products must be dropped.

A. Equation Setup

$$P_{it}^M = \alpha_6 + \alpha_3 GRP_3 + \alpha_5 GRP_5 + \beta' P_{it}^{US} + \gamma' NEQUIV_{it}^M$$
$$+ \delta' UTIL_{it}^M + \phi' QUOTA_{it}^M + \mu t + \epsilon_{it}. \tag{11}$$

Following the approach in Chapter Four, a test for the possible existence of differences in quality can be developed by first assuming that such differences are constant over time. It is then possible to control for the unmeasurable fixed difference in quality between U.S. and Mexican products in each group (that is, the proportion of the spread between the price of the two products that is due to fixed differences in quality), by inserting group–specific dummies in equation (1). In addition, including a time trend captures any constant change in the quality difference between the two periods. At this stage, Groups 1, 2, and 4 are dropped since composition effects cannot be ruled out in these products. The regression equation for the remaining groups is:

$$P_{it}^M = \alpha_6 + \alpha_3 GRP_3 + \alpha_5 GRP_5 + \beta' P_{it}^{US} + \gamma' NEQUIV_{it}^M$$
$$+ \delta' UTIL_{it}^M + \phi' QUOTA_{it}^M + \mu t + \epsilon_{it}, \tag{12}$$

where GRP_3 and GRP_5 are the dummies for the respective groups.

Several tests can be performed to gauge the importance of the presumed quality difference. If the fixed quality difference can explain all the spread between the U.S. and Mexican prices then the coefficient on P_{it}^{US} would be equal to 1, and all other coefficients, excluding the dummies and the intercept, would

TABLE 6.6. Mexico: F–tests for Composition Effect

H_0:	$\sum_j \theta_{ij} = 0$ No marginal effect	$\theta_{ij} = 0$ No composition effect	$\gamma_i + \sum_j \theta_{ij} = 0$ No rent sharing
Group 1	$F(1,34) = 3.559$ cannot reject	$F(5,34) = 15.71$ reject	$F(6,34) = 22.25$ reject
Group 2	$F(1,34) = 2895$ reject	(?)	(?)
Group 3	$F(1,34) = 3.860$ cannot reject	$F(2,34) = 2.194$ cannot reject	$F(3,34) = 25.111$ reject
Group 4	$F(1,34) = 7.287$ reject	(?)	(?)
Group 5	$F(1,34) = 0.638$ cannot reject	$F(5,34) = 1.721$ cannot reject	$F(6,34) = 40.774$ reject
Group 6	$F(1,34) = 1.550$ cannot reject	$F(2,34) = 0.824$ cannot reject	$F(3,34) = 13.534$ reject

Note: All rejections are at the 1 percent level. Failure to reject is at the 5 percent level.

be equal to zero. Tests for this hypothesis are presented below Table 6.7. The t–test and F–test for $\beta N = 1$ are rejected at the 1 percent level. The F–test for $\beta N = 1$ and the coefficients on all other variables except the dummies equal to zero is also rejected at the 1 percent level. The fact that there is one group (Group 3) whose exports are not quota bound may be an explanation for the lack of significance of the coefficient on P_{it}^{US}. To see whether rent sharing exists for those groups that are quota bound, Group 3 was dropped from the sample and the regression was re–estimated. A test for the log specification of equation (11) was also run with the bound groups, Groups 5 and 6.

B. Regression Results

The results of regression (11) for Groups 3, 5, and 6 are presented in Table 6.7. The coefficients on GRP_3 and GRP_5, as well as the intercept terms, α_6, $(\alpha_6 + \alpha_3)$, and $(\alpha_6 + \alpha_5)$ are significant at the 1 percent level, indicating that quality differences, fixed over time, may be a significant component of the difference between the U.S. and the Mexican price for these groups. The time trend

TABLE 6.7. Mexico: Fixed Effects Quality Difference Regression, Groups 3, 5, and 6

Dependent variable = P_{it}^M

Independent Variables	Coefficient	t–statistic	Intercepts $\alpha_6+\alpha_i$	F– statistic (1,22)
Constant	1.299 (0.4913)	2.644[a]		
P_{it}^{US}	-0.136 (0.1913)	-0.711		
NEQUIV$_{it}^M$	0.006 (0.0023)	2.603[a]		
UTIL$_{it}^M$	-0.661 (0.4902)	-1.348		
QUOTA$_{it}^M$	-1.712×10^{-9} (2×10^{-8})	-0.878		
t	0.082 (0.0809)	1.019		
GRP$_3$	11.303 (1.4815)	7.629[a]	12.602	67.37[a] reject
GRP$_5$	3.413 (0.8368)	1.019[a]	4.712	26.12[a] reject

Adjusted R^2 = 0.98,

Number of observations = 30.

Standard errors in parentheses.

[a] Significant at 1 percent.

Results of hypothesis testing:

t–statistic for test of $\beta N=1$:

t = -5.938; reject at the 1 percent level.

F–statistic for test of $\beta N=1$:

$F(1,22) = 154.778$; reject at the 1 percent level.

F–statistic for test of $\beta N=1$, $\gamma N=\delta N=\phi N=0$:

$F(4,22) = 48.97$; reject at the 1 percent level.

coefficient is not significant. Unfortunately, the difference between the fixed quality effect and the fixed rent sharing effect[12] cannot be distinguished. However, the coefficient on the U.S. price in Table 6.7 is close to zero and not significant.

---

12. Although this constant term has been referred to as the fixed rent sharing effect throughout the chapter, it is possible that other considerations aside from rent sharing or constant quality differences may explain part of this difference between the prices; an example might be fixed costs in the quota allocation system.

The results of regression (8) for Groups 5 and 6 only are presented in Table 6.8. The coefficient on P_{it}^{US} is now positive at 0.514 and significant at the 1 percent level. Of the other coefficients, those on the numbers equivalent and the time trend are significant. The negative time trend coefficient indicates an increasing discrepancy between the Mexican and U.S. prices over time which may be due to increasing quality differentials. The fact that neither the intercept term, α_6, nor the coefficient on GRP_5, nor the intercept $(\alpha_6+\alpha_5)$ are significant suggests that this effect is not specific to either of the groups in the sample. The tests presented below Table 6.8 also reject the hypothesis that fixed quality differences are the sole explanation for the differences between the price of U.S. production and the price of imports from Mexico.

The results of Table 6.8 indicate that the price difference in Groups 5 and 6 cannot be explained solely by fixed quality differences between U.S. and Mexican apparel. Furthermore, while the fixed component of rent sharing and the fixed quality effect cannot be distinguished, the results seem to indicate that for the quota-bound group, this fixed effect is not very important. One interpretation of the coefficient on the U.S. price is that for these two groups (woven shirts and underwear), an increase of one dollar in the U.S. price is associated with an average increase of 51 cents in the Mexican price. This may be an indication that U.S. retailers are receiving up to 49 percent of the rent from the MFA quota restrictions in these two groups of apparel.

Tests reveal that the linear specification fits the data better. Nevertheless, the results of the regression in logs, presented in Table 6.9, are consistent with the previous results in Table 6.8. Coefficients on the fixed effect dummies and the constant are not significantly different from zero, suggesting no fixed quality effect is operating. These results are supported by the hypotheses tests which reject the existence of fixed quality differences as the sole explanation for the price differences at the 1 percent level. The coefficient on the U.S. price is significant at the 1 percent level, with an elasticity of price transmission, all other variables held constant, of 0.59.

TABLE 6.8. Mexico: Fixed Effects Quality Difference Regression, Bound Groups 5 and 6

Dependent variable = P_{it}^M

Independent variables	Coefficient	t–statistic	Intercepts	F–statistic H_0: $\alpha_6 + \alpha_i = 0$
Constant	1.502 (0.9162)	1.640[c]		
P_{it}^{US}	0.514 (0.0612)	8.402[a]		
$NEQUIV_{it}^M$	0.008 (0.0045)	1.788[b]		
$UTIL_{it}^M$	-0.412 (0.9133)	-0.451		
$QUOTA_{it}^M$	7.2×10^{-9} (4×10^{-8})	0.201		
t	-0.249 (0.1275)	-1.956[b]		
GRP_5	-1.293 (1.0282)	-1.258	0.209	0.025 cannot reject

Adjusted R^2 = 0.93,
Number of observations = 20.
Standard errors in parentheses.
[a] significant at the 1 percent level.
[b] significant at the 5 percent level.
[c] significant at the 10 percent level.

Results of hypothesis testing:
t–statistic for test of $\beta N = 1$:
t = -4.616; reject at the 1 percent level.
F–statistic for test of $\beta N = 1$:
$F(1,23) = 63.050$; reject at the 1 percent level.
F–statistic for test of $\beta N = 1$, $\gamma N = \delta N = \phi N = 0$:
$F(4,23) = 83.107$; reject at the 1 percent level.

TABLE 6.9. Mexico: Fixed Effects Quality Difference Regression, Bound Groups 5 and 6, Log Specification

Dependent variable = $\log P_{it}^{M}$

Independent Variables	Coefficient	t–statistic	Intercepts $\alpha_6+\alpha_i$	F–statistic H_0: $\alpha_6+\alpha_i =0$
Constant	0.0374 (0.4339)	0.086		
$\log P_{it}^{US}$	0.591 (0.1048)	5.638[a]		
$\log NEQUIV_{it}^{M}$	0.189 (0.1280)	1.482[c]		
$\log UTIL_{it}^{M}$	-0.101 (0.0519)	-1.943[b]		
$\log QUOTA_{it}^{M}$	-0.186 (0.0680)	-2.734[a]		
$\log t$	-0.004 (0.0169)	0.249		
GRP_5	0.106 (0.1819)	0.583	-0.068	0.056 cannot reject

Adjusted R^2 = 0.98, Number of observations = 20.

Standard errors in parentheses.

[a] significant at the 1 percent level.

[b] significant at the 5 percent level.

[c] significant at the 10 percent level.

Results of hypothesis testing:

t–statistic for test of $\beta N = 1$:

t = 3.904; reject at the 1 percent level.

F–statistic for test of $\beta N = 1$:

$F(1,23) = 15.247$; reject at the 1 percent level.

F–statistic for test of $\beta N = 1$, $\gamma N = \delta N = \phi N = 0$:

$F(4,23) = 9.854$; reject at the 1 percent level.

Test of Log Specification:

Sum of squared residuals for the linear specification = 0.2893

Sum of squared residuals for the log specification = 0.3426

PART III
Quota Implementation

CHAPTER SEVEN

The Importance of Implementation Practices

I. Introduction

The focus of the book now shifts from rent sharing to quota implementation policies and their consequences. The two topics are not unrelated, as the way in which quota licenses are allocated among agents can affect the distribution of the quota rents between the exporting and importing countries. As mentioned earlier, the MFA outlines a set of country pair and product specific quota levels but leaves the details of their implementation up to the individual exporting countries. Since the allocation of the quota licenses is the responsibility of the exporting countries, it is generally believed that these countries would retain any ensuing quota rent by allocating the quota licenses to domestic agents rather than to agents in the importing country. However, the MFA exporting countries have taken many different routes in allocating their quota licenses. As a result, they have had very different experiences in exporting their products and reaping quota rents.

Under the MFA, quantitative levels for each apparel category are agreed upon in bilateral negotiations between the exporting country and each country of destination. These country/category levels are set in terms of volume of apparel and represent the maximum quantity the exporting country is allowed to ship within a quota year (which is usually a twelve-month period, though not necessarily a calendar year). The exporting country government is responsible for formulating a policy for distributing the quota licenses among domestic agents, usually the apparel producing firms and/or the apparel exporting firms. Most of the quota licenses are allocated at the beginning of the quota year; however, adjustments to the allocations may be made during the year and in some countries, a certain portion of the quota licenses may be set aside for later release. A quota license, once allocated, is normally valid for use any time during the quota year; aside from limited carry-over or carry-forward provisions, quota licenses may not be transferred between years.

Although different exporting countries have chosen different methods of implementing quotas, some common features can be found among the varied experiences. Some of these features are discussed below. A chain of events that reoccurs is that of, often well meaning intervention that has unanticipated and undesirable side effects. These side effects are then targeted by another layer of regulations and intervention and so on. In some countries this process converges before the distortions imposed become overwhelming, while in others, the balance goes the other way.

II. Some Key Features of Quota Implementation

A. Allocation criteria

Most exporting countries distributed initial quota allocations under the MFA on the basis of historical share in the period preceding the imposition of these quotas. To a large extent, the initial allocations on the basis of historical share are a consequence of political economy considerations: by allocating quota in this manner, existing producers obtained quota rents which compensated them for current and potential losses in terms of reduced exports.

However, as the prospect of creating a rentier class living off the proceeds of these licenses alone is not politically palatable, continued allocations are often tied to firms' performance in utilizing their quota allocations. In Hong Kong, for example, historical share was the main allocation criterion when a quota was implemented for the first time; subsequent allocations are based on export performance in the preceding quota year, with bonuses or penalties depending on the firms' quota utilization during that period. In Korea, some 85 percent of the total quota allocation is distributed on the basis of past performance, and in India the share is 60 percent.

A problem with allocating quota licenses primarily on the basis of past performance is that the license holdings would tend to be concentrated in the hands of the established firms, while new entrants with no export history for the category/destination concerned would be essentially shut out. Several MFA exporting countries have tried to resolve this problem by setting aside a portion of quota to be allocated on the basis of criteria other than past performance. In Korea, for example, 15 percent of the total quota is open to all firms with proven production capabilities, with preference given to firms with past export performance to unrestricted countries, firms producing high-value products, and firms which have made recent investments in their production facilities. In India, 20 percent of the total quota is allocated on the basis of firms' export performance to unrestricted countries (or in unrestricted categories) and 18 percent is allocated to manufacturer-exporters, partly on the basis of production capacity. Some countries, such as India and Bangladesh, also set aside a small fraction of the total quota for government corporations; others, such as Pakistan and Indonesia, give some preference to firms located in economically weak areas.

Finally, some countries have a small amount of free or open quota, which is distributed on a first-come-first-served basis to firms with proof of an export order the rationale for free quota is usually to enable firms that are not eligible for past performance allocations to obtain quota for export. In Hong Kong, any quota in excess of that distributed on the basis of past performance, is designated free quota. In India prior to 1992, a fraction of the total quota—as high as 55 percent in 1981, down to 10 percent in 1991—was allocated as free quota. In Bangladesh, approximately 10 percent of the total quota is distributed as free quota. As discussed earlier, the implementation of free quota, namely its allocation being tied to proof of an export order, also changes the balance of power between importers and exporters and can result in importers obtaining the quota rents.

B. Transferability

An important feature of quota implementation is whether the quota licenses may be traded among firms following the initial allocation by the government agency concerned. The MFA exporting countries vary significantly in the degree of transferability that they allow. In some countries, like Hong Kong, there are practically no restrictions on quota transfers and both permanent and temporary transfers are allowed. In Indonesia, past performance quota may be transferred through an auction system although the transactions carry a penalty for the transferor and a reward for the transferee; illegal quota transfers are said to be quite common. In Korea, quota transfers are regulated by the export associations which allocate the quotas, and involve quite an onerous penalty system. Limits on transferability are often implemented to hinder the creation of a rentier class living on quota rents alone.

Transferability has a number of important implications with regard to the price of the license, the amount of revenue from the quota, and the welfare of the agents. These implications are examined in Chapter Eight. Under fairly general conditions, while one might guess that transferable licenses would be more valuable than nontransferable ones, the opposite turns out to be the case if the quota is quite restrictive. However, if surplus and revenue are given equal weight in welfare, then transferability dominates.

C. Subcategorization

Another interesting aspect of quota implementation is the practice of subcategorization. The apparel categories that are restricted under the MFA differ according to country of destination but they are usually very tightly defined, right down to the type and purpose of the apparel and the fabric used, in the case of exports to the United States. Within these specific MFA-defined categories, some exporting countries further subdivide their quotas in order to meet certain distribution objectives. India, for example, subcategorizes the cotton apparel categories into knitted, hand loomed, and power loomed groups, with the quota entitlements calculated separately; it also sets aside portions of the total quota for woolen and acrylic apparel even when the United States imposes no specific limits for these categories. Bangladesh, in an effort to encourage the use of domestically-produced fabrics, sets aside 10 percent of its total quota to be allocated to firms which make use of such material. One might ask what the benefit of further subcategorization might be; in Chapter Ten, it is shown that subcategorization may be desirable under certain circumstances.

III. Looking Ahead

The following eight chapters look at these features of quota implementation in greater detail. Chapter Eight deals with the issue of license transferability and its effect on the license price. Chapter Nine focuses on the practice of allocating a certain amount of quota free of charge to firms on a first come first served basis (free quota): using a simple model, it analyzes the implications such an allocation mechanism on the price of licenses on the secondary market. Chapter Ten discusses the possible rationales for quota subcategorization, and, using a targeting model, compares the outcomes under this system with the market determined outcome.

Chapters Eleven and Twelve are empirical in nature. In Chapter Eleven, firm-level quota allocation data are used to examine the impact of the Korean quota allocation system on new entry and license market concentration. In Chapter Twelve, license market (auction) data are used to shed light on concentration and entry barriers in the Indonesian license market.

Chapters Thirteen and Fourteen focus on implications of the twelve-month validity of MFA quota licenses. Chapter Thirteen presents some theoretical models to explain the forces underlying the time path of the license price during the quota year. The models highlight the importance of various components of the license price, such as the option value component, the asset market component, and the renewal value component. Chapter Fourteen is the empirical counterpart to Chapter Thirteen: in this chapter, monthly license price and utilization data from Hong Kong are used to estimate a dynamic model of license prices based on the insights developed in Chapter Thirteen.

Chapter Fifteen approaches the study of license markets from a completely different angle, by looking at a common practice found in the literature of using available quota license prices from one country to impute quota license prices in other countries. This chapter compares actual license prices in Indonesia with their imputed values based on Hong Kong license prices, and presents some explanations for the discrepancies observed, in the process providing indirect evidence on the functioning of license markets.

Finally, detailed descriptions of the quota allocation systems in Hong Kong, Korea, Indonesia, India, Pakistan, and Bangladesh are contained in the Appendices I through VI.

CHAPTER EIGHT

License Transferability

I. Introduction

One striking observation that emerges from Chapter Seven is the significant variation across exporting country participants of the MFA in the degree of quota transferability permitted. For example, quotas may be traded freely between firms on either a permanent or temporary basis in Hong Kong, whereas in other countries, only a certain portion of quotas may be transferred, and even so, only subject to official regulation (e.g., in Korea), or only permanently (e.g., in India, Pakistan and Bangladesh). In fact, a surprisingly large number of countries either do not permit license transfers, or actively discourage them. A thumbnail sketch of some countries' regulations on MFA quota license transfers is presented in Table 8.1.

Most economists argue that transferable licenses will fetch higher prices and consequently, lead to improved welfare in the exporting country. The intuition is that if transferability is allowed, licenses will go to agents who value them the most, and this will result in a higher license price. Moreover, since transferable licenses will be allocated properly by the market under perfect competition, while nontransferable ones need not be, welfare in the exporting country (defined as the sum of license revenue and surplus) will necessarily be higher under transferability.

Both these presumptions are evaluated in this chapter, where it will be shown that the price of a transferable license will tend to be higher than the price of an otherwise identical nontransferable license only if the underlying quota is quite restrictive. Despite this, transferability is still preferable to non–transferability if consumer surplus and license revenue have equal weight in the welfare function.[1]

The analysis presented in this section differs from the standard analysis of transferability for two reasons: First, it compares the allocations which will result endogenously under the two systems. This is in contrast with the previous literature, which compares an existing, possibly arbitrary, allocation of licenses under nontransferability with that under transferability.

Second, it introduces uncertainty explicitly, providing a reason why agents who obtain licenses ex ante may wish to transfer them ex post. After all, if there

---

1. Spencer 1996 argues that, in certain cases, bureaucratic allocation of nontransferable quotas can actually help.

8.1. Extent of License Transferability in Eight Countries

Country	Scheme	Full Transferability	Limited Transferability	Non-Transferability
Bangladesh	Past Performance Quota, Free Quota		X	
	10 Percent Local Fabrics Quota			X
Hong Kong	Past Performance Quota	X		
	Free Quota			X
India	Past Performance Quota		X	
	Manufacturer Exporter Quota,			
	Public Sector Quota, Open Quota			X
Indonesia	1984-87 Permanent Quota		X	
	1987- Permanent Quota	X		
	Provisional Quota			X
Korea	Basic Quota (up to 80% and only to producers)		X	
	Open Quota			X
Pakistan	Performance Quota		X	
	Quota for newcomers, weak areas and best exporter			X
Thailand	Basic Quota	X		
	Supplementary Quota			X

is no uncertainty in the valuations of the agents involved, and if the ex ante allocation is endogenous, there will be no reason for agents to wish to trade ex post, so there will be no difference in the two systems.

The models used in this chapter are the simplest ones necessary to demonstrate the key points. Competitive models are employed throughout to abstract from the complications which arise when agents behave strategically. The key to the results lies in the observation that the price of a license under nontransferability depends on the distribution of ex ante valuations. However, the price under transferability depends on the ex post distribution of valuations.

II. The Traditional Analysis

The basic intuition behind the traditional presumption that transferable licenses are superior to nontransferable ones is nicely summarized in Faini et al 1992 where it is argued that constraints on license transferability are a source of inefficiency.[2] Their results may be recapitulated as follows.

Suppose there are two firms in a country producing a homogeneous good for export. Let the supply functions of the firms be S_1 and S_2 in Figure 8.1. Suppose the good is subject to a quota of V units, and that the initial allocation of this quota led to the firms being awarded V_1 and V_2 licenses respectively, such that their marginal costs were equalized with $V_1 + V_2 = V$. Now, suppose the firms' marginal costs change after this allocation is made. This could happen if, for example, Firm 1 invests in capital which lowers its marginal cost (i.e., its supply curve) to S_1', while Firm 2 does not. If the licenses are not transferable, Firm 1 will continue to produce V_1 at a total cost given by the area $OEAV_1$ and Firm 2 will continue to produce V_2 at a total cost given by the area $OFDV_2$. If the licenses are transferable, however, Firm 2, the higher marginal cost firm, will sell quota to Firm 1, the lower marginal cost firm, until their marginal costs are again equalized. Firm 1 will now increase its production to V_1' and its total cost to $OEBV_1'$, while Firm 2 reduces its output to V_2' and its total cost to $OFCV_2'$. Thus, the area $V_2'CDV_2 - V_1ABV_1'$ represents the net gain in welfare from permitting transferability.

Faini et al 1992 do not compare the license prices under transferability with those under nontransferability. However, it should be clear that if demand is given, and if there is no uncertainty regarding the supply curves of the two firms (i.e., if the supply curves are fixed at S_1 and S_2), then as long as the initial allocation of licenses is efficient in the sense that the marginal costs of the two firms are equalized, there will be no need for transfers to occur. In Figure 8.1, this license price would be given by GH, the difference between the demand

---

2. Lott 1987 presents a similar argument in the context of professional licensing to show that nontransferable licenses result in greater social losses than transferable ones.

price (where the demand curve intersects the quota level) and the supply price (where the horizontal sum of the supply, or marginal cost, curves intersects the quota level).

III. The Basic Model

In order to compare transferability and nontransferability in a meaningful way, it is necessary first to specify the underlying uncertainty in the valuations of licenses, and then to compare the two systems in the context of this uncertainty. Let ℓ denote the (stochastic) willingness to pay, or valuation, of an individual agent for a license; ℓ can be interpreted as the difference between the price in the restricted market and the marginal cost of the restricted suppliers (agents).

ASSUMPTIONS:

1. *There are two time periods. In the first period, ℓ is unknown so each agent is uncertain about his valuation; in the second period, this valuation is realized.*
2. *There is a continuum of agents with mass N. Each agent demands only one license at most.*
3. *All agents are identical ex ante, sharing a common distribution of valuations. (This assumption is relaxed later in the chapter.) Let $f(\ell)$ be*

FIGURE 8.1. Traditional Analysis of License Transferability

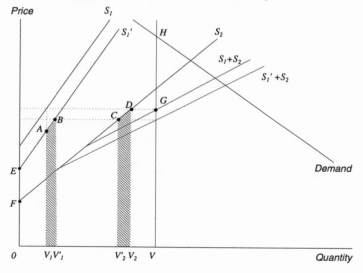

the density function, and F(ℓ) *the associated cumulative density function of the valuations. Let ℓ^{min} and ℓ^{max} be the lower and upper bounds of this distribution, with $\ell^{min} > 0$ so that licenses will always be used ex post, even if they are nontransferable. There is a continuum of valuations between ℓ^{min} and ℓ^{max}.*

4. *The valuations, ℓ, are independent of the size of the quota, V. This is possible if the exporting country is small, so that world prices are unaffected by the quota, and the supply price is constant. (This assumption is relaxed later in the chapter.)*

5. *Licenses are sold in the first period. If the licenses are nontransferable, then an agent who purchases a license in period one, when ℓ is unknown, cannot sell it in period two, when ℓ is realized. If the licenses are transferable, then the license holder may, if he wishes, sell his license in the second period at whatever the market clearing price happens to be at that time. The license price in the first period is called the ex ante price, and the license price in the second period is called the ex post price.*

6. *The ex post realizations are independent across all agents.*

A. Nontransferable Licenses

What is the market clearing price of a nontransferable license in this model? Since all agents are identical ex ante, they would all be willing to pay the same amount, namely, the expected value of ℓ. Hence, the demand curve for licenses would be horizontal at this price. Of course, the supply of licenses is fixed at V. Thus, as long as the quota is binding, that is, as long as there are more agents than quota, the equilibrium price of a license equals the expected valuation if the license is nontransferable:

$$L^{NT} = E(\ell). \tag{1}$$

Who actually receives a license is irrelevant since all agents are identical ex ante. Note that there is zero surplus from obtaining a license: agents pay exactly the amount they are willing to pay for a license. Note also that the license price is independent of the quota level as long as the quota is binding.

B. Transferable Licenses

Now consider what happens if the licenses are transferable. Given the assumptions of the model, the ex post distribution of realizations among the agents will be the same as the ex ante distribution of valuations for each agent. Thus, F(ℓ) may also be interpreted as the proportion of agents who have a valuation less than or equal to ℓ in the second period.

What determines the ex ante price with transferability? The value of a license in period one depends on the outcome in two, hence the model needs to be solved backwards. The ex post price is determined by equating total supply with total demand. This is equivalent to ensuring that the fraction of agents with valuations exceeding the ex post price equals the quota, V, relative to the size of the market, N. Denoting V/N by v, the ex post price, L_2, is defined implicitly as follows:

$$1 - F(L_2) = v. \tag{2}$$

Note that:

1. Although each agent's realization is stochastic, the ex post price, L_2, is non–stochastic.
2. The ex post price, L_2, depends on the level of the quota: the more restrictive the quota, the higher the ex post price.

Now, let us determine the price in period one. Since licenses are transferable, the surplus that an agent would obtain if he purchased the license in period one and sold it in period two (if it were in his interests to do so) must equal the surplus which he could obtain if he waited and purchased the license in period two (if it were in his interests to do so). In other words, the payoff from buying a license in period one must be the same as that from not buying at that time. This is what determines the ex ante price under transferability.

PROPOSITION 1

With a continuum of ex ante identical agents who have i.i.d. valuations which are independent of the quota level, there exists a critical quota level, V*, which, for a given size of the market, N, defines a critical degree of restrictiveness, v*, such that: for quotas smaller than V* (that is, for restrictive quotas), the ex ante price with transferability will exceed that without transferability; but for quotas larger than V* (that is, for not very restrictive quotas), the reverse will be true.

Proof

Denote the ex ante license price by L^T and the ex post price by L_2. If an agent buys a license in period one, he has two possible courses of action:

1. Use it in period two and realize his valuation, ℓ, if ℓ exceeds the ex post price, L_2.
2. Sell it for L_2 in period two, if his realized valuation falls short of the ex post price.

Thus, his payoff from purchasing a license in period one is simply the higher of the two values, net of the ex ante price paid for the license, that is, max $[\ell, L_2] - L^T$.

If the agent does not purchase the license in period one, he has two possible courses of action in period two:

1. Purchase a license for L_2, if his realized valuation, ℓ, is higher than the ex post price.
2. Not purchase a license, if his realized valuation falls short of the ex post price.

Thus, his payoff from not purchasing a license in period one is simply max $[(\ell - L_2), 0]$.

The agent is indifferent between the two options, that is, purchasing a license in period one versus not purchasing a license in period one, if the two payoffs are equal, that is, if:

$$max[\ell, L_2] - L^T = max[(\ell - L_2), 0]. \qquad (3)$$

Since max $[\ell, L_2] = $ max $[(\ell - L_2), 0] + L_2$, equation (3) implies that:

$$L_2 = L^T. \qquad (4)$$

This makes intuitive sense since the ex ante price depends on the outcome in period two. In the absence of transactions costs and their associated rigidities, if the ex post price in period two falls short of the ex ante price, then everyone would have the incentive to wait until period two to purchase a license. Conversely, if the ex post price exceeds the ex ante price, then everyone would want to purchase a license in period one. Hence, the ex ante price of a transferable license, L^T, must equal its ex post price, L_2, in equilibrium.

Recall that the ex post price is implicitly defined by equation (2). Therefore, the ex ante price of a transferable license is given by:

$$1 - F(L^T) = v \qquad (5)$$

A graphical depiction of the price under transferability and under nontransferability is provided in Figure 8.2, which depicts $F(\ell)$, the cumulative density function of ℓ. The price of a transferable license, L^T, is the point on the horizontal axis at which the distance between $F(\ell)$ and the value 1 is equal to v. The price of a nontransferable license, on the other hand, is $E(\ell)$, the expected value of ℓ. Recall that v=V/N. Define v* as:

$$1 - F(E(\ell)) = v^*. \qquad (6)$$

Then if $v > v^*$, that is, if the quota is not very restrictive, then $L^T < E(\ell)$, that is, the transferable license is cheaper than the nontransferable license. However, if the quota is restrictive enough that $v = v' < v^*$, then $L^T > E(\ell)$, that is, the transferable license is more expensive than the nontransferable license.   QED

IV. Variations of the Basic Model

The model described in the previous section rests on the restrictive assumptions that all agents are ex ante identical but different ex post, and that agents' valuations are not affected by the restrictiveness of the quota. In this section, it is shown that the spirit of Proposition 1 applies in more general cases as well.

A. Valuations Depending on the Restrictiveness of the Quota

It seems reasonable to expect that the agents' valuations should be affected by the restrictiveness of the quota. Assume, therefore, that each agent has a continuum of valuations, denoted by ℓ, which is identically and independently distributed over the interval $[\ell^{min}(v), \ell^{max}(v)]$, according to the density function, $f(\ell \mid v)$. The expected value of ℓ conditional on a given level of v is denoted by $E(\ell \mid v)$ and is assumed to rise as v falls. In other words, a more restrictive quota,

FIGURE 8.2. Transferable and Nontransferable License Prices

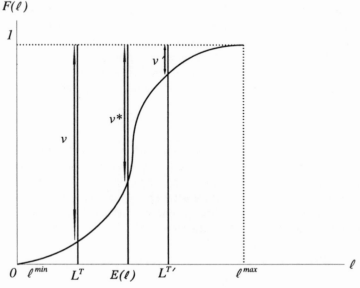

in and of itself, raises the expected gain from owning a license. As agents are identical ex ante, the license price under nontransferability will be:

$$L^{NT} = \begin{cases} E(\ell|v) & \text{if } v < 1, \\ 0 & \text{if } v \geq 1. \end{cases} \tag{7}$$

These functions are depicted in Figure 8.3.

PROPOSITION 2

With a continuum of ex ante identical agents who have valuations which are i.i.d., there exist two critical quota levels, V^{**} and V^{***}, which, for a given size of the market, N, define two critical levels of restrictiveness, v^{**} and v^{***}, such that: for quotas less than V^{**} (that is, for restrictive quotas), the ex ante price with transferability will exceed that without transferability; but for quotas larger than V^{***} (that is, for not very restrictive quotas), the reverse will be true.

Proof

Under transferability, the ex post cumulative distribution of valuations in the population, for a given v, is again given by $F(\ell\,|v)$, and the price, $L^T(v)$, is

FIGURE 8.3. License Prices when Valuations Depend on v

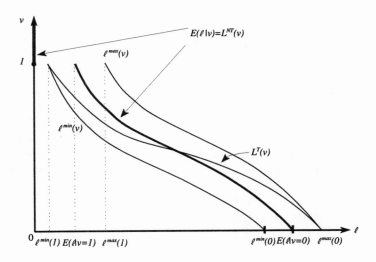

implicitly defined by:

$$1 - F(L^T|v) = v. \tag{8}$$

For v close to 1, this requires that $L^T(v)$ be close to $\ell^{min}(v)$ which is clearly less than $E(\ell\ |v)$. For v close to 0, this requires that $L^T(v)$ be close to $\ell^{max}(v)$ which is clearly greater than $E(\ell\ |v)$. Thus, one would expect, assuming that the distribution of ℓ changes continuously with v, that $L^T(v) > L^{NT}(v)$ for low values of v and $L^T(v) < L^{NT}(v)$ for high values of v. Of course, $L^T(v)$ may intersect $L^{NT}(v)$ more than once, so that a weaker form of Proposition 1 holds.   QED

Note that Proposition 1 holds in a special case where valuations are made up of a component which rises with the restrictiveness of the quota, as well as a purely random component of valuations which is unaffected by changes in the restrictiveness of the quota. In this example, the total valuation of an agent can be denoted by $>(v) + \ell$, where $>'(v) < 0$ and ℓ is distributed according to $f(\ell)$. It follows, given the usual assumptions, that $L^{NT} = >(v) + E(\ell)$ and that $1 - F(L^T - >(v)) = v$ defines the price under transferability. Thus, $L^T(v) = F^{-1}(1-v) + >(v)$. However, $L^T(v) - L^{NT}(v) = F^{-1}(1-v) - E(\ell)$, which is the same result as that obtained when valuations did not depend on v. Hence, Proposition 1 applies in this special case.

B. Heterogeneous Agents

Now let us suppose that there are a number of different types of agents in the economy. Let x denote agent type, such that the higher the value of x, the greater the expected willingness of the agent to pay for a license.

ASSUMPTIONS:

1. *The distribution of agent types in the population is given by g(x), with lower and upper bounds denoted by x^{min} and x^{max} respectively.*
2. *Each agent knows his own type, x, ex ante.*
3. *There is a continuum of valuations for each agent type. As before, suppose that the valuation of an agent of type x, denoted by $\ell(x)$, is distributed according to $f(\ell\ |x)$. This distribution is identical for, and independent across all agents of a given type, so it also represents the distribution of realizations ex post for agents of that type, since there is a continuum. $\ell^{min}(x)$ and $\ell^{max}(x)$ denote the lower and upper limits of $\ell(x)$ for each type x.*
4. *The expected value of a license for an agent of type x is given by $E(\ell\ |x)$. As before, assume each agent demands either zero or one license.*

PROPOSITION 3

With a continuum of ex ante identical agents of each type, who have valuations which are i.i.d., there exist two critical quota levels, V^o and V^{oo}, which, for a given size of the market, N, define two critical levels of restrictiveness, v^o and v^{oo}, such that: for quotas smaller than V^o (that is, for restrictive quotas), the ex ante price with transferability will exceed that without transferability; but for quotas larger than V^{oo}, (that is, for not very restrictive quotas) the reverse will be true.

Proof

If the licenses are nontransferable, an agent will be willing to pay $E(\ell\,|x)$ for the license. Hence, the ex ante distribution of valuations in the economy depends on $g(x)$. Equilibrium will obtain when the fraction of agents with ex ante valuations exceeding x^* is exactly equal to v, that is:

$$1 - G(x^*) = v \tag{9}$$

where $G(\cdot)$ denotes the cumulative distribution function of x. The marginal agent in this case will be of type x^*, where $x^* = G^{-1}(1-v)$. The nontransferable license price is thus:

$$L^{NT} = E(\ell\,|\,G^{-1}(1-v)). \tag{10}$$

This is bounded below by $E(\ell\,|x^{min})$ and above by $E(\ell\,|x^{max})$. Once we allow for heterogeneous agents, therefore, the nontransferable license price is no longer independent of the restrictiveness of the quota. Note that the nontransferable license price depends only on the ex ante variability of the agents and not on the ex–post variability of ℓ.

What if the licenses are transferable? It is known that the equilibrium will be such that the proportion of agents with ex post valuations exceeding the license price is exactly equal to v. Let $L^T(v)$ denote the transferable license price. Then, for an agent of type x, his ex post valuation will be larger than $L^T(v)$ only if $\ell(x) > L^T(v)$. The probability of this occurrence, as the density of agents of type x is $g(x)$, is given by $g(x)[1 - F(L^T(v)\,|x)]$. Integrating over agents of different types gives the condition:

$$\int_{x^{min}}^{x^{max}} g(x)[1 - F(L^T(v)|x)]dx = v \tag{11}$$

which implicitly defines the transferable license price. Unlike the nontransferable license price, the transferable license price depends on the ex post distribution of valuations.

Figure 8.4 is used to provide a sketch of the argument.[3] Agent types, x, are plotted along the vertical axis, with x^{min} and x^{max} being, respectively, the lower and upper limits. The valuations, $\ell(x)$, are plotted along the horizontal axis, with $\ell^{min}(x)$ and $\ell^{max}(x)$ denoting the lower and upper limits of $\ell(x)$ for each type x.

1. Consider, first, the license price under nontransferability and transferability as $v \to 0$, that is, as the quota becomes very restrictive. In this case, the nontransferable license price, $L^{NT}(v)$, would approach $E(\ell \mid x^{max})$, whereas the price under transferability, $L^{T}(v)$, would approach $\max_x[\ell^{max}(x)]$. But $\max_x[\ell^{max}(x)] \geq \ell^{max}(x^{max}) > E(\ell \mid x^{max})$. At a price of $E(\ell \mid x^{max})$, therefore, there would be excess demand for licenses in the transferable system.

FIGURE 8.4. License Prices with Heterogeneous Agents

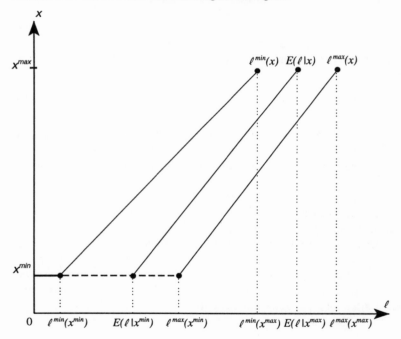

_____

3. Although $\ell^{min}(x)$ and $\ell^{max}(x)$ are drawn to be increasing in x in Figure 8.4, this is not needed for the proof.

2. Next, consider the opposite extreme, as $v \to 1$. In this case, $L^{NT}(v)$ would approach $E(\ell \,|x^{min})$, whereas the $L^T(v)$ would approach $\min_x [\ell^{min}(x)]$. But $\min_x [\ell^{min}(x)] \le \ell^{min}(x^{min}) < E(\ell \,|x^{min})$. At a price of E $(\ell \,|x^{min})$, therefore, there would be a shortage of demand for licenses in the transferable system.

3. By continuity, for quotas which are restrictive enough, $L^T(v) > L^{NT}(v)$; but for not very restrictive quotas, $L^T(v) < L^{NT}(v)$.[4] Hence, a weaker form of Proposition 1 holds after allowing for heterogeneous agents.

QED

V. Welfare Comparisons

The next step is to analyze the welfare implications of Proposition 1, using the basic model of Section III for simplicity. Does a higher license price necessarily imply higher welfare? Is transferability always better than nontransferability? Using the basic model of Section III, it can be shown that the answer to the first question is no; the answer to the second is yes, if license revenue and surplus are given equal weight in the welfare function, and no, if unequal weights are permitted. Welfare consists of:

1. The surplus accruing to agents.
2. Revenue from license sales.

In the case of nontransferable licenses, however, the surplus is all competed away, therefore, welfare consists of license revenue only.

A. Welfare Under Nontransferability

Consider the welfare of a typical agent. Since all agents are ex ante identical, national welfare will be proportional to the welfare of a typical agent. Assuming that license revenues are returned in a lump sum manner to all agents, the welfare of an agent will be equal to his surplus ex ante, plus his share, $1/N$, of the license revenue of $VE(\ell)$. Since his surplus is zero, the welfare of the representative agent under nontransferability will be given by:

$$W^{NT} = \frac{V}{N} E(\ell) = vE(\ell). \tag{12}$$

---

4. However, $L^T(v)$ and $L^{NT}(v)$ could cross more than once. In the case where $g(\cdot)$ and $f(\cdot)$ are uniform distributions, they cross only once. This example is available on request.

B. Welfare Under Transferability

If transfers are allowed, a typical agent will purchase the license if his valuation exceeds the ex ante price, and he will receive some surplus from this action. In addition, he will receive his share of the license revenue, $(1/N)VL^T$. Thus, welfare with transferability will be equal to the sum of surplus and revenue accruing to the typical agent. This is given by:

$$W^T = \int_{L^T}^{\ell^{max}} (\ell - L^T) f(\ell) \, d\ell + vL^T. \tag{13}$$

PROPOSITION 4

When surplus and revenue are given equal weight in welfare, transferability yields higher welfare than nontransferability. If the weight on revenue is high enough and the quota is not very restrictive, that is, the license price under transferability is less than that under nontransferability, then nontransferability can result in higher welfare.

Proof

Subtracting (12) from (13) gives:

$$W^T - W^{NT} = \int_{L^T}^{\ell^{max}} (\ell - L^T) f(\ell) \, d\ell + v[L^T - E(\ell)] \tag{14}$$

If the price under transferability is more than that under nontransferability (i.e., if $L^T - E(\ell) > 0$), then both terms on the right-hand side of (14) will be positive; hence, transferability will yield higher welfare than nontransferability in this case.

If the reverse is true, that is, if $L^T - E(\ell) < 0$, then the sign of (14) is not immediately apparent since the first term on the right-hand side is positive while the second is negative. However, using the fact that $1 - F(L^T) = v$, and then integrating by parts, (14) can be rewritten as:

$$W^T - W^{NT} = (1-v)[E(\ell) - L^T] + \int_{\ell^{min}}^{L^T} F(\ell) \, d\ell. \tag{15}$$

If $L^T - E(\ell) < 0$, both terms on the right-hand side of (15) will be positive.

Thus, if both surplus and revenue are given equal weight in welfare, transferability is always better than nontransferability. This makes intuitive sense, since license revenue is obtained at the expense of surplus, and transferability allows agents with higher surplus ex post to obtain the licenses.

What if revenue and surplus receive unequal weights? From (14), it is clear that:

1. If $L^T - E(\ell) < 0$, that is, if the quota is not very restrictive, and if the weight on revenue is high enough, and then $W^T - W^{NT} < 0$, that is, welfare under nontransferability is higher than it would be under transferability.
2. If $L^T - E(\ell) > 0$, that is, if the quota is restrictive enough, increasing the weight on revenue makes transferability even more attractive than in the case with equal weights.
3. Raising the weight on surplus above unity can never make nontransferability better than transferability, since there is no surplus under nontransferability.   QED

VI. Effect of Increased Uncertainty

This section analyzes how the results of the basic model are affected by exogenous changes in the distribution of ℓ. In particular, it shows how increasing uncertainty, modeled as a simple mean–preserving spread, affects the comparison between transferable and nontransferable licenses.

A simple mean preserving spread affects the density function by moving weight to the tails of the distribution while leaving the mean unchanged. If two density functions, $g(\ell)$ and $f(\ell)$ differ by a simple mean preserving spread, $h(\ell)$, so that $g(\ell) - f(\ell) = h(\ell)$, then by definition, with $G(\ell)$ and $F(\ell)$ denoting the corresponding cumulative density functions:[5]

1. $H(\ell) = G(\ell) - F(\ell)$ for all ℓ.
2. $H(\ell^{min}) = H(\ell^{max}) = 0$.
3. There exists $\ell^\dagger$ such that $H(\ell) \geq 0$ if $\ell \leq \ell^\dagger$, and $H(\ell) \leq 0$ if $\ell > \ell^\dagger$.
4. If

$$T(u) = \int_{\ell^{min}}^{u} H(\ell) \, d\ell, \text{ for } \ell^{min} \leq u \leq \ell^{max}, \text{ then:}$$

---

5. See Rothschild and Stiglitz 1970, 1971, and Hirshleifer and Riley 1992 for further details.

(a) $T(\ell^{\min}) = T(\ell^{\max}) = 0;$[6] and

(b) $T(u) \geq 0$ for $\ell^{\min} \leq u \leq \ell^{\max}.$[7]

These properties are illustrated in Figure 8.5, where $G(\ell)$ is obtained by adding a simple mean preserving spread, $H(\ell)$, to $F(\ell)$:

1. For values of ℓ less than $\ell^{\dagger}$, $G(\ell)$ lies above $F(\ell)$; for values of ℓ greater than $\ell^{\dagger}$, $G(\ell)$ lies below $F(\ell)$.
2. The distance between $G(\ell)$ and $F(\ell)$ is $H(\ell)$; this distance is zero at both end points.
3. The area between $G(\ell)$ and $F(\ell)$ to each side of $\ell^{\dagger}$ is the same, as the areas above $G(\ell)$ and $F(\ell)$ must be equal for the means to be equal.

PROPOSITION 5

Let $v^{\dagger}$ be defined by $F(\ell^{\dagger}) = 1 - v^{\dagger}$. Let $V^{\dagger}$ be the quota level corresponding to $v^{\dagger}$. If the quota level, V, exceeds $V^{\dagger}$, then an increase in uncertainty lowers the ex ante price with transferability. If V is less than $V^{\dagger}$, then an increase in uncertainty raises the ex ante price with transferability.

Proof

With the distribution function $F(\ell)$, L^{T} is the ex ante price with transferability, as explained earlier, with $F(L^{T}) = 1 - v$.

1. If L^{T} lies below $\ell^{\dagger}$, say, at L_{1}^{T}, then, after the introduction of a simple mean–preserving spread, it will fall to $L_{1}^{T'}$, where $G(L_{1}^{T'}) = 1 - v$.

---

6. $T(\ell^{\min}) = 0$ follows by definition. $T(\ell^{\max}) = 0$ is less obvious. By definition of a simple mean preserving spread,

$$\int_{\ell^{\min}}^{\ell^{\max}} \ell h(\ell)\, d\ell = 0.$$

Integrating by parts gives:

$$\int_{\ell^{\min}}^{\ell^{\max}} \ell h(\ell)\, d\ell = \ell H(\ell)\Big|_{\ell^{\min}}^{\ell^{\max}} - \int_{\ell^{\min}}^{\ell^{\max}} H(\ell)\, d\ell$$

$$= -\int_{\ell^{\min}}^{\ell^{\max}} H(\ell)\, d\ell$$

$$= -T(\ell^{\max})$$

$$= 0.$$

7. This follows from points (3) and (4a).

Recall that L^T is low when v is high, that is, when the quota is not very restrictive.

  2. If L^T lies below $\ell^\dagger$, say, at $L_2{}^T$, then, after the introduction of a
     simple mean–preserving spread, it will rise to $L_2^{T\prime}$, where $G(L_2^{T\prime}) =$
     $1 - v$. Recall that L^T is high when v is low, that is, when the quota
     is quite restrictive.

Since the price without transferability is unaffected by a simple mean preserving spread, and since the ex ante price with transferability exceeds the price without transferability only when the quota is quite restrictive, it can be deduced from the above that increasing uncertainty is likely to accentuate this difference in either case. $\qquad$ QED

Figure 8.5. The Effect of Uncertainty

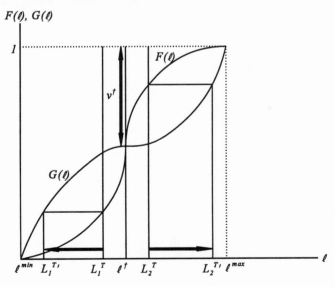

VII. Revenue-Maximizing Quota

Our basic model also affords an interesting insight into revenue-maximizing quota policy: it shows that if agents are ex ante identical, then revenue is maximized by making licenses nontransferable. Recall that the nontransferable price is defined by the expected value of ℓ, $E(\ell)$. The maximum revenue in this case is obtained by setting $v = 1$. Hence, the maximum revenue from the nontransferability policy is $E(\ell)$, where $E(\ell)$ is equal to the area above the $F(\ell)$ curve in Figure 8.2.[8] The transferable license price, on the other hand, is given by $F^{-1}(1- v)$: all possible revenues from the transferability policy may be traced out by taking each point on $F(\ell)$ and calculating the area of the rectangle formed by the horizontal coordinate of that point, which defines the transferable price, and the distance above $F(\ell)$, which defines v. However, the areas of these rectangles must always be less than the area above $F(\ell)$. Thus, if there are no costs of production for the producer (as is assumed here), nontransferability must raise more revenue than transferability.

Is it possible for transferability to raise more revenue than nontransferability? The answer is yes, under certain circumstances. One possibility would be if there were costs of disposal so that in some states the valuation of an agent could be negative. Consider the example of a continuum of agents who value the license at either 10 dollars or -10 dollars, with both valuations equally likely: the expected value of a license and, by extension, the nontransferable license price, would be zero, but under transferability, 5 dollars of revenue would be obtained if v is set at 1/2.

---

8. This comes from integrating by parts.

CHAPTER NINE

Free Quota

I. Introduction

Although past export performance (however defined) in the relevant category /country is the main criterion for quota allocation, many countries also set aside quota to be allocated according to various other criteria. These criteria may include export performance to a non–restricted country, investment in production facilities, or, most commonly, first–come–first–served to eligible firms.

This chapter looks at the practice of allocating a portion of the total quota free of charge on a first–come–first–served basis to agents with proof of an order. Hong Kong, India and Bangladesh, among other countries, have this free quota scheme. The rationale for this scheme is to facilitate entry by new firms which are not eligible for past performance quota allocations and may otherwise have to purchase quota from existing license holders. Unlike past performance quotas, which are traded on the secondary market in some countries, free quotas, once allocated, are usually not transferable.

An important point to note about free quota is that it is usually not transferable and is tied to an order in the sense that it is allocated only to exporters with documented proof of an order. As such, it alters the relative bargaining strengths of the importer and the exporter, with the result that the rents associated with such quota need not go to the exporter! Since the exporting firms which obtain free quota receive it free of charge, and only with proof of an order, their export prices—in a competitive market—will not reflect the quota price. The quota rents in such a system may go to the importers or be dissipated in the costs of acquiring the free quota.

Another interesting aspect of the free quota is that the availability of such quota tends to limit the premium charged on transferable past performance quotas. In a static model, it is only when the free quota is exhausted that the price for a temporary transfer becomes positive. Khanna 1991 claims that this was the case in India, noting that the moment free quota was made available, the premium for transferable past performance quota almost disappeared.

This chapter highlights the implications of the free quota on the price for tradeable quota licenses on the secondary market. A simple model is developed to show that the effect depends on:

1. The amount of free quota.
2. The restrictiveness of the total quota.
3. The distribution of valuations across the agents involved.

II. Model Setup

Consider a situation where there is a continuum of potential buyers of licenses.

ASSUMPTIONS:

1. *The buyers have different valuations for the licenses, possibly due to differences in their cost of production. Buyers are indexed by their valuation, ℓ.*
2. *There is no uncertainty on the part of the buyers regarding their individual valuations.*
3. *ℓ is distributed over the interval [0, 1] according to the density function $f(\ell)$. The mass of buyers, and hence, the demand for licenses at license price 0, is N.*
4. *The total quota level is set at V, where V < N. This means that the quota is binding, that is, there is excess demand for licenses when the license price is zero. Denote the restrictiveness of the quota, V/N, by v; v < 1.*
5. *Of the total quota V, Y is allocated as free quota and the rest, (V-Y), is sold. Denote Y/N by y; $y \le v < 1$.*
6. *The free quota licenses are not transferable. The remaining (V-Y) licenses, once sold, may not be re-sold—one can think of these licenses as being allocated according to some criterion, e.g., past performance, but allowed to be transferred once. In India, for example, open (i.e., free) quotas cannot be traded and closed quotas may be transferred only on a permanent basis.*
7. *There are two time periods:*
   a. *In period one, (V-Y) licenses are sold.*
   b. *In period two, the free quota, Y, is distributed and export takes place, (i.e., the licenses are used).*
8. *The proportion of buyers applying for free quota in period two (relative to N) is n, where $0 \le n \le 1$.*
9. *Costs increase substantially if production is expanded beyond the normal level,[1] hence, each buyer has a fixed, say unit, supply of goods available for export.*

---

1. For example, a firm with an unusually large order may have to subcontract part of it so as to be able to deliver on time.

III. License Price in the Absence of Free Quota

If there is no free quota, (i.e., y = 0), then all the V licenses are sold, with the license price determined by the intersection of demand and supply. Thus, the equilibrium license price, $L^{y=0}$, is defined implicitly by:

$$1 - F(L^{y=0}) = V/N = v$$

$$\Rightarrow L^{y=0} = F^{-1}(1 - v)$$

(1)

where F(·) denotes the cumulative density function associated with f(·). Although it is assumed that licenses may not be traded, since there is no uncertainty in the valuations of buyers, no transfers would be desired ex post anyway in the absence of free quota.

IV. License Price in the Presence of Free Quota

If there is free quota of Y, with 0 < y < v < 1, each buyer must decide on one of the following two courses of action:

1. Purchase a license in period one, thus guaranteeing his ability to export in the next period.
2. Not purchase a license in period one and apply for free quota in period two, taking the chance that he may be unsuccessful and consequently unable to supply.[2]

A buyer's payoff from purchasing the license in period one is simply his valuation of the license, net of the price paid for the license; his payoff from applying for free quota in period two is the probability of his obtaining the license multiplied by his valuation of the license (net of the price paid, which is zero). Only buyers with high enough valuations will choose to purchase a license in period one; the rest will choose to apply for free quota in period two.[3] No one will wish to do both, as long as the license price is positive, since

---

2. Since all licenses are nontransferable, he will not be able to purchase a license at that point in time.

3. To see this, consider the payoffs from both options for a buyer with valuation ℓ. If the license price that clears the market in period one is L, then:

Payoff if purchase a license $= \ell - L$

Payoff if apply for free quota $= \ell \min[(y/n), 1]$

Payoff if purchase a license – Payoff if apply for free quota

$= \ell(1 - \min[(y/n), 1]) - L$

$= \ell \max[1 - (y/n), 0] - L.$

licenses may not be re–sold in period two and each buyer's ability to supply is limited.

To determine the equilibrium license price in this environment, it is necessary to consider the marginal buyer, who is indifferent between the option of purchasing the license in period one and that of applying for free quota in period two.[4] Let ℓ^* denote the valuation of this marginal buyer. All buyers with valuations below ℓ^* will apply for free quota. Since n is the proportion of such buyers:

$$n = F(\ell^*). \tag{2}$$

All buyers with valuations above ℓ^* will purchase a license in period one. Since V-Y is the quantity available for sale in period one, equating demand with supply implicitly defines ℓ^*:

$$1 - F(\ell^*) = (V - Y)/N = v - y. \tag{3}$$

From (2) and (3):

$$\ell^* = F^{-1}(1 - v + y)$$

$$n = F(\ell^*) = 1 - v + y. \tag{4}$$

Now, for the marginal buyer to be indifferent between the two options open to him, the equilibrium license price, $L^{y>0}$, must be implicitly defined by:

$$\ell^* - L^{y>0} = \ell^*(y/n)$$

$$\Rightarrow L^{y>0} = \ell^*[1 - \frac{y}{F(\ell^*)}] = F^{-1}(1 - v + y)[\frac{1 - v}{1 - v + y}]. \tag{5}$$

The difference between the license price with no free quota and the license price with free quota is:

$$L^{y=0} - L^{y>0} = F^{-1}(1 - v) - F^{-1}(1 - v + y)[\frac{1 - v}{1 - v + y}]$$

$$= (1 - v)[\frac{F^{-1}(1 - v)}{1 - v} - \frac{F^{-1}(1 - v + y)}{1 - v + y}]. \tag{6}$$

If ℓ is uniformly distributed, then $F(\ell) = \ell$, and $L^{y=0} = L^{y>0}$. But if $f(\ell)$ is not a uniform distribution, then $(L^{y=0} - L^{y>0})$ may be greater or less than zero. Figure 9.1 is drawn for a roughly bell shaped distribution of ℓ. Note that for a quota level of V, $F^{-1}(1-v) / (1-v)$ is simply the inverse of the slope of the ray from the point E on the cumulative distribution function, and that (1-v+y) lies above

---

4. Note that $y < n$ if there is a binding quota.

(1- v) on the vertical axis. Figure 9.2 illustrates how the introduction of a free quota scheme can result in either a higher or a lower equilibrium license price.

If the quota is very restrictive, that is, if $v < v^*$ so that $(1-v) > (1-v^*)$ on the vertical axis, then $F^{-1}(1-v+y) / (1-v+y)$ will be larger than $F^{-1}(1-v) / (1-v)$, and, from (6), $L^{y>0}$ will be larger than $L^{y=0}$.

If the quota is not very restrictive, that is, if $v < v^*$ so that $(1-v) < (1-v^*)$ on the vertical axis, then $F^{-1}(1-v+y) / (1-v+y)$ will be smaller than $F^{-1}(1-v) / (1-v)$, and, from (6), $L^{y>0}$ will be smaller than $L^{y=0}$ only if y is not too large. If a large amount of free quota is distributed, then $F^{-1}(1-v+y) / (1-v+y)$ will be larger than $F^{-1}(1-v) / (1-v)$, and, from (6), $L^{y>0}$ will be larger than $L^{y=0}$. In Figure 9.2, for a small amount of free quota, y_1, the slope of the ray, OE_1, is greater than OE, but for a large amount of free quota, y_2, the slope of OE_2 is smaller than OE.

Hence, the introduction of free quota will tend to raise the price of the remaining transferable licenses if the total quota is very restrictive. But if the total quota is not too restrictive, and/or the share of free quota is not too large, then the free quota may actually undermine the value of owning transferable

FIGURE 9.1. Comparing License Prices with and without the Free Quota Scheme

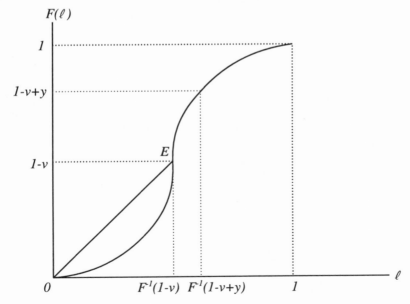

quota licenses,[5] thereby reducing the quota rent appropriated by exporters. In this analysis, the amount of free quota, y, affects $L^{y>0}$ in two ways:

1. Increasing y, for a given v, improves the chances of obtaining free quota, since y / n = y / (1-v+y) in equilibrium. This works to lower $L^{y>0}$.
2. Increasing y, for a given v, reduces the available licenses for sale and hence raises ℓ^*, the valuation of the marginal buyer of licenses—this works to raise $L^{y>0}$.

If ℓ is uniformly distributed, the second effect exactly counteracts the first so that the equilibrium license price, $L^{y>0}$, is unaffected by y. However, if ℓ is not uniformly distributed, then the introduction of a free quota scheme can either increase or lower the price of the remaining quota license.

Figure 9.2. License Prices and Quota Restrictiveness

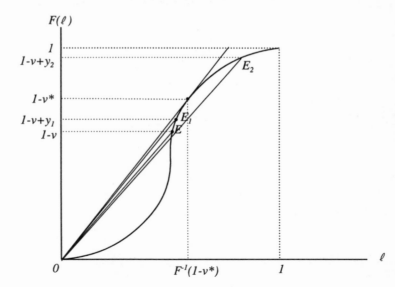

CHAPTER TEN

Quota Subcategorization[1]

I. Introduction

This chapter examines the implications of quota subcategorization, a key feature of India's quota allocation system. As mentioned in Chapter Seven, even though the categories of restricted apparel under the MFA are quite detailed (specified by fabric and garment type in the case of exports to the United States), in India, they are often further split into subcategories, e.g., children's and adult garments, or knitted, handloomed and mill–made/powerloomed garments, with the entitlements calculated separately. Special quantities are reserved for garments made of 100 percent cotton handloom fabrics; portions of quota are also set aside for woollen and acrylic garments and knitwear, even when the importing country imposes no specific limits for these categories.

The conventional wisdom holds that subcategorization is an undesirable policy since it can lead to situations where the quota is not binding in certain subcategories and very binding in others, resulting in underutilization of the total quota despite a positive license price. Such an argument may be found in Khanna 1991. In this chapter, a series of stylized targeting models is used to show that, depending on the environment and the objective of the authorities, subcategorization may be theoretically desirable.[2] Some early work on the consequences of quota subcategorization can be found in Corden 1971, although his approach differs from the targeting approach used here.

II. Subcategorization

Consider a particular MFA category, say cotton dresses, produced in India.

ASSUMPTIONS:

1. *Cotton dresses are produced in India under conditions of perfect competition.*

2. *Cotton dresses are produced in India for export only.*

---

1. This chapter is based on Krishna and Tan 1997a.

2. It is interesting to note the similarity of the results to the strategic trade literature: a particular policy may be welfare–improving under some circumstances and welfare–reducing under other circumstances.

3. *India is a large exporter of cotton dresses, that is, it faces a downward sloping foreign demand for this good.*
4. *There are two types of cotton dresses:*
   Those made from handloomed fabric—referred to as good 1,
   Those made from powerloomed fabric—referred to as good 2.
5. *Handloomed dresses are homogeneous goods, as are powerloomed dresses, but the two types of dresses are not substitutes.*
6. *The total quota on Indian exports of cotton dresses is exogenously set at V units.*

The analysis begins with how competitive forces will distribute the given quota of V units between handloomed and powerloomed cotton dresses. Then several possible objectives behind the imposition of separate subquotas on handloomed and powerloomed dresses are considered. The point of this exercise is to demonstrate that there may be a theoretical case for sub-categorization, given the overall quota; depending on the objective function of the Indian authorities, some intervention may be required on their part to bring the market distribution in line with the desired distribution.

In the rest of this section, the following notation will be used:

Q_i =   the quantity of good i
$P_i(Q_i)$ =   the inverse demand function for good i
$C_i(Q_i)$ =   the total cost function for good i
$C_i'(Q_i)$ =   the marginal cost function for good i

The subscript i=1 denotes handloomed cotton dresses and i=2 denotes powerloomed cotton dresses. For notational simplicity, all other variables entering into the P_i and C_i functions are dropped; in particular, the assumption of no substitution between handloomed and powerloomed dresses allows P_i and C_i to be written as functions of Q_i only.

III. Market Outcome

Suppose that the quota of V units on cotton dresses is binding. Left to competitive market forces, how will this quota eventually be divided between handloomed and powerloomed dresses?

If the quota is binding, it will introduce a wedge between the demand price, $P_i(Q_i)$, which foreign consumers are willing to pay for the restricted cotton dresses, and the supply price, or marginal cost, $C_i'(Q_i)$, of producing the dresses. This wedge, $P_i(Q_i)-C_i'(Q_i)$, measures the per unit quota rent, that is, the value of a quota license to export one dress of type i, i = 1, 2. If the quota licenses are freely transferable among producers of handloomed and powerloomed cotton dresses,[3] arbitrage will ensure that the competitive market will allocate production between the two types of dresses such that, at the margin, the value of a quota license for handloomed dresses is equal to the value of a quota license for powerloomed dresses. To see this, note that if $P_1(Q_1)-C_1'(Q_1) > P_2(Q_2)-C_2'(Q_2)$, power loom producers will sell their licenses to hand loom producers, hence the production of handloomed dresses will rise and the production of powerloomed dresses will fall. Conversely, if $P_1(Q_1)-C_1'(Q_1) < P_2(Q_2)-C_2'(Q_2)$, production will shift from handloomed dresses toward powerloomed dresses. Only when $P_1(Q_1)-C_1'(Q_1) = P_2(Q_2)-C_2'(Q_2)$ will there be no incentive for handloom and power loom producers to trade licenses.

The equilibrium condition under competitive market allocation, therefore, is:

$$P_1(Q_1) - C_1'(Q_1) = P_2(Q_2) - C_2'(Q_2). \tag{1}$$

Since the total quota, V, is assumed to be binding, all the licenses will be used:

$$Q_1 + Q_2 = V. \tag{2}$$

Equations (1) and (2) implicitly define the equilibrium output of handloomed and powerloomed dresses under competitive market conditions, subject to the total quota, V. Denote these quantities as V_1^m and V_2^m, respectively.

IV. Welfare Maximization Objective

Now suppose the Indian authorities decide to impose separate quotas, V_1 and V_2, on handloomed and powerloomed dresses, respectively, with the objective of maximizing welfare.

Using a partial equilibrium framework, and assuming cotton dresses are produced only for export,[4] this objective is tantamount to maximizing the sum of producer surplus and license revenue from the production and export of the two types of cotton dresses. Assuming the quotas are binding, for each type of restricted cotton dress (denoted by i):

1. producer surplus is given by: $C_i'(V_i)V_i - C_i(V_i)$, that is, the difference between sales revenue, $C_i'(V_i)V_i$, and the total cost of producing V_i units, $C_i(V_i)$;

---

3. As discussed in Part IV of the Appendix, since the late 1980s, some 60–65 percent of quota licenses were allocated to firms based on their past performance. According to Kumar and Khanna 1990, these licenses were freely transferable and an active secondary market existed in which the licenses were bought and sold. In 1991, the rules were changed to allow only permanent transfers.

4. This assumption is made for simplicity. Allowing for domestic consumption (and thereby including consumer surplus in the welfare function) will not alter the nature of the results.

2. license revenue is given by: $[P_i(V_i)-C_i'(V_i)]V_i$, that is, the per unit quota rent, $P_i(V_i)-C_i'(V_i)$, multiplied by the number of dresses exported, V_i. Thus, the sum of producer surplus and license revenue is given by $P_i(V_i)V_i-C_i(V_i)$ for each dress type i.

Given the exogenously specified quota level of V, the Indian authorities' objective function would be to:

$$\max_{V_1, V_2} \quad P_1(V_1)V_1 - C_1(V_1) + P_2(V_2)V_2 - C_2(V_2)$$

$$s.t. \quad V_1 + V_2 \leq V.$$

(3)

Assuming the objective function is concave, the first order conditions for welfare maximization dictate that:

$$P_1'(V_1)V_1 + P_1(V_1) - C_1'(V_1) = P_2'(V_2)V_2$$
$$+ P_2(V_2) - C_2'(V_2) = \lambda^w$$

(4)

where λ^w is the Lagrange multiplier.[5] In other words, the welfare maximizing subcategorization equates the difference between marginal revenue and marginal cost for the two sectors. Equation (4) implicitly defines the optimal levels of V_1 and V_2 for welfare maximization. Denote these quantities by V_1^w and V_2^w.

PROPOSITION 1

The competitive market allocation will achieve welfare maximization, that is, $V_1^m=V_1^w$ and $V_2^m=V_2^w$, if and only if $P_1(V_1^m)/\epsilon_1(V_1^m) = P_2(V_2^m)/\epsilon_2(V_2^m)$, where $\epsilon_i = -P_i(V_i)/P_i'(V_i)V_i$, the elasticity of demand for good i, defined as a positive number. If $P_1(V_1^m)/\epsilon_1(V_1^m) > P_2(V_2^m)/\epsilon_2(V_2^m)$, then $V_1^m>V_1^w$ and $V_2^m<V_2^w$, that is, the competitive market outcome results in an overproduction of handloomed dresses and an underproduction of powerloomed dresses for the purpose of welfare maximization. If $P_1(V_1^m)/\epsilon_1(V_1^m) < P_2(V_2^m)/\epsilon_2(V_2^m)$, then $V_1^m<V_1^w$ and $V_2^m>V_2^w$, that is, the competitive market outcome results in an underproduction of handloomed dresses and an overproduction of powerloomed dresses for the purpose of welfare maximization.

---

5. Note that λ^w could be equal to zero, in which case less than the entire quota may be used. This is discussed further in Proposition 2.

Proof

The first order condition for welfare maximization (equation (4)) can be written as:

$$[P_1(V_1) - C_1'(V_1)] - [P_1(V_1)/\epsilon_1(V_1)] =$$

$$(5)$$

$$[P_2(V_2) - C_2'(V_2)] - [P_2(V_2)/\epsilon_2(V_2)]$$

using the definition of ϵ_i given above. From equation (1), we know that at the competitive market quantities, $P_1(V_1^m) - C_1'(V_1^m) = P_2(V_2^m) - C_2'(V_2^m)$, so equation (5) holds at the competitive market equilibrium only if $P_1(V_1^m)/-\epsilon_1(V_1^m) = P_2(V_2^m)/\epsilon_2(V_2^m)$. This situation is illustrated in Figure 10.1. If $P_1(V_1^m)/\epsilon_1(V_1^m) > P_2(V_2^m)/\epsilon_2(V_2^m)$, then at (V_1^m, V_2^m), the left hand side of equation (5) is smaller than the right hand side, that is, the difference between marginal revenue and marginal cost is smaller for handloomed dresses than it is for powerloomed dresses, indicating an overproduction of the former and underproduction of the latter for the purpose of welfare maximization. This situation is illustrated in Figure 10.2. The opposite is true if $P_1(V_1^m)/\epsilon_1(V_1^m) < P_2(V_2^m)/\epsilon_2(V_2^m)$; this situation is illustrated in Figure 10.3. QED

FIGURE 10.1. $V_1^m = V_1^w$, and $V_2^m = V_2^w$

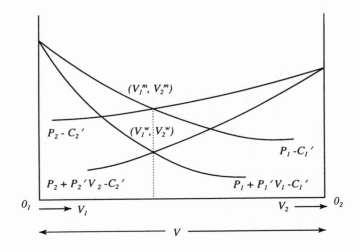

FIGURE 10.2. $V_1^m > V_1^w$ and $V_2^m < V_2^w$

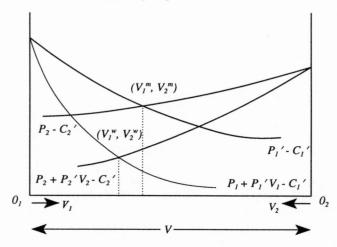

(V_1^m, V_2^m)

$P_2 - C_2'$

(V_1^w, V_2^w)

$P_2 + P_2'V_2 - C_2'$

$P_1' - C_1'$

$P_1 + P_1'V_1 - C_1'$

0_1 ⟶ V_1 V_2 ⟵ 0_2

⟵ V ⟶

FIGURE 10.3. $V_1^m < V_1^w$ and $V_2^m > V_2^w$

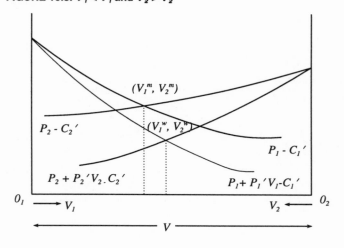

(V_1^m, V_2^m)

$P_2 - C_2'$

(V_1^w, V_2^w)

$P_1 - C_1'$

$P_2 + P_2'V_2.C_2'$

$P_1 + P_1'V_1 - C_1'$

0_1 ⟶ V_1 V_2 ⟵ 0_2

⟵ V ⟶

PROPOSITION 2

Given an exogenously determined total quota, V, sub–categorization of V generically leads to an improvement in welfare over the market allocation of V between the two types of dresses.

Proof

If the Indian authorities were able to set the total quota on cotton dresses rather than accept an exogenously given level, V they would maximize the country's welfare by choosing the subquotas V_1^{w*} and V_2^{w*} such that equation (4) is satisfied with $\lambda^w = 0$. In other words, the first best welfare maximizing policy for India would be to set the subquotas so as to equate marginal cost with marginal revenue in the handloom and power loom sectors. Given the assumption of India being a large country, and using reasoning analogous to the optimal tariff argument, we know that the chosen subquotas V_1^{w*} and V_2^{w*} would add up to the optimal quota on cotton dresses which would maximize India's welfare. Call this optimal quota, V^{w*}. Comparing the first best result with the situation where the quota is exogenously fixed at V, note that if V is larger than the optimal quota, V^{w*},[6] then the opportunity exists for the authorities to create an unusable dummy subcategory in order to exploit their monopoly power in the world market. By setting the quota size for the dummy subcategory at $V-V^{w*}$, the authorities could effectively restrict their exports to the optimal quota level! If $V < V^{w*}$, there is no room for subcategorization to enhance the country's monopoly power, although subcategorization would still be required in order to achieve welfare maximization at the given total quota level, V.   QED

PROPOSITION 3

If India were a small country, that is, a price–taker, in the world market for cotton dresses, then the competitive market allocation will achieve welfare maximization.

Proof

If India were a price–taker in the world market for cotton dresses, P_i will not be a function of V_i. Hence, $P_i{}'(V_i)V_i = 0$ for i = 1, 2, and the market outcome will be identical to the welfare–maximizing outcome.   QED

---

6. This would be the case if, in Figure 10.1, the two curves, $(P_1(V_1) - C_1{}'(V_1))$ and $(P_2(V_2) - C_2{}'(V_2))$ intersected below the horizontal axis (i.e., $\lambda^w = 0$).

V. Foreign Exchange Maximization Objective

Next, let us consider a different objective for imposing separate quotas on handloomed and powerloomed dresses, namely that of maximizing foreign exchange earnings. Given V, the Indian authorities would then have the following objective function (assumed to be concave):

$$\max_{V_1, V_2} \quad P_1(V_1)V_1 + P_2(V_2)V_2$$

$$s.t. \quad V_1 + V_2 = V. \tag{6}$$

The first order conditions for revenue maximization dictate that:

$$P_1{}'(V_1)V_1 + P_1(V_1) = P_2{}'(V_2)V_2 + P_2(V_2) = \lambda^f \tag{7}$$

where λ^f is the Lagrange multiplier. In other words, the revenue maximization objective is met if the marginal revenues are equalized in both sectors. Equation (7) implicitly defines the optimal levels of V_1 and V_2 for foreign exchange (revenue) maximization, which are denoted by V_1^f and V_2^f, respectively.

PROPOSITION 4

The competitive market allocation will maximize revenue if and only if $[P_1(V_1^m)/\epsilon_1(V_1^m) - P_2(V_2^m)/\epsilon_2(V_2^m)] + [C_1{}'(V_1^m) - C_2{}'(V_2^m)] = 0$. If $P_1(V_1^m)/\epsilon_1(V_1^m) = P_2(V_2^m)/\epsilon_2(V_2^m)$, so that the competitive market allocation is also the welfare maximizing allocation, but $C_1{}'(V_1^m) > C_2{}'(V_2^m)$, then $V_1^m < V_1^f$ and $V_2^m > V_2^f$, that is, the market equilibrium will result in underproduction of handloomed dresses and overproduction of powerloomed dresses for the purpose of revenue maximization. If $P_1(V_1^m)/\epsilon_1(V_1^m) = P_2(V_2^m)/\epsilon_2(V_2^m)$ and $C_1{}'(V_1^m) < C_2{}'(V_2^m)$, then $V_1^m > V_1^f$ and $V_2^m < V_2^f$, that is, the market equilibrium will result in overproduction of handloomed dresses and underproduction of powerloomed dresses for the purpose of revenue maximization.

Proof

We can write the first order condition for revenue maximization (equation (7)) as:

$$[P_1(V_1) - C_1{}'(V_1)] - P_1(V_1)/\epsilon_1(V_1) + C_1{}'(V_1) =$$

$$[P_2(V_2) - C_2{}'(V_2)] - P_2(V_2)/\epsilon_2(V_2) + C_2{}'(V_2). \tag{8}$$

At the competitive market equilibrium, $P_1(V_1^m) - C_1{}'(V_1^m) = P_2(V_2^m) - C_2{}'(V_2^m)$, so equation (8) holds at (V_1^m, V_2^m) if and only if $[P_1(V_1^m)/\epsilon_1(V_1^m) - P_2(V_2^m)/\epsilon_2(V_2^m)]$

+ $[C_1'(V_1^m)-C_2'(V_2^m)] = 0$. If $P_1(V_1^m)/\epsilon_1(V_1^m) = P_2(V_2^m)/\epsilon_2(V_2^m)$, we know from Proposition 1 that the competitive market solution maximizes welfare. However, if $P_1(V_1^m)/\epsilon_1(V_1^m) = P_2(V_2^m)/\epsilon_2(V_2^m)$, but $C_1'(V_1^m) > C_2'(V_2^m)$, then at (V_1^m, V_2^m), the left-hand side of equation (8) is larger than the right-hand side, that is, the marginal revenue from handloomed dresses is greater than the marginal revenue from powerloomed dresses, indicating an underproduction of former and overproduction of the latter for the purpose of revenue maximization. The opposite is true if $P_1(V_1^m)/\epsilon_1(V_1^m) = P_2(V_2^m)/\epsilon_2(V_2^m)$ and $C_1'(V_1^m) < C_2'(V_2^m)$.   QED

PROPOSITION 5

Given an exogenously determined total quota, V, sub–categorization of V generically leads to higher revenue (foreign exchange earnings) than under the market allocation of V between the two types of dresses.

Proof

The first best revenue maximizing policy (if the Indian authorities were free to set the total quota rather than take it as given) would be to set the sub–quotas such that marginal revenue is zero in each sector (i.e., such that equation (7) is satisfied with $\lambda^f = 0$), with the sub–quotas adding up to V^{f*}, the optimal quota from the revenue maximizing perspective.[7] As before, comparing the first best result with the situation where the quota is exogenously fixed at V, note that if V is larger than the optimal quota, V^{f*}, the authorities could create an unusable dummy subquota of size V-V^{f*} in order to effectively restrict their exports to the optimal quota level. Of course, if $V < V^{f*}$, subcategorization cannot be used to attain the optimal quota, although subcategorization would still be required in order to achieve revenue maximization at a given total quota, V.   QED

VI. Quota Rent Maximization

A third possible objective could be the maximization of quota rents from the restricted export of cotton dresses. In this case, given V, the Indian authorities

---

7. Note that, due to the fact that marginal costs are not a consideration here, the optimal quota for foreign exchange maximization is always larger than the optimal quota for welfare maximization, that is, $V^{f*} > V^{w*}$. This can also be deduced from a diagram similar to Figure 10.1, whereby if the curves $(P_1'V_1+P_1)$ and $(P_2'V_2+P_2)$ intersect at the horizontal axis so that the distance between the two vertical axes measures the revenue maximizing optimal quota V^{f*}, then the curves $(P_1'V_1+P_1-C_1')$ and $(P_2'V_2+P_2-C_2')$ must intersect below the horizontal axis. Hence, in order to obtain V^{w*}, we can think of having to push the right vertical axis leftward until $(P_1'V_1+P_1-C_1')$ and $(P_2'V_2+P_2-C_2')$ intersect at the horizontal axis; this new, narrower distance between the two axes now measures V^{w*}.

would want to set subquotas V_1 and V_2 so as to satisfy the following objective function (assumed to be concave):

$$\max_{V_1, V_2} \quad [P_1(V_1) - C_1'(V_1)]V_1 + [P_2(V_2) - C_2'(V_2)]V_2 \tag{9}$$

$$s.t. \quad V_1 + V_2 = V.$$

The first order conditions for maximization dictate that:

$$[P_1'(V_1)V_1 + P_1(V_1)] - [C_1''(V_1)V_1 + C_1'(V_1)] = $$
$$[P_2'(V_2)V_2 + P_2(V_2)] - [C_2''(V_2)V_2 + C_2'(V_2)] = \lambda^r \tag{10}$$

where λ^r is the Lagrange multiplier. Equation (10) implicitly defines the rent maximizing allocation of handloomed and powerloomed dresses, which we denote V_1^r and V_2^r, respectively.

PROPOSITION 6

The competitive market allocation will maximize quota rent if and only if $[P_1(V_1^m)/\epsilon_1(V_1^m) - P_2(V_2^m)/\epsilon_2(V_2^m)] + [C_1(V_1^m)/\eta_1(V_1^m) - C_2(V_2^m)/\eta_2(V_2^m)] = 0$, where $\eta_i = C_i(V_i)/C_i''(V_i)V_i$, the price elasticity of supply for good i. If $P_1(V_1^m)/\epsilon_1(V_1^m) = P_2(V_2^m)/\epsilon_2(V_2^m)$, so that the competitive market allocation is also the welfare maximizing allocation, but $C_1(V_1^m)/\eta_1(V_1^m) > C_2(V_2^m)/\eta_2(V_2^m)$, then $V_1^m > V_1^r$ and $V_2^m < V_2^r$, that is, the market equilibrium will result in overproduction of handloomed dresses and underproduction of powerloomed dresses for the purpose of rent maximization. If $P_1(V_1^m)/\epsilon_1(V_1^m) = P_2(V_2^m)/\epsilon_2(V_2^m)$ and $C_1(V_1^m)/\eta_1(V_1^m) < C_2(V_2^m)/\eta_2(V_2^m)$, then $V_1^m < V_1^r$ and $V_2^m > V_2^r$, that is, the market equilibrium will result in underproduction of handloomed dresses and overproduction of powerloomed dresses for the purpose of rent maximization.

Proof

Rearranging equation (10), we have:

$$[P_1(V_1) - C_1'(V_1)] - P_1(V_1)/\epsilon_1(V_1) - C_1(V_1)/\eta_1(V_1) = $$
$$[P_2(V_2) - C_2'(V_2)] - P_2(V_2)/\epsilon_2(V_2) - C_2(V_2)/\eta_2(V_2) \tag{11}$$

using the definition of η_i given above. At the competitive market equilibrium, $P_1(V_1^m)$-$C_1'(V_1^m)P_2(V_2^m)$-$C_2'(V_2^m)$, so equation (10) holds at (V_1^m, V_2^m) if and only if $P_1(V_1^m)/\epsilon_1(V_1^m)+C_1(V_1^m)/\eta_1(V_1^m)=P_2(V_2^m)/\epsilon_2(V_2^m)+C_2(V_2^m)/\eta_2(V_2^m)$. If $P_1(V_1^m)/\epsilon_1(V_1^m)=P_2(V_2^m)/\epsilon_2(V_2^m)$, we know from Proposition 1 that the competitive market solution maximizes welfare. However, if $P_1(V_1^m)/\epsilon_1(V_1^m)=P_2(V_2^m)/\epsilon_2(V_2^m)$, but $C_1(V_1^m)/\eta_1(V_1^m)> C_2(V_2^m)/\eta_2(V_2^m)$, then at (V_1^m, V_2^m), assuming marginal costs are increasing, the left-hand side of equation (11) is smaller than the right-hand side, indicating an overproduction of handloomed dresses and underproduction of powerloomed dresses for the purpose of rent maximization. The opposite is true if $P_1(V_1^m)/\epsilon_1(V_1^m) = P_2(V_2^m)/\epsilon_2(V_2^m)$ and $C_1(V_1^m)/\eta_1(V_1^m) < C_2(V_2^m)/\eta_2(V_2^m)$. A similar point is made in Corden 1971, p.224.[8] QED

PROPOSITION 7

Given an exogenously determined total quota, V, subcategorization of V generically results in a larger amount of quota rent than would be the case under the market allocation of V between the two types of dresses.

Proof

If the authorities were free to set the total quota to maximize their collection of quota rent, they would choose subquota levels that satisfy equation (10) with $\lambda^r = 0$ such that the subquotas add up to the optimal quota, V^{r*}.[9] As before, comparing the first best result with the situation where the quota is exogenously fixed at V, note that if V is larger than the optimal quota, V^{r*}, the authorities could create an unusable dummy subquota of size $V-V^{r*}$ in order to effectively restrict their exports to the optimal quota level. Of course, if $V < V^{r*}$, no such opportunity exists for attaining the optimal quota, although sub–categorization would still be required in order to achieve rent maximization under a given total quota, V. QED

---

8. Corden 1971, p.224 analyzes the situation where there are separate import quotas on two items (bags and hats) and concludes that allowing for interchangeability between bag and hat quotas may raise or lower total quota profits.

9. Assuming marginal costs are increasing, a comparison of equation (10) and equation (3) shows that $V^{r*} < V^{w*}$. This can also be seen by noting that in a diagram similar to Figure 10.1, if the curves $(P_1'V_1+P_1-C_1')$ and $(P_2'V_2+P_2-C_2')$ intersect at the horizontal axis so that the distance between the two vertical axes measures the welfare maximizing optimal quota, V^{w*}, then the curves $(P_1'V_1+P_1-C_1'-C_1'')$ and $(P_2'V_2+P_2-C_2'-C_2'')$ must intersect below the horizontal axis if C_1'' and C_2'' are positive. Hence, in order to obtain V^{r*}, we can think of having to push the right vertical axis leftward until $(P_1'V_1+P_1-C_1'-C_1'')$ and $(P_2'V_2+P_2-C_2'-C_2'')$ intersect at the horizontal axis; this new, narrower distance between the two axes now measures V^{r*}.

CHAPTER ELEVEN

Some Observations on Quota Holdings and Transfers in Korea

I. Introduction

In this chapter, data on quota holdings and transfers in Korea are used to determine license concentrations in the different MFA categories and how these change over time. The data were obtained from the Korean export associations, which record the quota allocations to individual firms, as well as their net change in holdings, on an annual basis. The time period covered by the data is 1982 through 1988 (with the exception of 1987).

II. Quota Holdings

Upon examining the data, the most notable fact is that quota license holdings are quite concentrated in Korea. They are considerably more concentrated compared to Hong Kong, for example. This evidence is presented in Figure 11.1 which depicts the 1982 numbers equivalent data for Hong Kong and Korea. In addition, it is evident that holdings of categories with MFA numbers in the 600s (manmade fibers) and 300s (cotton), are generally less concentrated than the holdings of categories in the 400s (wool).

The second observation is that the number of license holders in each category appears to be increasing over time. The numbers equivalent of the Herfindahl index of concentration of holdings in each MFA category also seems to be rising, albeit slowly, over time, suggesting that license holdings are becoming less and less concentrated. The data are presented in Figure 11.2. In a sense, this is not too surprising, since the concentration in license holdings tends to weaken (i.e., the numbers equivalent tends to rise) with the entry of more and more new license holders. However, it is also interesting to consider if this slightly rising trend of the numbers equivalent is due, in any part, to reduced concentration amongst the existing license holders, (i.e., a smaller variation in license holdings across firms).[1] Table 11.1 presents the results of a simple regression of the numbers equivalent ($NEQUIV_{it}$) against 32 category dummies, and time:

---

1. Recall that a reduction in the variation among firms with the number of firms constant will raise the numbers equivalent.

FIGURE 11.1. Korea: 1982 Numbers Equivalent in Korea and Hong Kong

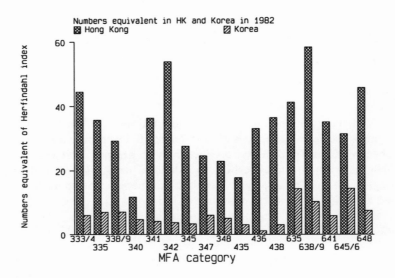

FIGURE 11.2. Korea: Behavior of Numbers Equivalent Over Time

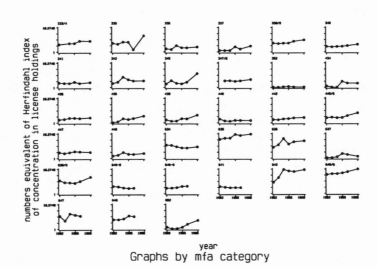

$$NEQUIV_{it} = \alpha_0 + \sum_{i=1}^{32} \alpha_i CAT_i + \beta t + \epsilon_{it} \qquad (1)$$

the coefficient on the time variable is significant and positive at 0.40, implying that the numbers equivalent increases by one approximately every two and a half years. Table 11.2 presents the results of the same regression with the inclusion of a new variable, the number of license holders (NUM):

$$NEQUIV_{it} = \alpha_0 + \sum_{i=1}^{32} \alpha_i CAT_i + \beta t + \gamma NUM_{it} + \epsilon_{it} \qquad (2)$$

Holding the number of license holders constant, the coefficient on the time variable drops to 0.28, although it is still statistically significant. Therefore, the numbers equivalent increases by about one every three and a half years. Hence, there seems to be a natural tendency towards greater dispersion in license holdings.

TABLE 11.1. Korea: Regression of Numbers Equivalent on Time

Dependent variable = $NEQUIV_{it}$

Independent Variable	Coefficient	t–statistic
Constant	-786.8493 (98.3394)	-8.001[a]
t	0.4001 (0.0495)	8.077[a]

Number of observations = 191
R^2 = 0.9169, Adjusted R^2 = 0.8995
32 category dummies included.
Standard errors are in parentheses beneath the parameter estimates.
[a] Significant at the 1 percent level.

TABLE 11.2. Korea: Regression of Numbers Equivalent on Time and Number of Holders

Dependent variable = $NEQUIV_{it}$

Independent Variable	Coefficient	t–statistic
Constant	-555.9858 (120.752)	-4.604[a]
t	0.2834 (0.0609)	4.651[a]
NUM_{it}	0.0308 (0.0098)	3.134[a]

Number of observations = 191
R^2 = 0.9219, Adjusted R^2 = 0.9048
32 category dummies included.
Standard errors are in parentheses beneath the parameter estimates.
[a] Significant at the 1 percent level.

III. Quota Transfers

The pattern of license transfers may be considered from alternative perspective, by asking the following questions:

1. Do firms holding more than the average quantity of licenses tend to transfer their holdings out?
2. Do firms holding fewer than the average quantity of licenses tend to transfer them in?

The simple correlation of transfer amount with deviation of size of holdings from the average size turns out to be a positive, albeit quite small number, 0.15. This suggests a mean dispersion tendency amongst the license holders. At first glance, this may seem inconsistent with the earlier observation of reduced license holding variation among firms. However, the transfer data include both temporary as well as permanent transfers, whereas the numbers equivalent data reflect only permanent transfers.

Next, the transfer activity among the firms was observed and how it was related to the license holding concentration. Figure 11.3 plots the unweighted average activity per license against the numbers equivalent ($NEQUIV_{it}$). The vertical axis represents:

$$\frac{\sum_j |TRANSF_{ijt}|}{\sum_j HLDG_{ijt}} \tag{3}$$

where:

$TRANSF_{ijt}$ = amount of transfer made by firm j in category i at time t, and
$HLDG_{ijt}$ = license holdings of firm j in category i at time t.

There is a slight upward trend which suggests that more transfer activity occurs in the less concentrated categories. Figure 11.4 plots the average activity per license per firm against the numbers equivalent, with the vertical axis representing:

$$\sum_j \left| \frac{TRANSF_{ijt}}{HLDG_{ijt}} \right| . \tag{4}$$

Again, a weak upward trend may be observed.

FIGURE 11.3. Korea: Average Transfer Activity Plotted Against Numbers Equivalent

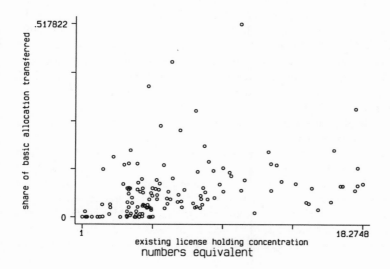

FIGURE 11.4. Korea: Average Transfer Activity Per Firm Plotted Against Numbers Equivalent

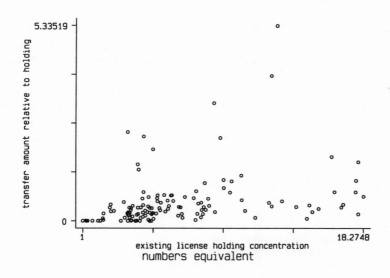

IV. Allocation of Open Quota

The analysis of quota holdings in Korea may be concluded by looking at the allocation of the open quota in 1988 and 1990. As mentioned in Part II of the Appendix, the Korean allocation procedure dictates that approximately 15 percent of the annual quota in each category be set aside as open quota. Table 11.3 lists, for 26 MFA categories, the proportion of total quota[2] allocated in the form of open quota in 1988 and 1990. The proportion of open quota, in fact, ranges from approximately 2 percent to 43 percent, with an average of 15 percent in 1988. Moreover, it increased between 1988 and 1990 for all categories except 341 and 345.

The bulk of the open quota is distributed according to the applicants' past export performance to non-quota areas, with the remainder allocated to firms which made recent investments in their production facilities, and firms which exported relatively expensive items. Table 11.4 shows, for the same 26 categories, the proportion of the open quota allocated on the basis of past export performance to non-quota areas in 1988 and 1990. The fraction of the open quota allocated on this basis ranged from approximately 24 percent to as much as 97 percent, with an average of 68 percent in 1988 and 81 percent in 1990. Also, the relative importance of this criterion for all categories except 352 and 641-Y rose between 1988 and 1990.

The next step was to look at the recipients of the open quota: were they mostly new entrants[3] or existing firms? Table 11.5 suggests that the open quota was largely and increasingly captured by new entrants. Table 11.6 provides further insight by showing the new entrants' share of the portion of open quota distributed according to the past export performance criterion and their share of the remaining portion of open quota distributed according to the other two criteria. The figures point to a distinct and increasing preference for new entrants in the allocation of past export performance based open quota compared to the other criteria.

Finally, the two channels by which newcomers could obtain quota—namely, open quota and temporary transfer from existing firms—may be compared.[4] How successful were new entrants in obtaining open quota as compared to temporary transfers? Table 11.5 sheds some light on this question. New entrants captured a significantly greater share of the open quota compared to basic quota transfers. Furthermore, their share of open quota over the period covered was rising whereas their share of basic transfers was falling.

---

2. The total quota is the sum of the total basic allocation and the total open allocation.

3. A firm is considered a new entrant if it did not receive any basic allocation that year.

4. Note that quota obtained by the first method counts towards the firm's export performance in the subsequent round of basic allocations, whereas quota obtained by the second method does not.

TABLE 11.3. Korea: Proportion of Total Quota Allocated as Open Quota

MFA Category	1988	1990
333/4	0.3081	0.4331
335	0.2179	0.2654
336	0.1641	0.3244
338/9	0.2874	0.3562
341	0.4073	0.2931
342	0.1585	0.2654
345	0.2475	0.1971
347/8	0.2508	0.3315
352	0.2098	0.2679
434	0.0616	0.3728
435	0.0339	0.0913
436	0.2223	0.2959
438	0.2909	0.4038
440	0.1294	0.3491
442	0.1268	0.2011
445/6	0.0167	0.1292
447	0.0985	0.2024
448	0.1531	0.2001
634	0.0612	0.1112
635	0.0497	0.0886
636	0.0511	0.2563
638/9	0.1091	0.137
641-P	0.0233	0.1018
641-Y	0.0279	0.0157
645/6	0.0568	0.0878
647/8	0.1453	0.2365
Average	0.1503	0.2313

TABLE 11.4. Korea: Proportion of Open Quota Allocated on the Basis of Past Export Performance in Non–Quota Markets

MFA category	1988	1990
333/4	0.6667	0.8494
335	0.6668	0.6921
336	0.6666	0.8501
338/9	0.6667	0.8000
341	0.6652	0.8501
342	0.6667	0.8000
345	0.6668	0.8000
347/8	0.6667	0.8000
352	0.9653	0.8500
434	0.7526	0.8499
435	0.6677	0.8506
436	0.2353	0.4439
438	0.7501	0.8500
440	0.5637	0.8367
442	0.7502	0.8534
445/6	0.7536	0.8505
447	0.6669	0.8001
448	0.7504	0.8502
634	0.6667	0.8348
635	0.6666	0.7653
636	0.7501	0.8500
638/9	0.6666	0.8000
641-P	0.7497	0.8505
641-Y	0.7572	0.7541
645/6	0.6667	0.8000
647/8	0.6667	0.8000
Average	0.6838	0.8051

TABLE 11.5. Korea: Newcomers' Share of Basic Quota Transfers and Open Quota

MFA Category	New Entrants' Share of Basic Transfers		New Entrants' Share of Open Quota	
	1988	1990	1988	1990
333/4	0.0301	0.0218	0.5738	0.7998
335	0.0816	0.0066	0.5814	0.6645
336	0.0000	0.0092	0.6260	0.8473
338/9	0.0156	0.0000	0.4748	0.5582
341	0.0450	0.0003	0.7128	0.8338
342	0.0091	0.0000	0.6260	0.7489
345	0.0000	0.0000	0.5099	0.4533
347/8	0.0309	0.0235	0.6152	0.7205
352	0.0000	0.0000	0.6986	0.5877
434	0.0000	0.0000	0.7456	0.8051
435	0.0000	0.0000	0.6716	0.8221
436	0.1184	0.0000	0.2565	0.3856
438	0.0181	0.0120	0.7238	0.9711
440	0.0001	0.0000	0.2705	0.3577
442	0.0019	0.0115	0.6922	0.7572
445/6	0.0015	0.0000	0.6000	0.8028
447	0.0538	0.0219	0.3456	0.4456
448	0.0167	0.0453	0.8812	0.5024
634	0.0148	0.0145	0.3527	0.4197
635	0.0127	0.0200	0.4953	0.5645
636	0.0207	0.0414	0.5263	0.7127
638/9	0.0134	0.0099	0.3135	0.4507
641-P	0.0090	0.0010	0.3621	0.4210
641-Y	0.0000	0.0000	0.5304	0.7541
645/6	0.0035	0.0009	0.2019	0.2487
647/8	0.0243	0.0207	0.3853	0.4740
652	0.1069	0.0053		
Average	0.0233	0.0098	0.5297	0.6196

TABLE 11.6. Korea: New Entrants' Share of Open Quota Distributed According to Past Export Performance to Non–Quota Markets and Other Criteria

MFA category	New Entrants' Share of Basic Transfers		New Entrants' Share of Open Quota	
	1988	1990	1988	1990
333/4	0.8320	0.9300	0.0575	0.0618
335	0.7914	0.9305	0.1612	0.0664
336	0.8798	0.9910	0.1189	0.0320
338/9	0.6502	0.6766	0.1242	0.0846
341	0.9547	0.9488	0.2323	0.1820
342	0.8548	0.9158	0.1683	0.0814
345	0.7299	0.5502	0.0697	0.0658
347/8	0.8976	0.8359	0.0505	0.2589
352	0.6878	0.6864	1.0000	0.0279
434	0.8519	0.9473	0.4225	0.0000
435	1.0000	0.9587	0.0119	0.0442
436	1.0000	0.4118	0.0277	0.3648
438	0.9645	0.9952	0.0013	0.8345
440	0.4798	0.4153	0.0000	0.0625
442	0.8953	0.8806	0.0822	0.0620
445/6	0.7836	0.9175	0.0386	0.1502
447	0.5078	0.5570	0.0209	0.0000
448	0.9997	0.5763	0.5250	0.0831
634	0.5280	0.4968	0.0022	0.0348
635	0.7315	0.7202	0.0232	0.0567
636	0.6839	0.8560	0.0532	0.0000
638/9	0.4325	0.5455	0.0754	0.0716
641-P	0.4768	0.4912	0.0182	0.0211
641-Y	0.6498	1.0000	0.1579	0.0000
645/6	0.2597	0.3022	0.0864	0.0347
647/8	0.5588	0.5912	0.0383	0.0053
Average	0.7339	0.7357	0.1372	0.1033

V. Summary

To summarize, the data indicate that newcomers were more successful in obtaining open quota than they were in obtaining basic transfers, and that they were more likely than existing firms to be awarded open quota on the basis of their past export performance to non–quota countries. These observations, together with the fact that the open quota seems to be expanding relative to the basic quota and that the past export performance criterion seems to be taking on a greater significance relative to the other criteria for allocating open quota, lead to the inference that the open quota allocation system in place in Korea works to increase competition in the market by favoring new entrants. This is in direct contrast to the situation in India, as discussed in Appendix IV, where the trend has been a steady reduction in the open quota relative to the closed quota.

CHAPTER TWELVE

Patterns of Quota Transfer in Indonesia[1]

I. Introduction

In this chapter, data on MFA quota transactions in Indonesia are used to analyze quota trading patterns and changes in the market structure for quota licenses over time. These questions are of interest because they can provide further insight into the determinants of license prices and the competitiveness of license markets.

In July 1987, the Indonesian authorities established the Textile Quota Exchange (TQE), a separate bourse in the Indonesian Commodity Exchange in which MFA quota licenses could be legally traded under an auction system. In the first two years of the TQE's operation, quota transfers through the exchange entailed a reduction in the transferor's allocation and a corresponding increase in the transferee's quota by 20 percent of the transferred amount in the subsequent quota period. As of September 1990, in the third year of operation, all transactions undertaken in the TQE represent permanent transfers, that is, the transferred amount is deducted from the transferor's performance and credited to the transferee in the next allocation round. According to Pangestu 1987, temporary transfers are effected through an illegal quota market called the *bursa pasar pagi*.

II. The Data

The data used in this chapter were obtained from Indonesian sources through Carl Hamilton and James Anderson. They pertain to the first four years of TQE auctions, from July 1987 through June 1991, and cover 28 MFA categories.[2] Each observation contains the following information:

1. Date of transaction
2. Buying firm
3. Selling firm
4. License price
5. Quantity sold
6. MFA category

---

1. Written with Paul Jensen and Elaine McCormick Watt.

2. The quota license year in Indonesia runs from July 1 to June 30, hence the data cover four license periods.

In all, there were 10,697 transactions involving export licenses to the United States during the period covered.

The transacting firms are identified by numbers which appear to be assigned chronologically. In this numbering scheme, firms participating in the first auction have smaller numbers than firms that entered in the second auction, and so on. Firm numbers ranged from 1 to 256 in the first auction, 342 in the second auction, 425 in the third, and 522 in the fourth. Table 12.1 provides some summary data on the participating firms and the transactions. Note that not all the firm numbers are represented in the transactions data. Presumably, there were firms that registered with the TQE in a particular year but did not participate in the auction that year.

III. Quota License Transactions and Trading Clubs

What, if anything, do the transaction data reveal about concentration and entry barriers in the license market? Recall that each transaction records the firm identification number of the buyer and that of the seller. Figure 12.1 plots the buying firm number against the selling firm number for each of the four quota years, with each point representing a single transaction. Since the firm numbers seem to be chronologically assigned, with earlier auction participants receiving smaller numbers than latecomers, the scattergrams are suggestive of some sort of concentration in the license market as the majority of the transactions are between older firms (i.e., those with lower firm numbers). The simple correlation coefficients of the transacting firm numbers are slightly positive in all four quota years, at 0.0294 in 1987/88, 0.0597 in 1988/89, 0.0535 in 1989/90 and 0.0945 in 1990/91.

Of course, this pattern could simply reflect the tendency for firms to trade with other members of their cohort, with whom they have established business contacts. Alternatively, it is also consistent with the existence of an old boys' network of established firms which seeks to create barriers to the entry of new firms. If this is the case, determining the nature of these trading clubs could shed some light on the evolution of the structure of the market for quota licenses.

A. Age of Firm and Frequency of Transactions

One explanation for the pattern of trades might be that old firms have a larger presence in the market (due to larger allocations and/or greater activity), and this could account for the observed concentration of transactions among such firms compared to newer firms. If older firms trade more often than newer firms,

FIGURE 12.1. Indonesia: Buyers and Sellers

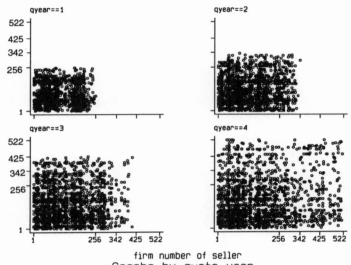

firm number of seller
Graphs by quota year

FIGURE 12.2. Indonesia: Number of Purchases by Firm Number

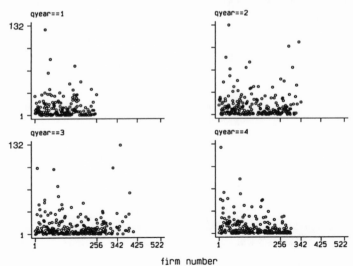

firm number
Graphs by quota year

TABLE 12.1. Indonesia: Summary of TQE Participation

	1987–88	1988–89	1989–90	1990/91
Range of firm numbers	1–256	1–342	1–425	1–522
Number of participants	180	235	247	330
Number of new entrants	180	42	13	46
Percentage of new entrants	100.00%	17.87%	5.26%	13.94%
Number of transactions	2069	2592	2930	3106
Number of MFA traded categories	18	28	35	34

TABLE 12.2. Indonesia: Breakdown of Transactions in 1990–91

	Old Buyer	New Buyer	Row Total
Old seller			
frequency:	1919	511	2430
row %:	78.97%	21.03%	100.00%
column %:	79.56%	73.63%	78.24%
cell %:	61.78%	16.45%	78.24%
New seller			
frequency:	493	183	676
row %:	72.93%	27.07%	100.00%
column %:	20.44%	26.37%	21.76%
cell %:	15.87%	5.89%	21.76%
Column total			
frequency:	2412	694	3106
row %:	77.66%	22.34%	100.00%
column %:	100.00%	100.00%	100.00%
cell %:	77.66%	22.34%	100.00%

then there is a greater possibility for any given firm—conditional on its entering into a transaction—that its trading partner will be an older firm. Figure 12.2 plots the frequency of purchases for each firm, and Figure 12.3 plots the frequency of sales for each firm, by quota year. Clearly, older firms tend to buy licenses and sell licenses more frequently than newer firms. In other words, they tend to engage in more transactions than newcomers do. This can be seen from Figure 12.4.

To examine this more closely, define—somewhat arbitrarily—old firms to be those firms that were registered in quota year one; these are firms one through 256. All other firms are considered new. Using only the observations from the last year of the sample, Table 12.2 shows the breakdown of the patterns in the transactions between firms. Note that in the fourth year, there were 191 old and 159 new active firms.

The most striking feature of this table is the large percentage of transactions that involve the old firms. Transactions between old firms account for 61.78 percent of all transactions while transactions involving only new firms make up just 5.89 percent of the sample. In addition note that, conditional on entering into a transaction, an old firm will sell to another old firm 78.97 percent of the time, and buy from another old firm 79.56 percent of the time, whereas a new firm will sell to an old firm 72.93 percent of the time, and buy from an old firm 73.63 percent of the time. These configurations generally support the idea that older firms have a greater presence and are more likely to participate in license transactions than are newer firms.

B. Age of Firm and Volume of Transactions

The next step was to examine patterns in the volume of licenses traded. Since the quota levels and the units in which they are specified vary substantially across MFA categories, in order to maintain comparability, the volume of each transaction was measured relative to the quota level of the MFA category concerned. For 1990/91, the simple correlation between the percentage of quota volume traded and the age of the buying firm was -0.0385. The correlation between the percentage of quota volume traded and the age of the selling firm was 0.0877, where the age of the firm was determined by the number of years for which the firm had been registered with the TQE.[3] This suggests that older firms tend to purchase smaller quantities and sell larger quantities relative to the quota size.

---

3. In other words, firms with numbers 256 and below were four years old, firms with numbers between 256 and 342 were three years old, firms with numbers between 342 and 425 were two years old, and firms with numbers 522 and above were one year old in 1990/91.

FIGURE 12.3. Indonesia: Number of Sales by Firm Number

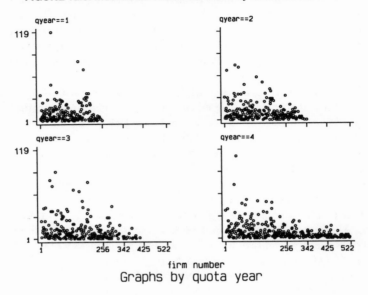

firm number
Graphs by quota year

FIGURE 12.4. Indonesia: Number of Transactions by Firm Number

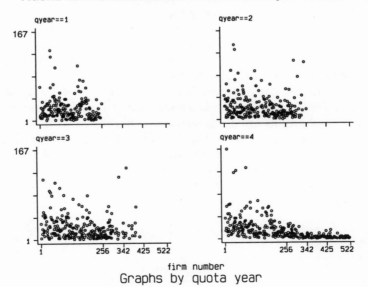

firm number
Graphs by quota year

A more detailed breakdown is given in Table 12.3, which, following Table 12.2, divides firms into old and new depending on whether they were registered in 1987/88. Table 12.3 shows that the average sale by an old seller is between 0.21 and 0.28 percent of quota, compared to a range of 0.11 to 0.13 percent of quota by a new seller, whereas the average purchase by an old buyer is between 0.13 and 0.21 percent of quota relative to a range of 0.11 to 0.28 percent of quota by a new buyer.[4]

Table 12.4 shows the results from regressing the percentage of quota volume traded on several explanatory variables, including the age of the buying firm and the age of the selling firm involved:[5]

$$VOL_{it} = \alpha + \beta_1 AGE\_B_{it} + \beta_2 AGE\_S_{it} + \beta_3 TIME_t + \beta_4 TIME_t^2$$

$$+ \sum_{i=1}^{24} \gamma_i CAT_i + \epsilon_{it}. \tag{1}$$

The variables are defined as follows:

VOL_{it} = Number of licenses traded in category i at time t, expressed as a percentage of the quota for category i

AGE_B_{it} = Age of the buying firm (ranging from one to four, as defined above)

AGE_S_{it} = Age of the selling firm (ranging from one to four, as defined above)

$TIME_t$ = Number of months remaining for which the license is valid (since licenses are valid for twelve months, $TIME = 13 - t$)

CAT_i = MFA category dummies[6]

The square of the time variable was included to allow for a non–linear pattern of license trades over time. The regression results indicate a significant negative relation between buyer age and volume traded, and a significant positive relation between seller age and volume traded.

These observations are consistent with the idea that older firms are allocated larger quantities of licenses and thus, they are able to sell larger

---

4. Note that less than 1 percent of the total quota tends to be traded.

5. Note that, due to data limitations, the set of explanatory variables is by no means exhaustive. However, since the purpose is to determine the effect of firm age on volume transacted, the omission of other independent variables does not pose too much of a problem as long as the omitted variables do not jointly affect both firm age and volume transacted.

6. From the sample of 3,106 transactions in 36 categories in 1990/91, 36 observations from several different categories had to be dropped due to either a lack of quota information or insufficient trading (i.e., only one transaction in that year).

TABLE 12.3. Indonesia: Average Volume of Quota Traded in 1990–91

	Old Buyer	New Buyer
Old seller	0.21%	0.28%
New seller	0.13%	0.11%

Based on a smaller sample of 3,071 transactions of categories for which quota information was available.

TABLE 12.4. Indonesia: Regression of Transaction Volume on Firm Age

Dependent variable = VOL_{it}

Independent Variable	Coefficient	t–statistic
Constant	0.2116	2.481[b]
	(0.0853)	
AGE_B_{it}	-0.0409	-3.573[a]
	(0.0114)	
AGE_S_{it}	0.0457	3.0703[a]
	(0.0149)	
$TIME_t$	0.0415	2.639[b]
	(0.0157)	
$TIME_t^2$	-0.0026	-2.211[b]
	(0.0012)	

Number of observations = 3,070

24 category dummies included.

$R^2 = 0.2556$

Standard errors in parentheses.

[a] Significant at the 1 percent level.

[b] Significant at the 5 percent level.

quantities of licenses and need to purchase fewer licenses.[7] The idea that older firms tend to have larger allocations follows from the Indonesian allocation rules, particularly the rule that 80 percent of the licenses issued by the Department of Trade are allocated on the basis of past utilization (see Appendix III). Hence, it is not unreasonable to suppose that older firms do indeed receive larger license allocations. However, the negative correlation between buyer age and size of transaction suggests that any existing concentration in license holding may be slowly eroding since older firms seem to be buying relatively smaller quantities and selling relatively larger quantities than newer firms.

C. Age of Firm and License Price

The evidence thus far is not too supportive of the idea of an old boys' club that seeks to keep new entrants out. Table 12.1 shows that some 5–18 percent of newcomers are admitted to the TQE each quota year, and Table 12.3 shows that older firms in general tend to purchase smaller shares of quota and sell larger shares of quota than newer firms. The explanation for the fact that older firms are more likely to trade amongst themselves than with newer firms most likely rests on the presumption that older firms have larger license allocations due to the 80 percent allocation rule, and simply have greater presence in the license market.

As a final check for the possibility of a trading club, the data are examined for evidence of price discrimination in the license market. If the presence of a network of old firms is the result of a desire to restrict entry of new firms into the market in an attempt to preserve some market power, aided by the 80 percent allocation rule, one would expect to find some evidence of price discrimination against the newer firms in the market.

Before continuing, note that there were 3,108 transactions in the sample period that were recorded with a zero price. All but two of these transactions occurred in the first two years of the sample period, and the zero price transactions only involve firms with numbers below 337. It is possible that zero prices simply mean that the licenses were given away for free. However, another possible explanation is that they represent license swaps across different MFA categories. A swap is assumed to have occurred if Firm One is observed to have sold licenses for a particular MFA category to Firm Two, and, in a separate

---

7. Unfortunately, comparable data on quota allocations were not available as the firm numbers assigned at the TQE are not the same as the ETTPT numbers assigned to quota holders.

sold licenses for a particular MFA category to Firm Two, and, in a separate transaction, bought licenses for a different category from Firm Two, with both transactions recorded at a price of zero. From this group of transactions, some 45 percent appear to be the result of such quid pro quo trades between firms.[8] It is difficult to infer the market value of licenses from different categories from the zero price transactions, hence these observations are omitted from any price analysis (although they were included in the previous portions of the analysis that did not involve license prices).

Table 12.5 shows the results for the regression of license price (LIC_{it}) on several explanatory variables, one of which is the age of the buyer (AGE_B_{it}):

$$LIC_{it} = \alpha + \beta_1 AGE\_B_{it} + \beta_2 AGE\_S_{it} + \beta_3 TIME_t \\ + \beta_4 TIME_t^2 + \sum_{i=1}^{31} \gamma_i CAT_i + \epsilon_{it} \tag{2}$$

As before, the age of the firm (one to four years) is determined by the year it is first registered at the TQE. AGE_S_{it} denotes the age of the seller. The time variable, $TIME_t$, measures the number of months remaining for which the license is valid. Also included is time squared as the dynamic behavior of the license price over the quota year is likely to be non–linear.[9]

The results from the regressions indicate that the age of the buyer has no significant effect on the price of the license. This would suggest that there is no evidence of price discrimination in the license market, based on the age of the firm. Therefore, after examining the evolution of the distribution of active firms in the market and looking for evidence of price discrimination, it appears that there is no evidence to support persistence in market structure as new firms appear to have access to the market and they are not discriminated against once in the market.

---

8. This may be an underestimation of the actual percentage of transactions that were swaps, as it is assumed that each swap is represented by only two transactions. For example, if Firm 1 sold to Firm 2 in four separate transactions, and Firm 2 sold to Firm 1 once, then these transactions are counted as one swap and three unmatched transactions. However, it is possible that Firm 1 needed multiple transactions involving several MFA categories in order to repay Firm 2. If allowing for these multiple transactions in a trade, then one could argue that a larger proportion of the zero price transactions represent swaps.

9. See Chapter Thirteen for more details on how license prices may be expected to behave over the quota year.

TABLE 12.5. Indonesia: Regression of Transaction Price on Firm Age

Dependent variable = $100*LIC_{it}$

Independent Variable	Coefficient	t–statistic
Constant	813,213 (46134)	17.627[a]
AGE_B_{it}	968 (6184)	0.156
AGE_S_{it}	17,118 (8036)	-2.130
$TIME_t$	13,770 (8502)	-1.620
$TIME_t^2$	377 (632)	0.596

Number of observations = 3,102

31 category dummies included.

$R^2 = 0.9016$

Standard errors in parentheses.

[a] Significant at the 1 percent level.

CHAPTER THIRTEEN

The Time Path of Quota License Prices[1]

I. Introduction

In a static perfectly competitive model, a quota license has a scarcity value, as the quota—as long as it is binding—will raise the domestic price of the restricted good above the world price, creating profits proportional to the price difference for the license holders. The size of this price difference depends on the extent of scarcity created by the quota in the domestic market, hence it can be thought of as the scarcity component of the license price.

As described in Chapter Seven, however, MFA export licenses are usually allocated among firms in the beginning of the quota year, for use any time within the quota period, which is generally twelve months. In such a dynamic setting, the license price has at least two additional components, both of which are related to the fact that the license is valid for an entire year.

The first of these is the asset market component. A quota license may be viewed as an asset with a life of one year. Like any other asset, the price path of the license must be such that the license is held voluntarily. For this to occur in a world without uncertainty, the price of the asset must rise at the rate of interest as the latter represents the opportunity cost of holding the asset. Therefore, the asset market component predicts that the price of a license will rise over the year. In the literature on nonrenewable resources, this is commonly known as the Hotelling Rule.[2]

The second component, which arises in an environment of uncertainty, is the option value component. At any point in time during the year, a quota holder can either use his license (by shipping the goods himself or by making a temporary transfer to someone else), or defer his license application in the hope of a higher price in the future if demand realizations are high. A license allows the decision on use to be deferred until the state of demand is known. Therefore, the value of a license held today (before the tomorrow's state is known) can exceed the expected price of the license at any time in the future. In other words, a quota license has an option value.

In addition, the details of the quota allocation system can create other complications which affect the license price. For example, quota allocations

---

1. A portion of this chapter is based on Krishna and Tan 1996b.

2. This condition was first noted by Hotelling 1931, and further developed in other papers e.g., Solow 1974 and Dasgupta and Heal 1979.

may be tied to past performance, whereby firms with a high quota utilization are rewarded with an increased allocation in the next quota round. In this case, the license price would also include a renewal value component.

In this chapter, some simple models are presented which help to explain the forces underlying license price paths during the quota period. Model one focuses on the option value component. Model two demonstrates that the option value component disappears in interior solutions when the license price is made endogenous. It can be modified to show that the option value component may reappear in the presence of corner solutions, and to allow for imperfect competition. Model three incorporates the past performance criterion, that is, the renewal value component.

II. Model One: The Option Value Component

A. Assumptions

Consider trade between two countries, say, the United States (the importer) and Hong Kong (the exporter). The following assumptions apply:

1. *The good being traded is a homogeneous good.*
2. *There are no transport costs or tariffs.*
3. *The United States imposes a quota of V units on imports of the good from Hong Kong.*
4. *The U.S. price of the good in question can take on only two exogenously given values: a^H (high price), and a^L (low price). This would be the case if demand in the United States is uncertain and if Hong Kong supply is such a small part of total supply to the U.S. market that any change in the supply from Hong Kong would not affect the U.S. price.*[3]
5. *The supply price from Hong Kong is exogenously given and fixed at S. This assumes that the U.S. market is a small enough part of the total sales of Hong Kong that changes in supply to the United States do not affect the supply price in Hong Kong. This assumption of infinite elasticity of supply and demand is crucial since it makes the value of using a license in any state an exogenous variable. Thus, if U.S. demand is high, the value of using a license is L^H, where: $L^H = a^H - S$; if U.S. demand is low, the value of using a license is L^L, where: $L^L = a^L - S$, and $a^H > a^L$. Assume that $L^L > 0$, that is, $S < a^L$.*
6. *The quota license is valid for three time periods.*

---

3. Note that other assumptions which result in the same license price realizations (such as supply side uncertainty) can also be used to motivate the model.

7. *At each point in time, there is a realization of demand, either high or low. The high demand state (denoted by the superscript H) is assumed to occur with probability π and the low demand state (denoted by the superscript L) with probability (1!π). The expected value of using a license in any given time period is therefore a constant and equals E(L) where:*

$$E(L) = \pi L^H + (1-\pi)L^L. \tag{1}$$

However, the holder of a license decides whether or not to use his license after the state is realized. Thus, the value of a license need not equal E(L).

B. Solution

The model is solved backward, based on the stream of choices and values depicted in Figure 13.1.

1. Period Three

In period three, if the license is not used, the payoff is zero; if it is used, the payoff is the value of the license in the state realized. Recall that both L^H and L^L are non–negative. This means all available licenses will be used in the final period. The expected license price in period three, $E(L_3)$, is thus $E(L)$.

FIGURE 13.1. Model One: Stream of Choices and Payoffs in Three Period Model

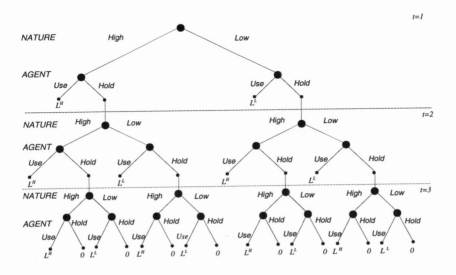

2. Period Two

If period two is a high demand state, all the licenses will be used, since $L^H >$ $\delta E(L_3)$ where δ is the discount factor. If period two is a low demand state, then as long as δ is not too small (i.e., as long as $L^L < \delta E(L_3)$) none of the licenses will be used.[4] In this case, the lowest price at which any transaction will occur is $\delta E(L_3)$, and this, not L^L, is the value of owning a license in the low demand state. If the discount factor is very small (i.e., if $L^L > \delta E(L_3)$), all the licenses will be used, even if period two is a low demand state. Thus, at the beginning of period two, before uncertainty about the state of nature is resolved, the value of a license will equal $E(L_2)$, where:

$$E(L_2) = \pi L^H + (1 - \pi)\max[L^L, \delta E(L_3)]. \tag{2}$$

3. Period One

Similarly in period one, if a high demand state occurs, all the licenses will be used since $L^H > \delta E(L_2)$. If a low demand state occurs and $L^L < \delta E(L_2)$, no licenses will be used but the value of a license will be $\delta E(L_2)$, and not L^L. If $L^L > \delta E(L_2)$, then all the licenses will be used and the value of a license is L^L. Before uncertainty is resolved in period one, therefore, the expected value of a license, $E(L_1)$, will be given by:

$$E(L_1) = \pi L^H + (1 - \pi) \max[L^L, \delta E(L_2)]. \tag{3}$$

C. The Option Value Component

1. How Does it Arise?

The option value arises because the license holder can defer his decision on whether or not to use a license until after the uncertainty is resolved. Deferring this decision has no value if there is no choice left as to whether or not to use the license, or if the optimal decisions are not state–contingent, rendering the choice effectively worthless. One reason why the utilization decision may not be state–contingent would be if the discount factor is so small that periods, in effect, separate, and all the licenses are used at the beginning, irrespective of the state of demand. Another reason, explored later in this chapter, is that

---

4. Specifically, this holds as long as:

$$\delta > \frac{L^L}{\pi L^H + (1 - \pi)L^L}.$$

endogenous forces may make both using and not using the license equally attractive.

In period three, using the license is the only sensible choice, so there is no option value to a license. In periods one and two, however, it may be valuable to be able to defer the decision on use until after the uncertainty is resolved. If the optimal strategy involves such a state-contingent choice (e.g., holding the license in low demand states and using it in the first high demand state), then an option value component exists. The option value component at any given period is given by the difference in the expected license price before the revelation of uncertainty and the expected license price before the revelation of uncertainty subject to the constraint that the decision on use is made now.[5] The latter price is given by E(L). Thus, if δ is not too small, the option value component equals $E(L_i)-E(L)$ in period i for i=1 or 2; there is no option value component in period three.

To summarize, the option value component of the license price exists because quota licenses are issued at the beginning of period one and are valid for three periods. The value of a license prior to any information being revealed exceeds the expected price of the license at any time in the future. This occurs since a license allows the decision on use to be deferred until the state is known. This is what is meant by the option value of the license.

2. How Does it Affect the License Price Over the Year?

Note that the license price falls over time, due to that fact that the option price component diminishes with time. This is most clearly seen by observing that if δ is large enough for the option value to be positive:

$$E(L_3) = E(L)$$

$$E(L_2) = E(L_3) + (1 - \pi)[\delta E(L) - L^L] \tag{4}$$

$$E(L_1) = E(L_2) + (1 - \pi)^2 \delta[\delta E(L) - L^L]$$

and the option value component in each period is:

$$E(L_3) - E(L) = 0$$

$$E(L_2) - E(L) = (1 - \pi)[\delta E(L) - L^L] \tag{5}$$

$$E(L_1) - E(L) = (1 - \pi)[1 + (1 - \pi)\delta][\delta E(L) - L^L].$$

---

5. For another application of option values, see van Wijnbergen 1985.

In the first two periods, the license holder has the option of not using his license, and this option has value. In the third (terminal) period, this option value disappears. From (5), it is clear that $E(L_1)-E(L) > E(L_2)-E(L) > E(L_3)-E(L)$, that is, the option value component is greater in earlier periods when there is more time remaining in which the license can be used. Also, from (4), the option value component declines over time at an increasing rate, that is, $(E(L_2)-E(L_1))/E(L_1) > (E(L_3)-E(L_2))/E(L_2)$.

3. How Does it Affect Quota Utilization Over the Year?

Note that this model consists of corner solutions only. All licenses are used in a high demand state, and no licenses are used in a low demand state unless it is in the terminal period, if δ is large. The utilization path is not necessarily monotonic. For a quota of size V, the expected utilization will be:

1. πV in period one.
2. $(1-\pi)\pi V$ in period two.
3. $(1-\pi)^2 V$ in period three.

III. Model Two: The Asset Market Component

A. ASSUMPTIONS

Model one assumes that the gain from using a license in any state was exogenously given. This assumption is obviously very special. Now, consider a model where:

1. *Hong Kong supply is such a small part of total supply to the U.S. market that the Hong Kong exporters/license holders face an infinitely elastic U.S. demand for their product.*[6]
2. *The U.S. market forms a large part of the total sales of Hong Kong so that its inverse export supply curve is given by the linear function:*

$$P^S = \theta Q^S \tag{6}$$

where θ is the slope of the supply function.
3. *The only source of uncertainty is U.S. demand, which can be in either one of two possible states:*

---

6. The model works just as well with a downward sloping demand curve.

$$P^D = \begin{cases} a^H & \text{if demand is high,} \\ a^L & \text{if demand is low} \end{cases} \tag{7}$$

where $a^L < a^H$. The high demand state occurs with probability π, and the low demand state with probability $(1 - \pi)$.

4. The model consists of two periods, which constitute the quota year. V licenses are issued at the beginning of the first period and they are valid for two periods.
5. The quota is binding even in the low demand period, that is, $V \leq a^L/\theta$.
6. License holders behave in a perfectly competitive manner.

B. Solution

1. Period Two

Consider the second period first. Suppose there are V_2 licenses left over from the first period, where $V_2 \leq V$. All the V_2 licenses will be used since this is the last period. If the second period is a high demand period, the license price will be the difference between the high demand price in the United States and the Hong Kong supply price of V_2 units:

$$L_2^H = a^H - \theta V_2 \tag{8}$$

and if it is a low demand period, then the license price will be:

$$L_2^L = a^L - \theta V_2. \tag{9}$$

The expected period two license price is therefore:

$$\begin{aligned} E(L_2 | V_2) &= \pi L_2^H + (1 - \pi) L_2^L \\ &= \pi a^H + (1 - \pi) a^L - \theta V_2 \end{aligned} \tag{10}$$

at the beginning of period two. Notice that the more licenses are remaining in period two, the lower will be the actual and expected period two license price. This reflects the scarcity value of the license.

2. Period One

Now return to period one. If license holders are perfectly competitive, then in equilibrium, the value of using the license must equal the value of not using it. Exactly enough licenses will be used in period one in each state so that the period one license price is equal to the discounted value of the expected period two license price, where the discount factor is given by $\delta = 1/(1+r)$. In other words, V_1^H and V_1^L will be chosen so as to satisfy:

$$a^H - \theta V_1^H = \delta E(L_2 \mid V_2 = V - V_1^H) \quad \textit{if Period 1 demand is high,}$$

$$a^L - \theta V_1^L = \delta E(L_2 \mid V_2 = V - V_1^L) \quad \textit{if Period 1 demand is low.} \tag{11}$$

In Figure 13.2, with O_1 as the origin for V_1, and O_2 as the origin for V_2, the equilibrium period one utilization and license price are thus given by the intersection points. It is easy to solve the equations (11) for the equilibrium period one utilization and license price. Letting $K = \pi a^H + (1-\pi)a^L$, for simplicity of notation, the equilibrium period one utilization is:

$$V_1^{H*} = \frac{1}{\theta(1+\delta)}(a^H - \delta K + \delta\theta V) \quad \textit{if Period 1 demand is high,}$$

$$V_1^{L*} = \frac{1}{\theta(1+\delta)}(a^L - \delta K + \delta\theta V) \quad \textit{if Period 1 demand is low,} \tag{12}$$

and the equilibrium period one license price is:

$$L_1^{H*} = \frac{\delta}{1+\delta}(a^H + K - \theta V) \quad \textit{if Period 1 demand is high,}$$

$$L_1^{L*} = \frac{\delta}{1+\delta}(a^L + K - \theta V) \quad \textit{if Period 1 demand is low.} \tag{13}$$

Therefore, the expected license price in period one is:

$$E(L_1) = \pi L_1^{H*} + (1-\pi)L_1^{L*} \tag{14}$$

and from (11), it follows that the expected period two license price at the beginning of period one is simply:

$$E(L_2) = \pi E(L_2 \mid V_2 = V - V_1^{H*}) + (1-\pi)E(L_2 \mid V_2 = V - V_1^{L*})$$

$$= \pi(L_1^{H*}/\delta) + (1-\pi)(L_1^{L*}/\delta) \tag{15}$$

$$= E(L_1)/\delta.$$

Since $\delta < 1$, it is evident that $E(L_1) < E(L_2)$, that is, the ex ante expected license price rises over time if the discount factor is less than one. According to this simple model, the rate of growth of the license price, $(1-\delta)/\delta$, equals the rate of interest if there is discounting. In other words, Hotelling's Rule obtains. If there is no discounting, then the license price stays constant. In either case, the option value component of the license price is eliminated by the equilibrating mechanisms in the license market and only the scarcity and asset value components remain.[7] A similar result is obtained by Pindyck 1980 in the context of nonrenewable resources with stochastic demand and constant or linear extraction costs. No conclusions can be drawn about the direction of the license utilization path as it depends on the precise form of the demand function.

C. Implications

This simple model suggests that:

1. The license price in any period is negatively related to the number of licenses available in that period, as evident from (8) and (9).
2. The expected license price is positively related to the time period.
3. The expected license price is negatively related to the quota level, as seen from (13), (14), and (15).

Note that the option price component is missing in this model since it is

FIGURE 13.2. Model Two: Equilibrium License Prices with Perfect Competition

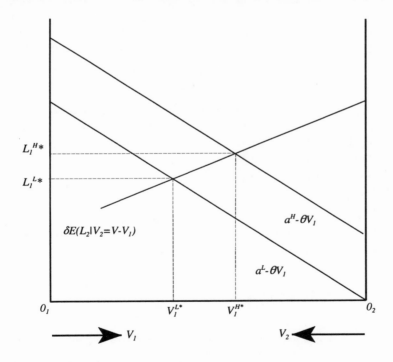

---

7. This result holds even assuming persistence of demand states.

Note that the option price component is missing in this model since it is assumed that all solutions are interior. In a model with many possible states, some of which lead to corner solutions (for example, if some states exist where even if all existing licenses are used, it is strictly preferable to use a license rather than hold onto it), the option value component will re–emerge as there will be a disparity between the value of using and not using a license. This option price component could result in license prices falling over time.

That quota licenses may be viewed as options is not a new insight. For example, Anderson 1987 likens a quota license to an American–type put option, although he notes that the endogeneity of license prices in any period makes the analogy with the option pricing literature suspect. Eldor and Marcus 1988 extend Anderson's analysis, drawing upon the financial literature to obtain an explicit formula for the value of a quota license in a stochastic environment. However, their formula rests critically on the assumption that licenses are continuously replenished as they are exercised, resulting in a constant number of licenses at all times and making future license prices independent of the number of licenses used today.[8] In the model presented here, the number of licenses in the next period is allowed to vary, hence, the price realizations in the next period will also vary. This endogeneity of the license price is what equates the value of current exercise and holding the asset until further information is revealed, and this eliminates the option price component for interior solutions in this model.

D. Modification of the Model: Corner Solutions

A slight modification of model two is sufficient to show how the existence of a corner solution may result in the option value component of the license price reasserting itself.[9] Suppose now that a high demand state in period one denotes such a high demand that $V_1^{H*} > V$.

It is clear from (12) that $V_1^{H*} > V$ if:

$$a^H > \delta K + \theta V. \tag{16}$$

In Figure 13.2, this would be depicted by the $(a^H!\theta V_1)$ line intersecting the $\delta E(L_2 * V_2)$ line at a point to the right of the origin Q . Since the number of licenses used cannot exceed the total quota, all V licenses will be used in this state, and:

---

8. In this sense, their assumption of constant replenishment of licenses serves the same purpose as the assumption of infinitely elastic demand and supply in model one.

9. The shape of the demand function is crucial here, as the example would not work with a function where price is asymptotically high for very small quantities demanded.

$$L_1^{H**} = a^H - \theta V. \tag{17}$$

In the event of a low demand state, L_1^{L*} is defined as in (13). Letting B = $a^H - \delta K - \theta V$ for simplicity of notation, the expected license price in period one will thus be:

$$E(L_1) = \pi L_1^{H**} + (1 - \pi)L_1^{L*}$$

$$= \frac{1}{1+\delta}(\pi B + 2\delta K - \delta\theta V). \tag{18}$$

Note that B is the distance between the points where the $(a^H - \theta V_1)$ line and the $\delta E(L_2 | V_2)$ line intersect the right vertical axis. From (16), it follows that B > 0. The expected period two license price at the beginning of period one is then:

$$E(L_2) = \pi E(L_2 | V_2 = 0) + (1 - \pi)E(L_2 | V_2 = V - V_1^{L*})$$

$$= \frac{1}{1+\delta}(2K - \theta V - \pi B) \tag{19}$$

from (10) and (12). A comparison of (18) and (19) reveals that if δ is not too small, then $E(L_1)$ may exceed $E(L_2)$. For example, if $\delta = 1$, then $E(L_1) - E(L_2) = \pi B > 0$. Once the possibility of corner solutions is allowed, therefore, the value of a license cannot be completely arbitraged by intertemporal adjustments in utilization. Consequently, the license price path over the year may no longer be governed by Hotelling's Rule. In fact, it can be seen from (18) and (19) that:

$$E(L_1) = \delta E(L_2) + \pi B \tag{20}$$

that is, the expected license value in period one consists of the asset market component, $\delta E(L_2)$, and a residual term, πB, where B is the corner solution surplus of the high demand state and π is the probability of receiving it. This residual term is interpreted as the option value component at the beginning of period one.[10] Hence, if there is a corner solution in the high demand state (and an interior solution in the low demand state) in period one, there is an addition to the asset market component of the amount πB. If B = 0, then there is no option value component and Hotelling's Rule obtains.

It is also possible to consider the case of a corner solution in the low demand state (and an interior solution in the high demandstate) in period one, if demand is so low that $V_1^{L*} < 0$. In this case the asset market component will

---

10. The authors are grateful to a referee for pointing this out. Note that the form of the demand function is critical. If it does not intersect the price axis, as with the constant demand elasticity function, there can be no corner solution and hence no option value!

be reduced by the amount $(1-\pi)B'$, where B' is the corner solution loss of the low demand state, (i.e., the distance between the points where the $\delta E(L_2|V_2)$ line and the $(a^L-\theta V_1)$ line intersect the left vertical axis). Therefore, if the option value component is interpreted as the license value minus the asset market component, then this option value component can be either positive or negative.

E. Modification of the Model: Imperfect Competition

In this modification, the original model two assumptions are retained with the exception of perfect competition. Now assume there is only one license holder who obtains the product from the competitive suppliers and sells it in the quota–constrained U.S. market.

In model two, with perfectly competitive license holders, the expected license price in period one is given by equating the value of using the license in that state with the discounted value of holding on to the license for use in the next period, that is:

FIGURE 13.3. Model Two with Imperfect Competition

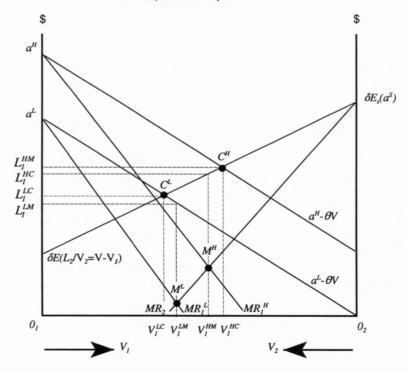

next period, that is:

$$a^{SI} - \theta V_1^{SI} = \delta E(L_2 | V - V_1^{SI}) \tag{21}$$

where S1 denotes the state of demand in period one, S1 = H or L. The left-hand side of the equation, $(a^{S1} - \theta V_1^{S1})$, is a negative function of V_1^{S1} while the right-hand side, $\delta E(L_2 | V - V_1^{S1})$, is a positive function of V_1^{S1} (i.e., a negative function of V_2). In Figure 13.3, their intersection at C^H determines the equilibrium utilization and price, (V_1^{HC}, L_1^{HC}), if period one is a high demand state, and their intersection at C^L determines the equilibrium (V_1^{LC}, L_1^{LC}), if period one is a low demand state.

Now consider the case of a monopolist license holder who realizes that using more licenses (i.e., exporting more of the quota constrained product) will raise the supply price of the product. In the competitive case, the equilibrium period one license utilization and price were found by equating the average revenue from using the licenses with the average revenue from holding them for the next period. The relevant consideration for the monopolist license holder is instead the marginal revenue from using his licenses in period one versus the marginal revenue from holding on to them. Now in period one, given the state of demand S1, the marginal revenue from using his licenses is:

$$MR_1^{SI} = a^{SI} - 2\theta V_1^{SI} \tag{22}$$

and the marginal revenue from holding his licenses (i.e., using them in period two) is:

$$MR_2 = \delta[E_{S2}(a^{S2}) - 2\theta V_2] \tag{23}$$

where S2 denotes the state of demand in period two, S2 = H or L. The license holder will choose his period one utilization so as to maintain indifference between the two choices of action. In Figure 13.3, the intersection M^H denotes the equilibrium if period one is a high demand state, and M^L denotes the equilibrium if period one is a low demand state. The corresponding license utilizations and prices are (V_1^{HM}, L_1^{HM}) if period one is a high demand state, and (V_1^{LM}, L_1^{LM}) if period one is a low demand state.

The exact location of the equilibrium points for the monopolist relative to the competitive situation depends of course on factors such as:

1. The discount rate.
2. The relative demand prices in the two states.
3. The probability of occurrence of the states.

For example, Dasgupta and Heal 1979 show that with a constant elasticity of demand (CED) function in the absence of uncertainty, the utilization path for an exhaustible resource (such as a quota) is actually the same under imperfect

curve (i.e., how the elasticity varies along the demand curve) is crucial in determining whether and how the utilization paths differ under perfect and imperfect competition. In summary, the utilization and price paths of the quota licenses may be quite different with imperfect competition than they are under perfect competition, even though the total utilization is the same in both cases.

IV. Model Three: The Renewal Value Component

A. ASSUMPTIONS

This model incorporates the effect of the past performance criterion on the value of a quota license. Consider a model analogous to model one, but with the following difference: obtaining a new license in the next quota year is a function of license usage in the current time period. For simplicity, a version of model one is used with only two periods in the quota year. It is illustrated in Figure 13.4. The value of a new license is denoted by R.

B. Solution

In period two, if a high demand state occurs, and the license is used, the holder obtains the license price as well as the (discounted) value of a new license in the next quota period, (i.e., $L^H+\delta R$). He obtains nothing if the license is not used. If a low demand state occurs, using the license yields $L^L+\delta R$. Not using the license again results in zero gain.

If a high demand state occurs in period one, and the license is used, the license owner obtains $L^H+\delta^2 R$. If the license is not used, the license holder waits for

FIGURE 13.4. Model Three: Stream of Choices and Payoffs in Two Period Model

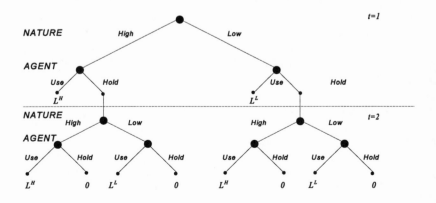

owner obtains $L^H + \delta^2 R$. If the license is not used, the license holder waits for period two which may be either a high demand state or a low demand state. If a low demand state occurs in period one, the payoffs are analogously defined. Note that by recursion, R must equal the value of holding a license at t=1 before uncertainty is realized, denoted by $E(L_1)$.

The problem is then solved backwards as usual. Since a license can always not be used, $R \geq 0$. In the last stage, therefore, licenses are always used as long as $L^L + \delta R > 0$. For now, assume that this is so. Regardless of the realization in the first period, the value of holding a license in the second period before the state is realized is denoted by $E(L_2)$ where:

$$E(L_2) = \pi(L^H + \delta R) + (1 - \pi)(L^L + \delta R)$$

$$= E(L) + \delta R \tag{24}$$

and E(L) is defined as before in model one as:

$$E(L) = \pi L^H + (1 - \pi)L^L. \tag{25}$$

If a high demand state occurs in period one, the license is always used as $L^H + \delta^2 R > \delta E(L_2)$. If a low demand state occurs in period one, the license will be used if $L^L + \delta^2 R > \delta E(L_2)$ (i.e., if $L^L > \delta E(L)$, or $\delta < L^L/E(L)$). If $L^L < \delta E(L)$, the license will not be used. Thus the value of a license is equal to $\max[L^L + \delta^2 R, \delta E(L_2)]$. This results in:

$$E(L_1) = \pi(L^H + \delta^2 R) + (1 - \pi)\delta E(L_2)$$

$$= E(L) + \delta^2 R + (1 - \pi)[\delta E(L) - L^L], \quad if\ \delta \geq \frac{L^L}{E(L)}, \tag{26}$$

$$E(L_1) = E(L) + \delta^2 R, \quad\quad\quad if\ \delta \leq \frac{L^L}{E(L)}.$$

C. The Renewal Value Component

1. The Renewal Value Component and the Option Value Component

Note that if δ is large, $E(L_1)$ contains an option value component, which is the difference between $E(L_1)$ and the best that can be obtained from choosing a given time to sell. The option value component is given by $(1-\pi)[\delta E(L)-L^L]$. It is equal to the probability of a low demand outcome in period one multiplied by the gain from waiting in the event of a low demand outcome. If δ is small, no option value component exists as all the licenses will be used up in period one irrespective of the state.

Using the fact that $E(L_1) = R$, we can solve for R:

$$R = \frac{[E(L)]}{1 - \delta^2} + \frac{(1-\pi)[\delta E(L) - L^L]}{1 - \delta^2}, \text{ if } \delta \ge \frac{L^L}{E(L)},$$

$$R = \frac{E(L)}{1 - \delta^2}, \qquad\qquad\qquad \text{if } \delta \le \frac{L^L}{E(L)}. \tag{27}$$

Note that R contains an option value component if δ is large. However, this is not the case if δ is small, as the new license will be used up in the first period of the next quota year. From (24) and (27):

$$E(L_2) = (\frac{1 - \delta^2 + \delta}{1 - \delta^2})E(L) + \frac{\delta(1 - \pi)[\delta E(L) - L^L]}{1 - \delta^2}, \text{ if } \delta \ge \frac{L^L}{E(L)},$$

$$E(L_2) = (\frac{1 - \delta^2 + \delta}{1 - \delta^2})E(L), \qquad\qquad \text{if } \delta \le \frac{L^L}{E(L)}. \tag{28}$$

If δ is large, an option value exists even in period two since it enters $E(L_2)$ through the renewal value component, R.

2. The Renewal Value Component and Temporary Versus Permanent Transfers

Now consider the case where $L^L < 0$, so that $\delta > L^L/E(L)$. In this case, the price for a temporary transfer of a license may be negative! If a transfer is made after the state is realized, say in period two, and it is a low demand state, the price of the license (call it P^T) must be such that using it is as beneficial as selling it at price P^T. Selling it yields $P^T + \delta R$ in period two and using it yields $L^L + \delta R$.[11] Thus, $P^T = L^L < 0$.

The price of a permanent transfer, however, cannot be negative. A permanent transfer would entail a choice between selling the license (at a price, say P^P) and using it, which yields $\max[0, L^L + \delta R]$. For the license holder to be indifferent between the two options, P^P must be equal to $\max [0, L^L + \delta R]$. Thus, P^P must be non–negative. Note that, in addition, the difference between the price of a permanent and temporary transfer, (P^P-P^T), equals δR, or the present value in period two of the renewal rights.[12] Thus, while temporary transfers can be associated with negative prices, permanent transfers, which are a transfer of the license and the renewal rights, cannot have negative prices.

---

11. It is assumed that all temporary transfers are used. This is an appropriate assumption as long as the transfer price is positive, since the only reason to buy a license would be to use it. This would not be a good assumption if the transfer price is negative, since renewal rights are not sold to the transferee, thus creating a moral hazard problem: transferees have an incentive to take the money and run. If there is no way to ensure use, then such temporary transfers will not be made; only permanent ones will be made. If temporary transfers are made, then their price will reflect the possibility of losing renewal rights and will exceed the use value of the license.

12. Note that the difference in permanent and temporary license prices is in general equal to the present value of renewal rights as this is the only difference in these two transfer forms.

CHAPTER FOURTEEN

The Dynamic Behavior of Quota License Prices in Hong Kong[1]

I. Introduction

This chapter expands on the theoretical discussion of license price paths in Chapter Thirteen by using monthly data on quota license prices and utilization in Hong Kong to estimate a dynamic model of license prices. The task is not a trivial one, for it is apparent from the discussion in Chapter Thirteen that the time path of a quota license price over a year is a complicated phenomenon to model. The problem is not the same as determining the price path of a nonrenewable resource, as there is a specific termination date beyond which the quota license is worthless, whereas no such condition exists in the case of exhaustible resources like petroleum and minerals. On the other hand, a strict analogy cannot be drawn with the option pricing literature either, since the quota license price at any time is likely to be affected by the amount of licenses utilized up to that time. However, theoretical considerations discussed in Chapter Thirteen suggest that even in the presence of uncertainty, quota license prices should follow Hotelling's Rule and rise at the prevailing interest rate as long as all solutions are interior.

A. Testing Hotelling's Rule

As a straightforward test of whether quota license prices follow Hotelling's Rule, the following regression was run separately for the years 1982 through 1988 using monthly data from Hong Kong for MFA licenses to export to the United States:

$$\log(LIC_{it}) = \alpha_i + \beta t + \gamma t^2 + \epsilon_{it}, \quad t = 1,...12 \tag{1}$$

where LIC_{it} denotes the license price for MFA category i at time t. According to Hotelling's Rule:

1. The constant α_i should represent the license price for category i at the beginning of the sample year.

---

1. A portion of this chapter is based on Krishna and Tan 1996b.

2. The estimated β should reflect the interest rate in the sample year.
3. γ should be zero.

The results are shown in Table 14.1. Of the seven sample years tested, only two yield a positive and statistically significant estimate of β. However, the sizes of these estimates imply monthly interest rates of 18 percent and 38 percent, which are highly implausible figures compared with the range of 6 to 11 percent per annum for U.S. treasury bills in those same years. Furthermore, the coefficient on t^2 is significantly different from zero in four of the seven years. The final column in Table 14.1 gives the results of regression (1) for the entire sample with 22 category dummies and six year dummies. The estimated coefficient for t in that regression is negative but not statistically significant. Thus, the evidence suggests that Hotelling's Rule does not hold within any given year.

B. Testing the Option Value Component

The next step is to examine the option value component of the license price. Allowing for the possibility of corner solutions, equation (20) in Chapter Thirteen indicates that the option value component at time t may be given by the difference between the expected value of the license at time t and the discounted expected value of the license in the next period. Now, the fitted value of the dependent variable from regression (1) is simply the expectation of the log of the license price conditional on the time period being t. Hence, the antilog of the fitted value from the whole sample regression of (1) may be used as an estimate of the expected value of the license at time t. To compute the discount rate δ_t, which is equal to $1/(1+r_t)$, the U.S. treasury bill rate (converted to a monthly rate) at time t was used to estimate r_t.[2] The following regression was run:

$$E(LIC_{it}) - \delta_t E(LIC_{i,t+1}) = \sum_{j=1}^{22} \alpha_j CAT_j + \sum_{k=1}^{6} \lambda_k YEAR_k$$
$$+ \beta t + \gamma t^2 + \epsilon_{it}, \ t=1,...,11 \tag{2}$$

where CAT_j, j=1,...,22 and $YEAR_k$, k=1,...,6 are category and year dummies respectively. The results are presented in Table 14.2. As a result of the unbalanced data panel and having to drop the last observation for each year, the

---

2. This is a reasonable approximation since Hong Kong interest rates are closely linked to U.S. interest rates, given the small open nature of the Hong Kong economy.

TABLE 14.1. Hong Kong: Test of Hotelling's Rule

Dependent variable = $\log(LIC_{it})$

Independent variable	1982	1983	1984	1985	1986	1987	1988	1982-88
t	-0.2924[a]	0.3755[a]	0.1847[b]	-0.0360	0.0446	0.1286	-0.1264[c]	-0.0187
	(0.0764)	(0.0436)	(0.0853)	(0.0820)	(0.0372)	(0.0786)	(0.0640)	(0.038)
t^2	0.0214[a]	-0.0194[a]	-0.0283[a]	0.0179[b]	0.0046	-0.0138[b]	-0.0013	0.0008
	(0.0057)	(0.0033)	(0.0085)	(0.0067)	(0.0030)	(0.0064)	(0.0052)	(0.003)
Category dummies	12	13	15	1	1	11	11	22
Year dummies	–	–	–	–	–	–	–	6
Number of observations	143	155	100	11	11	121	121	662
R^2	0.7557	0.8556	0.4701	0.9257	0.9472	0.5254	0.6667	0.7352

Standard errors in parentheses.
[a] Significant at the 1 percent level.
[b] Significant at the 5 percent level.
[c] Significant at the 10 percent level.

TABLE 14.2. Hong Kong: Time Path of Option Value Component

Dependent variable = $E(LIC_{it}) - \delta_t E(LIC_{i,t+1})$

Independent variable	Coefficient	t–statistic
t	-0.5345	-6.9888[a]
	(0.0765)	
t^2	0.0163	2.4945[b]
	(0.0065)	

Number of observations = 598
R^2 = 0.8623
22 category dummies and 6 year dummies included.
Standard errors in parentheses.
[a] Significant at the 1 percent level.
[b] Significant at the 5 percent level.

sample was reduced to 598 observations.[3] The coefficient on t is negative and statistically significant at the 1 percent level. The coefficient on t^2 is positive and statistically significant at the 5 percent level. Thus, the option value component is estimated to decline over the year at a decreasing rate.[4]

II. Model Setup

In what follows, a fuller model is developed which captures, as far as possible, the theoretical considerations raised in Chapter Thirteen. There are T time periods, indexed by t = 1,...,T, in a quota year. In each time period, there is a demand for and supply of licenses (to be used to ship merchandise) as a function of their price.

A. Demand

The demand for licenses to facilitate export is straightforward: it is based on the excess demand for apparel in the importing country (the United States), that is, demand in the importing country less supply from all other sources. This demand for licenses is denoted by:

---

3. Some of these estimated option value components are negative, indicating that the corner solution case in Chapter Thirteen may be applicable.

4. Although model one in Chapter Thirteen predicts that the option value component should fall at an increasing rate over the year, the corner solution version of model two (even when it is extended to three periods) is less precise regarding the declining path of the option value component, as the shape of the demand curve becomes an important consideration.

$$D_{it} = D(\overset{(-)}{L_{it}}, \overset{(-)}{C_{i,t-1}^{HK}}, \overset{(+)}{X_{it}}) \tag{3}$$

where:

L_{it} = the license price of category i at time t,
$C_{i,t-1}^{HK}$ = the cost of production in Hong Kong for category i at time $t-1$, and
X_{it} = a demand shift parameter, such as an index of retail sales in the United States.

The expected signs of the partial derivatives are indicated above the variables:

1. The demand for licenses should be negatively related to the license price. Demand depends on the full price of the good produced in Hong Kong. The full price of the good includes the supply price in Hong Kong and the license price. Since the full price of the Hong Kong produced good is inclusive of the license price, it is clear that an increase in the license price also reduces the demand for quota licenses.
2. The demand for licenses should be negatively related to the lagged cost of production of apparel in Hong Kong. The supply price is positively related to the cost of production in Hong Kong, so that as the cost of production rises in Hong Kong, the demand for licenses falls. The cost variable is lagged by one period to reflect the consideration that the actual production of clothing for export is not instantaneous. Therefore, the supply price of a piece of apparel exported at time t is a function of the cost incurred in its production during the previous period.
3. The demand for licenses should be positively related to the U.S. demand for Hong Kong made apparel. An increase in the U.S. demand for Hong Kong made apparel due, for example, to income or taste changes should lead to a higher demand for licenses to export such apparel.

B. Supply

Now consider the supply side. At each point in time, a license holder must decide whether to use his license or hold on to it for another period. Use implies the actual utilization of a license to facilitate the export of a piece of apparel to the United States. It is easiest to think of this as a license holder selling his license to an exporter who is ready to ship the goods to the United States. Note that selling the license to another holder to hoard is not considered using the license in this model. The supply of licenses in category i at time t is given by:

$$S_{it} = S(\overset{(+)}{L_{it}}, \overset{(+)}{A_{it}}, \overset{(?)}{T-t}) \tag{4}$$

where:

L_{it} = the license price of category i at time t,
A_{it} = the total availability of licenses at time t in category i, and
T-t = is the amount of time remaining for which the licenses are valid.

Again, the expected signs of the partial derivatives are indicated above the variables:

1. The supply of licenses should increase with the current license price, L_{it}.
2. The supply of licenses should also rise as A_{it} rises because an increased availability of licenses at a given point in time lowers their expected price in the future, and this in turn lowers the value of holding on to a license.
3. The supply of licenses also depends on the amount of time remaining for which the licenses are valid.

The option value argument suggests that other factors constant, supply will be larger towards the end of the year when there is less of an option value in holding on to a license. On the other hand, the asset market argument predicts the opposite, as in later months, higher license prices will be required to elicit supply from license holders who must be compensated for interest foregone in holding a license.

C. Equilibrium

In equilibrium, demand equals supply:

$$D_{it}(\cdot) = S_{it}(\cdot) = U_{it} \tag{5}$$

The equilibrium level of quota utilization is denoted by U_{it}. Both U_{it} and L_{it} are observed monthly. Equations (3) and (4) make up the structural form of the simultaneous equations model. The endogenous variables of the system are:

D_{it} = demand,

S_{it} = supply, and
L_{it} = license price.

The reduced form of the simultaneous equation system may be solved for the license price and quota utilization in any period as a function of the exogenous variables in the model. This gives:

$$U_{it}(\overset{(-)}{C^{HK}_{i,t-1}}, \overset{(+)}{X_{it}}, \overset{(+)}{A_{it}}, \overset{(?)}{T-t}) \tag{6}$$

$$L_{it}(\overset{(-)}{C^{HK}_{i,t-1}}, \overset{(+)}{X_{it}}, \overset{(-)}{A_{it}}, \overset{(?)}{T-t}) \tag{7}$$

Note the following implications:

1. An increase in the U.S. demand shift parameter, X_{it}, shifts $D_{it}(\cdot)$ out, raising the equilibrium license price, $L_{it}(\cdot)$, and quota utilization, $U_{it}(\cdot)$.
2. An increase in $C^{HK}_{i,t-1}$ will shift the demand for licenses inward. This will lower $L_{it}(\cdot)$ and $U_{it}(\cdot)$.
3. An increase in A_{it} shifts $S_{it}(\cdot)$ outward, reducing $L_{it}(\cdot)$ and raising $U_{it}(\cdot)$.
4. The effect of an increase in $(T-t)$ is ambiguous.

This model provides the basis for the reduced form and structural equations utilized in Section IV.

III. The Data

Hong Kong's textile quota system is described in Part I of the Appendix. The data utilized in this study cover the time period 1982–88. They are classified according to MFA categories. Data were not available for all categories for the entire period; however, the sample is sufficiently large to accomplish the stated objectives.[5] The license prices (LIC_{it}) are prices for temporary transfers and are expressed in Hong Kong dollars per dozen pieces. They are monthly averages unless otherwise stated. Aside from monthly license prices, data were also collected on:

---

5. Although quota licenses in Hong Kong are openly transferable, there is no systematic record of the transactions. Carl Hamilton at the University of Stockholm's Institute for International Economic Studies and Peter Ngan of the Federation of Hong Kong Garment Manufacturers contributed significantly to this work by providing monthly license prices for many MFA categories. Additional information was obtained from a Hong Kong–based trade journal, *Textile Asia*, which frequently tracks quota license prices.

1. monthly quota utilization (i.e., shipments),
2. cumulative (year to date) quota utilization, and
3. annual quota levels by MFA category.

These figures are published monthly in the *Notice to Exporters Series 1a (USA)* documented by the Trade Industry and Customs Department of Hong Kong. The quota level ($QUOTA_i$), monthly quota utilization ($UTIL_{it}$), and cumulative quota utilization ($\Sigma\ UTIL_{it}$) are expressed in dozens of pieces. From these, the availability of licenses is calculated for the remainder of the year, $AVAIL_{it}$, as:

$$AVAIL_{it} = QUOTA_i - \sum_{i=1}^{t-1} UTIL_{it}. \tag{8}$$

Monthly Hong Kong costs are measured by monthly wage rates in Hong Kong's apparel sector, $WAGE_t^{HK}$. These are approximated as the total monthly payroll in that sector divided by the number of persons engaged, using data published in the Hong Kong Monthly Digest of Statistics. The state of demand in the United States is proxied by monthly total retail sales, $SALES_t$.

IV. Estimation

A. The Reduced Form

The following log–linear model was run to capture the competitive model developed in the Section II:

$$\log(LIC_{it}) = \beta_1 \frac{AVAIL_{it}}{QUOTA_i} + \beta_2 TIME_t + \beta_3 TIME_t^2 + \beta_4 SALES_t$$

$$+ \beta_5 WAGE_{t-1}^{HK} + \sum_{j=1}^{22} \gamma_j CAT_j + \sum_{k=1}^{6} \lambda_k YEAR_k + \epsilon_{it}$$

$$\log(UTIL_{it}) = \beta_1' \frac{AVAIL_{it}}{QUOTA_i} + \beta_2' TIME_t + \beta_3' TIME_t^2 + \beta_4' SALES_t \tag{9}$$

$$+ \beta_5' WAGE_{t-1}^{HK} + \sum_{j=1}^{22} \gamma_j' CAT_j + \sum_{k=1}^{6} \lambda_k' YEAR_k + \epsilon_{it}'.$$

The data were pooled across time and categories, seven years and 22 categories in all. In the above equations:

1. The subscript i represents the MFA category.

2. The subscript t represents the month in which the observation was made, where t=1,...,12.
3. The variable $TIME_t$, denoting the amount of time remaining from the beginning of month t for which the license can be used, is computed simply as (13−t). The log–linear specification enables $-\beta_2$ to be interpreted as the rate of change of the license price, holding availability and all other variables constant.
4. The quadratic term, $TIME_t^2$, is included as an explanatory variable to allow for the possibility that the rate of change of quota utilization and license prices may not be constant.
5. The variable $AVAIL_{it}$ is scaled by the quota level, $QUOTA_i$, rendering it unit–free. This is done in order to maintain comparability between categories in the pooled data set. This variable captures the scarcity component of the license price.
6. The category dummies, CAT_j, j=1,...,22 are included to permit different levels of license prices and quota utilization across categories, and year dummies $YEAR_k$, k=1,...,6, to allow for annual variations.

The results of the OLS estimation of the reduced form equations are given in Tables 14.3 and 14.4. Also included in the tables are the expected signs of the coefficients on the independent variables which follow from equations (6) and (7) in Section II.

As predicted, an increase in availability with all else constant reduces the equilibrium license price and increases the equilibrium quantity utilized at any time t. An increase in Hong Kong costs (as proxied by the wage per worker in the apparel sector in the previous month) lowers the equilibrium license price and quota utilization. An increase in retail sales in the United States tends to increase the equilibrium license price but the effect on the equilibrium quota utilization is not statistically significant. The coefficients on $TIME_t$ and $TIME_t^2$ in Table 14.3 indicate that with availability (and all else) held constant, the path of the license price declines over the year at a decreasing rate.[6] The reduced form estimates suggest that the competitive demand and supply model describe the data quite well.

---

6. This is easily seen by noting that:

$$\frac{1}{LIC_{it}}\frac{\partial LIC_{it}}{\partial t} = -\beta_2 - 2\beta_3 TIME_t$$

$$= -0.15 - 0.03\,TIME_t = -0.50 + 0.03t\ .$$

TABLE 14.3. Hong Kong: Reduced Form License Price Equation

Dependent variable = $\log(LIC_{it})$

Independent Variable	Coefficient	t–statistic	Expected Sign of Coefficient
$AVAIL_{it}/QUOTA_i$	-2.7538 (0.3942)	-6.9856[a]	(−)
$TIME_t$	0.1541 (0.0611)	2.5236[b]	(?)
$TIME_t^2$	0.0134 (0.0040)	3.3056[a]	(?)
$SALES_t$	0.1308 (0.0216)	6.0578[a]	(+)
$WAGE_{t-1}^{HK}$	-0.0007 (0.0001)	-4.7877[a]	(−)

Number of observations = 598
$R^2 = 0.7757$
22 category dummies and 6 year dummies included.
Standard errors in parentheses.
[a] Significant at the 1 percent level.
[b] Significant at the 5 percent level.

TABLE 14.4. Hong Kong: Reduced Form Utilization Equation

Dependent variable = $\log(UTIL_{it})$

Independent Variable	Coefficient	t–statistic	Expected Sign of Coefficient
$AVAIL_{it}/QUOTA_i$	1.1789 (0.3095)	3.8092[a]	(+)
$TIME_t$	0.3653 (0.0479)	7.6183[a]	(?)
$TIME_t^2$	-0.0385 (0.0032)	-12.1129[a]	(?)
$SALES_t$	0.0005 (0.0170)	0.0311	(+)
$WAGE_{t-1}^{HK}$	-0.0005 (0.0001)	-4.0072[a]	(−)

Number of observations = 598
$R^2 = 0.8780$
22 category dummies and 6 year dummies included.
Standard errors in parentheses.
[a] Significant at the 1 percent level.

B. The Structural Form

As the next step, the structural demand and supply equations were estimated using two stage least squares. Using exclusion restrictions alone permits identification of the simultaneous equations system although the structural equations are overidentified.

The structural form equations estimated were:

$$\log(DEMAND_{it}) = \alpha_1 \log(LIC_{it}) + \alpha_2 WAGE_{t-1}^{HK} + \alpha_3 SALES_t$$

$$+ \sum_{j=1}^{22} \mu_j CAT_j + \sum_{k=1}^{6} \theta_k YEAR_k + \epsilon_{it}$$

$$\log(SUPPLY_{it}) = \alpha'_1 \log(LIC_{it}) + \alpha'_2 \frac{AVAIL_{it}}{QUOTA_i} + \alpha'_3 TIME_t \tag{10}$$

$$+ \alpha'_4 TIME_t^2 \sum_{j=1}^{22} \mu'_j CAT_j + \sum_{k=1}^{6} \theta'_k YEAR_k + \epsilon'_{it}.$$

The results, together with the expected signs of the coefficients from equations (3) and (4), are presented in Tables 14.5 and 14.6.

The supply equation relates the license utilization in a given month to that month's license price, the amount of quota remaining, as well as the number of months remaining for which the license is valid. The estimated equation is a remarkably good fit, with an R^2 value of 0.86, and statistically significant coefficients on all the relevant variables. All else constant, a 1 percent increase in the current license price increases the supply of licenses by 2½ percent and a 1 percent increase in the fraction of quota remaining increases the supply of licenses by 2 percent. With availability (and all else) held constant, license supply appears to follow a quadratic time path, rising to a peak in August before falling for the rest of the year.

The demand equation is of less interest here, although it is also a good fit. The coefficient on $\log(LIC_{it})$ is negative and significant in this equation, and the coefficients on $SALES_t$ and $WAGE_{t-1}^{HK}$ are statistically significant with the expected signs.

The estimation of both the structural and reduced forms of the simultaneous equations model have very high explanatory power. This suggests that the model has captured most of the relevant variables of concern in modeling the dynamic behavior of quota license prices and utilization, and that it may be useful in predicting their paths.

TABLE 14.5. Hong Kong: License Supply Equation

Dependent variable = $\log(\text{SUPPLY}_{it})$

Independent Variable	Coefficient	t–statistic	Expected Sign of Coefficient
$\log(\text{LIC}_{it})$	0.2526	2.2509[b]	(+)
	(0.1122)		
$\text{AVAIL}_{it}/\text{QUOTA}_i$	2.0043	4.6655[a]	(+)
	(0.4296)		
TIME_t	0.3617	6.5572[a]	(?)
	(0.0552)		
TIME_t^2	-0.0440	-14.3926[a]	(?)
	(0.0031)		

Number of observations = 598
$R^2 = 0.8562$
22 category dummies and 6 year dummies included.
Standard errors in parentheses.
[a] Significant at the 1 percent level.
[b] Significant at the 5 percent level.

TABLE 14.6. Hong Kong: License Demand Equation

Dependent variable = $\log(\text{DEMAND}_{it})$

Independent Variable	Coefficient	t–statistic	Expected Sign of Coefficient
$\log(\text{LIC}_{it})$	-0.5980	-5.6618[a]	(−)
	(0.1056)		
WAGE_{t-1}^{HK}	-0.0013	-9.8791[a]	(−)
	(0.0001)		
SALES_t	0.0514	3.9280[a]	(+)
	(0.0131)		

Number of observations = 598
$R^2 = 0.8043$
22 category dummies and 6 year dummies included.
Standard errors in parentheses.
[a] Significant at the 1 percent level.

V. Testing for Imperfect Competition

In this section, the imperfect competition model in Chapter Thirteen is considered using data on the distribution of licenses in Hong Kong. Information concentration in license holding is computed for each MFA category using these license allocation data. The numbers equivalent of the Herfindahl index is a proxy for the number of equal sized firms that own licenses. Thus it provides an indication of the extent of concentration in license holdings—the higher the concentration, the smaller the numbers equivalent. The numbers equivalent is denoted by $NEQUIV_i$. Since there are only data on the distribution of quota licenses in the beginning of each year, $NEQUIV_i$ varies only annually, and not monthly. Ideally, knowing the concentration of license holdings each month would be valuable, but unfortunately, the initial distribution is the only information available. The numbers equivalent figures in the sample range from twelve to 90.

If all license holders behave competitively, then the addition of one extra license holder should not make a difference, (i.e., $NEQUIV_i$ should not affect the supply path of licenses over a year). Since license holders are penalized for under–utilization with reduced allocations in the following year, there is no incentive to restrict the supply of licenses for the whole year in the hope of driving up the license price. In the case of imperfect competition in the license market, the past performance rule in the quota allocation mechanism should ensure that $NEQUIV_i$ would not affect the entire supply of licenses in a year. However, if the license market is not competitive, $NEQUIV_i$ could certainly affect the quota utilization path over the year and thereby affect license prices, even though the total utilization is not likely to be reduced.

A. The Reduced Form

The following equations reflect modifications of the log–linear regression model to capture this consideration:

$$\log(LIC_{it}) = b_1 \frac{AVAIL_{it}}{QUOTA_i} + b_2 TIME_t + b_3 TIME_t^2 + b_4 SALES_t$$

$$+ b_5 WAGE_{t-1}^{HK} + b_6 NEQUIV_i * TIME_t + \sum_{j=1}^{22} c_j CAT_j \qquad (11)$$

$$+ \sum_{k=1}^{6} d_k YEAR_k + \epsilon_{it}.$$

The interaction term $NEQUIV_i * TIME_t$ captures the effect of the concentration in license holdings as a function of time. This term is introduced to account for the possibility that in the absence of perfect competition, concentration in license holdings could affect the time path of quota utilization. The (percentage) effect of license holding concentration on the equilibrium utilization at time t is thus given in equation (12) as $b_6' \, TIME_t$. All the other variables can be explained and interpreted as before. The results of the OLS estimation of the reduced form equations are given in Tables 14.7 and 14.8.

The interaction term, $NEQUIV_i * TIME_t$ is significantly positive in the utilization equation and significantly negative in the license price equation.

This means that an increase in license holding concentration decreases the slope of the license price path, making it fall more steeply and rise more gradually than the competitive path.

The sign, size and significance of all the other variables are almost unchanged from Tables 14.2 and 14.3. Note from equation (11) and Table 14.7 that as before, with all else constant, the equilibrium license price declines at a decreasing rate, and equilibrium license utilization increases at a decreasing rate from January until some time around August when it starts to fall.

B. Structural Form

The structural demand and supply equations are:

$$\log(DEMAND_{it}) = a_1\log(LIC_{it}) + a_2 WAGE_{t-1}^{HK} + a_3 SALES_t$$

$$+ \sum_{j=1}^{22} f_j CAT_j + \sum_{k=1}^{6} g_k YEAR_k + \epsilon_{it}$$

$$\log(SUPPLY_{it}) = a_1'\log(LIC_{it}) + a_2' WAGE_{t-1}^{HK} + a_3' \frac{AVAIL_{it}}{QUOTA_i} \qquad (12)$$

$$+ a_4' TIME_t + a_5' TIME_t^2 + a_6 NEQUIV_i$$

$$* TIME_t + \sum_{j=1}^{22} f_j' CAT_j + \sum_{k=1}^{6} g_k' YEAR_k + \epsilon_{it}'.$$

The interaction term, $NEQUIV_i * TIME_t$ is introduced in the supply equation but not the demand equation as there is no convincing argument as to why license holding concentration should affect the structural supply equation using two stage least squares.

The interaction term in Table 14.9, $NEQUIV_i * TIME_t$, is positive and significant, indicating that a reduction in the numbers equivalent (i.e., an increase in concentration) lowers the supply of licenses in the beginning of the year more than in the latter part of the year. This is suggestive of imperfect competition in the license market. The structural demand equation is of less interest here, so the results of the estimation, are not presented except to note that they are almost identical to Table 14.5.

To summarize, the estimation of both the structural and reduced forms of the simultaneous equations model point to the fact that the degree of concentration in license holdings does have a significant impact on the time path of the license prices and quota utilization. This seems to suggest that license holders in Hong Kong do not behave in a perfectly competitive manner,although this conclusion should be viewed in light of the fact that the data on license holding concentration are somewhat limited.

TABLE 14.7. Hong Kong: Reduced Form License Price Equation (Imperfect Competition)

Dependent variable = $\log(LIC_{it})$

Independent Variable	Coefficient	t–statistic	Expected Sign of Coefficient
$AVAIL_{it}/QUOTA_i$	-2.7541 (0.3921)	-7.0231[a]	(−)
$TIME_t$	0.2044 (0.0637)	3.2100[a]	(?)
$TIME_t^2$	0.0131 (0.0040)	3.2421[a]	(?)
$SALES_t$	0.1276 (0.0215)	5.9261[a]	(+)
$WAGE_{t-1}^{HK}$	-0.0007 (0.0001)	-4.7917[a]	(−)
$NEQUIV_i*TIME_t$	-0.0013 (0.0005)	-2.6364[a]	0

Number of observations = 598
$R^2 = 0.7785$, Adjusted $R^2 = 0.7655$
22 category dummies and 6 year dummies included.
Standard errors in parentheses.
[a] Significant at the 1 percent level.

TABLE 14.8. Hong Kong: Reduced Form Utilization Equation (Imperfect Competition)

Dependent variable = $\log(\text{UTIL}_{it})$

Independent Variable	Coefficient	t–statistic	Expected Sign of Coefficient
$\text{AVAIL}_{it}/\text{QUOTA}_i$	1.1791 (0.3076)	3.8340[a]	(+)
TIME_t	0.3227 (0.0499)	6.4614[a]	(?)
TIME_t^2	-0.0382 (0.0032)	-12.0976[a]	(?)
SALES_t	0.0033 (0.0169)	0.1967	(+)
WAGE_{t-1}^{HK}	-0.0005 (0.0001)	-4.0549[a]	(−)
$\text{NEQUIV}_i*\text{TIME}_t$	0.0011 (0.0004)	2.8479[a]	(0)

Number of observations = 598
R^2 = 0.8797, Adjusted R^2 = 0.8727
22 category dummies and 6 year dummies included.
Standard errors in parentheses.
[a] Significant at the 1 percent level.

TABLE 14.9. Hong Kong: License Supply Equation (Imperfect Competition)

Dependent variable = $\log(\text{SUPPLY}_{it})$

Independent Variable	Coefficient	t–statistic	Expected Sign of Coefficient
$\log(\text{LIC}_{it})$	0.2758 (0.1144)	2.4115[b]	(+)
$\text{AVAIL}_{it}/\text{QUOTA}_i$	2.0628 (0.4333)	4.7610[a]	(+)
TIME_t	0.2988 (0.0607)	4.9243[a]	(?)
TIME_t^2	-0.0438 (0.0031)	-14.3258[a]	(?)
$\text{NEQUIV}_i*\text{TIME}_t$	0.0015 (0.0005)	3.2897[a]	0

Number of observations = 598
R^2 = 0.8563, Adjusted R^2 = 0.8482
22 category dummies and 6 year dummies included.
Standard errors in parentheses.
[a] Significant at the 1 percent level.
[b] Significant at the 5 percent level.

CHAPTER FIFTEEN

Comparing Actual and Imputed Quota License Prices in Indonesia[1]

I. Introduction

In this chapter, the license price data from Hong Kong and Indonesia described in Chapters Twelve and Fourteen are employed from a completely different angle, in an indirect test designed to shed some light on the functioning of license markets and the appropriate way in which to estimate license prices absent direct observations.

A common practice found in some MFA studies involves the use of Hong Kong license prices, which are relatively easily available, to impute license prices in other MFA–restricted exporting countries, where such data are not so easy to obtain. For example, Hamilton 1988 uses the import tariff equivalent for Hong Kong—calculated from Hong Kong quota license prices—to obtain lower bound estimates of import tariff equivalents in Korea and Taiwan, where quota license prices are less readily available. Trela and Whalley 1990, in their general equilibrium analysis of the effects of MFA restrictions on 34 exporting countries (including Hong Kong), compute the unit costs of quota restricted products from these exporting countries by multiplying the unit cost in Hong Kong with the ratio of the exporting country's relative wage in the textile and apparel sector, adjusted by productivity differences, to that of Hong Kong's.[2] The license prices are imputed as the difference between the f.o.b. prices and these unit costs.

This chapter uses data on Indonesian license prices, along with data on Hong Kong license prices, to investigate the accuracy of the imputation procedure discussed above. The findings show that the imputation procedure yields estimates of license prices which are considerably higher than the actual prices. Some possible explanations for this result are considered, including the possibility that:

1. The Cobb–Douglas functional form, on which the imputation procedure is based, is too restrictive.

---

1. This chapter is based on Krishna, Martin and Tan 1997.
2. A similar approach is taken by Hamilton and Kim 1990 in order to impute the import tariff equivalent in Korea using Hong Kong data.

2. The quality of Hong Kong and Indonesian apparel exports are quite different.
3. Hidden costs associated with the quota allocation system differ in the two countries, violating the underlying assumption of no frictions in the allocation system.
4. Market imperfections exist, making the competitive model, on which the imputation procedure is based, inappropriate.

II. The Theoretical Foundation

The perfectly competitive model as described in Chapter Two, may be recapitulated as follows, using Figure 15.1. RD represents residual demand from the importing country, which will be called the United States. This is given by subtracting domestic supply and supply from sources other than the exporting country of interest, i, from total demand in the United States. RS depicts the residual supply from country i, (i.e., supply from country i less demand from all sources other than the United States). The intersection of the two gives the world price in the absence of quotas and the level of imports from country i to the United States. If a quota is set allowing only V units to be imported, then the home price at which this level of imports is demanded is P^i, which exceeds C^i, the world price at which it is supplied. Their difference gives the license price L^i, which can be interpreted as the implicit specific tariff.

Figure 15.1. Indonesia: Calculating Quota Rent

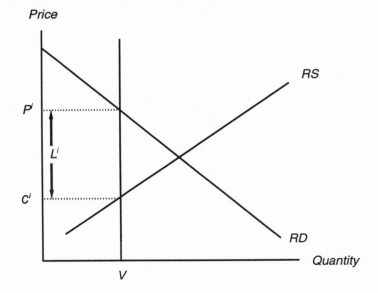

Therefore, if the apparel industry is perfectly competitive, the unit cost in country i is equal to C^i and it can be calculated by subtracting the license price (L^i) from the license price inclusive f.o.b. price of country i's exports to the United States (P^i):

$$C^i = P^i - L^i. \tag{1}$$

As discussed in Chapter Seven (and in greater detail in Part I of the Appendix), MFA quota licenses are freely traded in Hong Kong, and license price data are available from various sources. License prices are considerably harder to obtain for other countries, either because licenses are not legally transferable or because the data are not made public. Data on wages, productivity and f.o.b. export prices (license inclusive) are regularly published; however, data on production costs are limited and highly aggregated. The usual imputation procedure uses the information that is more easily obtainable to impute that which is not. First, Hong Kong f.o.b. prices and license prices are used to estimate costs of production in Hong Kong. These are used to impute production costs in Indonesia. F.o.b. prices in Indonesia, along with these production costs, are then used to derive license price data.

Suppose apparel goods are manufactured using labor (L) and capital (K). Let:

w = the cost per unit of labor
r = the cost per unit of capital
a_L = the number of units of labor required to produce one unit of output
a_K = the number of units of capital required to produce one unit of output

Then the unit cost in Hong Kong is given by:

$$C^{HK} = r^{HK} a_K^{HK} + w^{HK} a_L^{HK} \tag{2}$$

where a_L^{HK} and a_K^{HK} are both functions of w^{HK}/r^{HK}.

Similarly, the unit cost in Indonesia may be written as:

$$C^I = r^I a_K^I + w^I a_L^I \tag{3}$$

where a_L^I and a_K^I are functions of w^I/r^I. Then the ratio of the unit cost in Indonesia to that in Hong Kong is:

$$\frac{C^I}{C^{HK}} = \frac{r^I a_K^I + w^I a_L^I}{r^{HK} a_K^{HK} + w^{HK} a_L^{HK}.} \tag{4}$$

Let θ denote labor's share in total cost, that is:

$$\theta^I = \frac{w^I a_L^I}{C^I}, \qquad \theta^{HK} = \frac{w^{HK} a_L^{HK}}{C^{HK}}. \tag{5}$$

Then this implies that:

$$C^I = \frac{w^I a_L^I}{\theta^I}, \qquad C^{HK} = \frac{w^{HK} a_L^{HK}}{\theta^{HK}} \tag{6}$$

and the unit cost in Indonesia can be written as:

$$C^I = (\frac{w^I a_L^I}{\theta^I})(\frac{\theta^{HK}}{w^{HK} a_L^{HK}}) C^{HK}. \tag{7}$$

If a Cobb–Douglas technology is assumed in the apparel manufacturing sector then the share of labor, θ, is a constant. If the further assumption of identical Cobb–Douglas technology in Indonesia and Hong Kong is given, then $\theta^I = \theta^{HK}$, and:

$$C^I = (\frac{w^I a_L^I}{w^{HK} a_L^{HK}}) C^{HK}. \tag{8}$$

Note that $(1/a_L)$ is simply output per worker. Thus, in the perfectly competitive model with identical Cobb–Douglas production technology in the apparel sector in each country, the unit cost in Indonesia can be calculated as the unit cost in Hong Kong weighted by the ratio of wage divided by output per worker in Indonesia to wage divided by output per worker in Hong Kong.[3] This permits cost data on Indonesia to be derived. The Indonesian license price is then given by the license price inclusive f.o.b. price of Indonesian exports to the United States (P^I) less the unit cost in Indonesia (C^I).

III. Comparing Actual and Imputed License Prices

In this section, the methodology described in Section II is used to calculate Indonesian license prices for 1987 and 1988.

---

3. A referee has pointed out that θ would be locally the same in Hong Kong and Indonesia as long as both countries have constant returns to scale technologies with identical capital–labor ratios in efficiency terms. In the Cobb Douglas case, θ would be the same in both countries even after allowing for Hicks–neutral or factor–augmenting technical change in either input. And, with identical θ values, equation (8) would hold globally.

A. The Data

The f.o.b. prices of Indonesian and Hong Kong exports to the United States were obtained from *U.S. IA–245* import trade tapes. The prices are in U.S. dollars and include the license price. Data on monthly Hong Kong license prices (in Hong Kong dollars) by MFA categories were provided by Carl Hamilton at the University of Stockholm's Institute for International Economic Studies and Peter Ngan of the Federation of Hong Kong Garment Manufacturers. The license prices pertain to temporary transfers, whereby the transferred quota counts wholly toward the transferor's export performance. These monthly license prices were aggregated into an annual average and converted them to U.S. dollars using the fixed exchange rate of HK$7.80 to US$1.

Wage and value added data were obtained from the 1990 Handbook of Industrial Statistics published by UNIDO. The latest figures available were for 1986 in Indonesia and 1987 in Hong Kong. In Indonesia in 1986, wage per employee was US$600 and output per employee, calculated as wage per employee divided by the product of wages in value added and value added in output, was US$0.51. In Hong Kong in 1987, wage per employee was US$5800 and output per employee was US$2.81. Hence, using the methodology of Section II, the ratio of Indonesian unit cost to Hong Kong unit cost is $(600/0.51)/(5800/2.81) = 0.5742$. Assuming identical Cobb–Douglas technology in Indonesia and Hong Kong, therefore, the cost of producing one unit of Indonesian apparel is slightly more than half the cost of producing one unit of Hong Kong apparel.

Table 15.1 lists, for 23 MFA apparel categories in 1987 and 1988:

1. The license price inclusive f.o.b. price of Hong Kong exports to the United States (P^{HK}), in column (1).
2. The average annual Hong Kong license price per piece in U.S. dollars (L^{HK}), in column (2).
3. The estimated unit cost in Hong Kong ($C^{HK} = P^{HK} - L^{HK}$), in column (3).
4. The license price inclusive f.o.b. price of Indonesian exports to the United States (P^I), in column (4).
5. The estimated unit cost in Indonesia ($C^I = 0.5742\ C^{HK}$), in column (5).
6. The imputed Indonesian license price per piece, $L^I = P^I - C^I$, in column (6).[4]

---

4. Note that the imputed unit cost in Hong Kong is negative in the case of MFA category 342 (cotton skirts). This can be traced to the fact that for several months in 1987 and 1988, the license price for a cotton skirt far exceeded the price of the skirt itself. Note also that in some instances, the imputed Indonesian license price is negative, indicating that the unit costs in Indonesia have been overestimated.

TABLE 15.1. Part 1. Indonesia: Results of Imputation Procedures

MFA Category	Year	(1) P^{HK}	(2) L^{HK}	(3) C^{HK} (1)-(2)	(4) P^I	(5) C^I	(6) L^I (4)-(5)	(7) C^I	(8) L^I (4)-(7)	(9) C^I	(10) L^I (4)-(9)	(11) L^I
334	1987	16.30	5.26	11.04	8.63	6.34	2.29	11.43	-2.80	6.05	2.58	0.41
334	1988	17.15	3.00	14.15	9.94	8.12	1.82	14.65	-4.71	8.49	1.45	0.20
335	1987	10.60	6.69	3.91	8.86	2.24	6.62	4.05	4.81	3.38	5.48	n.a.
335	1988	11.11	3.00	8.11	10.73	4.66	6.07	8.40	2.33	8.11	2.62	0.06
336	1987	14.41	5.23	9.18	5.14	5.27	-0.13	9.51	-4.37	3.39	1.75	0.25
336	1988	14.09	2.86	11.23	5.17	6.45	-1.28	11.64	-6.47	4.27	0.90	0.12
337	1987	3.52	0.32	3.20	3.92	1.84	2.08	3.31	0.61	3.69	0.23	0.42
337	1988	3.92	0.23	3.69	4.12	2.12	2.00	3.82	0.30	4.01	0.11	n.a.
338	1987	6.70	2.87	3.83	3.69	2.20	1.49	3.97	-0.28	2.19	1.50	0.37
338	1988	7.03	1.58	5.45	4.31	3.13	1.18	5.64	-1.33	3.46	0.85	0.19
339	1987	4.21	2.87	1.34	3.04	0.77	2.27	1.39	1.65	1.01	2.03	0.37
339	1988	4.15	1.58	2.57	3.53	1.47	2.06	2.66	0.87	2.26	1.27	0.19
340	1987	6.49	2.55	3.94	3.74	2.26	1.48	4.08	-0.34	2.35	1.39	0.18
340	1988	7.75	1.17	6.58	4.33	3.78	0.55	6.82	-2.49	3.81	0.52	0.45
341	1987	5.37	1.46	3.91	3.38	2.25	1.13	4.05	-0.67	2.55	0.83	0.69
341	1988	7.37	0.38	6.99	4.41	4.02	0.39	7.25	-2.84	4.34	0.07	0.03
342	1987	8.98	9.00	-0.02	5.16	-0.01	5.17	-0.02	5.18	-0.01	5.17	1.06
342	1988	9.86	3.60	6.26	5.59	3.59	2.00	6.48	-0.89	3.67	1.92	0.17
345	1987	13.56	5.80	7.76	5.02	4.46	0.56	8.04	-3.02	2.98	2.04	n.a.
345	1988	14.54	3.94	10.60	6.14	6.09	0.05	10.98	-4.84	4.64	1.50	0.01
347	1987	7.28	3.27	4.01	5.23	2.30	2.93	4.15	1.08	2.98	2.25	0.59
347	1988	7.22	2.29	4.93	5.89	2.83	3.06	5.10	0.79	4.16	1.73	1.72

TABLE 15.1. Part 2. Indonesia: Results of Imputation Procedures

MFA Category	Year	(1) P^{HK}	(2) L^{HK}	(3) C^{HK} (1)-(2)	(4) P^I	(5) C^I	(6) $\hat{L}^I$ (4)-(5)	(7) C^I	(8) $\hat{L}^I$ (4)-(7)	(9) C^I	(10) $\hat{L}^I$ (4)-(9)	(11) L^I
348	1987	7.55	3.56	3.99	5.60	2.29	3.31	4.13	1.47	3.06	2.54	0.59
348	1988	7.76	2.16	5.60	6.61	3.22	3.39	5.80	0.81	4.94	1.67	1.72
335	1987	11.12	0.60	10.52	4.74	6.04	-1.30	10.90	-6.16	4.65	0.09	n.a.
335	1988	11.20	1.00	10.20	5.67	5.86	-0.19	10.56	-4.89	5.35	0.32	0.12
636	1987	17.66	2.14	15.52	4.01	8.91	-4.90	16.07	-12.06	3.65	0.36	0.59
636	1988	17.89	1.52	16.37	5.46	9.40	-3.94	19.95	-11.49	5.17	0.29	0.09
638	1987	4.68	1.23	3.45	3.07	1.98	1.09	3.58	-0.51	2.35	0.72	0.26
638	1988	4.46	0.23	4.23	3.87	2.43	1.44	4.38	-0.51	3.80	0.07	0.02
639	1987	4.09	1.23	2.86	2.14	1.64	0.50	2.97	-0.83	1.55	0.59	0.26
639	1988	4.01	0.23	3.78	2.66	2.17	0.49	3.91	-1.25	2.60	0.06	0.02
640	1987	3.99	0.27	3.72	2.73	2.13	0.60	3.85	-1.12	2.64	0.09	0.13
640	1988	4.68	0.21	4.47	3.02	2.57	0.45	4.63	-1.61	2.99	0.03	0.07
641	1987	7.77	1.19	6.58	3.43	3.78	-0.35	6.82	-3.39	3.01	0.42	0.33
641	1988	7.93	1.73	6.20	3.65	3.56	0.09	6.42	-2.77	2.96	0.69	0.17
642	1987	10.93	6.78	4.15	3.96	2.38	1.58	4.30	-0.34	1.56	2.40	1.06
642	1988	10.73	4.02	6.71	5.08	3.85	1.23	6.95	-1.87	3.29	1.79	0.17
645	1987	6.10	1.39	4.71	4.11	2.71	1.40	4.88	-0.77	3.29	0.82	0.01
645	1988	5.22	0.55	4.67	4.61	2.68	1.93	4.84	-0.23	4.28	0.33	0.05
646	1987	7.13	1.39	5.74	4.28	3.30	0.98	5.95	-1.67	3.57	0.71	0.01
646	1988	6.40	0.55	5.85	4.08	3.36	0.72	6.06	-1.98	3.87	0.21	0.05
647	1987	5.72	1.13	4.59	2.67	2.63	0.04	4.75	-2.08	2.22	0.45	0.49
647	1988	7.82	0.79	7.03	3.43	4.04	-0.61	7.28	-3.85	3.19	0.24	0.38
648	1987	4.81	0.79	4.02	2.13	2.31	-0.18	4.16	-2.03	1.84	0.29	0.18
648	1988	5.06	0.70	4.36	2.50	2.50	-0.00	4.51	-2.01	2.23	0.27	0.49

The Indonesian license prices were obtained from transactions data from the Textile Quota Exchange (TQE). A full description of this data set is contained in Chapter Twelve. The average annual Indonesian license price was computed by averaging all the transaction prices available for each year (zero price transactions were dropped).[5] Next, these were converted to U.S. dollars using the annual average exchange rates published in the *International Financial Statistics*. As the quota year for Indonesia runs from July to the following June, the average license prices are actually for 1987/88 and 1988/89.

B. Comparison

The actual Indonesian license prices are also shown in Table 15.1, column (11). Note that in 31 cases, fully three–quarters of the sample, the actual license price falls short of the imputed license price! Of the 46 license prices imputed, four could not be compared with their corresponding actual prices as the data were missing. In ten cases the imputed license price was negative; the methodology would impute a zero license price in these instances. In only eleven cases was the imputed license price smaller than the actual license price.

That the methodology tends to overestimate Indonesian license prices is most clearly seen in Figure 15.2, which is a scattergram of the imputed Indonesian license prices versus the actual Indonesian license prices, with negative imputed license prices set to zero. Most of the points lie above the 45 degree line, indicating that the imputed license prices exceed the actual license prices in most cases. Table 15.2 shows the results of regressing the imputed Indonesian license price on the actual Indonesian license price.[6] If the standard imputing procedure is accurate, we should obtain a zero estimated intercept and a coefficient of one on the actual license price.

The regression results indicate, however, that whereas the estimated slope coefficient is not significantly different from one, the estimated intercept is US$0.84 significant at the 1 percent level. The joint test of zero intercept and slope coefficient of 1 is easily rejected even at the 5 percent level of confidence.

The correlation coefficient between the actual and imputed license prices is only 0.42. Low as this figure may seem, there is reason to believe that it may even be an overestimate since the actual Indonesian quota prices used in our sample are likely to be biased upward. One reason for this is the fact that zero prices were omitted from the sample. Another reason is that the transactions on the Indonesian TQE are not strictly

---

5. There is considerable movement in license prices within any given quota year, and Chapter Thirteen addresses the issues underlying the dynamic behavior of quota license prices in detail. In this paper, the issue of daily or monthly license price volatility is sidestepped by making use only of average license prices over the quota year, so as to be consistent with the other pieces of information, such as production cost data which are available only annually.

6. In this and the following two regressions, the observation was dropped for category 342 in 1987 due to the negative estimated cost in Hong Kong.

TABLE 15.2. Indonesia: Regression of Imputed License Price on Actual License Price (Standard Imputation Procedure)

Dependent variable = $\hat{L}_{it}^{I}$

Independent Variable	Coefficient	t–statistic
Constant	0.8435	3.3607[a]
	(0.2510)	
L_{it}^{I}	1.1334	2.3009[b]
	(0.4926)	

Number of observations = 41
R^2 = 0.1195
Standard errors are in parentheses beneath the parameter estimates.
[a] Significant at the 1 percent level.
[b] Significant at the 5 percent level.

Results of hypothesis testing:
F–statistic for joint test of intercept = 0 and slope = 1:
F = 27.7391; reject the null hypothesis at the 5 percent level.
t–statistic for test of slope=1:
t = 0.2708; do not reject the null hypothesis.

FIGURE 15.2. Indonesia: Imputed Versus Actual Indonesian License Prices (Standard Imputation Procedure)

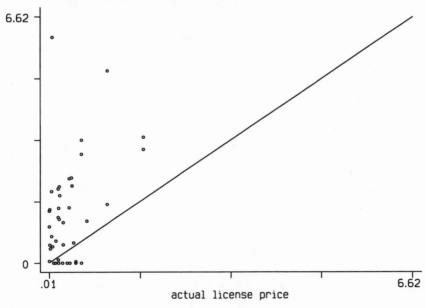

Imputed vs actual Indonesian license prices from Table 1 (in U.S. dollars per piece)

temporary transfers in the Hong Kong sense, as the transferor is penalized by 20 percent and the transferee rewarded by 20 percent of the transferred amount when licenses are allocated in the following quota year. This penalty scheme acts as an incentive for buyers, but a deterrent to sellers, thus having the effect of increasing the demand for and decreasing the supply of licenses on the exchange. The result is that quota prices from the bourse are likely to be on the high side.

IV. Alternative Hypotheses

This section examines some possible explanations for the empirical results. Four types of explanations are considered:

1. The first is related to the functional form used.
2. The second is based on quality differences.
3. The third is based on differences in the quota allocation mechanism and associated hidden costs.
4. The fourth is based on the possibility of market imperfections.

A. Functional Form

As outlined in Section II, the imputation procedure assumes that there are identical Cobb–Douglas technologies in the two countries. This assumption may be relaxed somewhat by allowing different labor shares (θ^{HK} and θ^I) in the two countries, (i.e. use the formula in equation (7) rather than that in equation (8). The formula of equation (8) is adjusted by multiplying it by (θ^{HK}/θ^I), the ratio of labor shares in Hong Kong and Indonesia.

Now, from Table 15.1, most of the estimates of Indonesian license prices are higher than the actual prices. Therefore, the labor shares adjustment would help to reduce this discrepancy if it raised our estimates of Indonesian costs. The Indonesian cost estimate would rise if this adjustment factor exceeds unity, that is, if the labor share in Hong Kong exceeds that in Indonesia. Given that the relative price of labor is higher in Hong Kong, this would occur if there is little substitutability between labor and capital.[7] In this event, an increase in the wage–rental ratio does not induce much substitution away from labor and consequently raises the share of labor in total costs

---

7. If a constant elasticity of substitution (CES) formulation is used, the share of labor rises with the wage–rental ratio if the elasticity of substitution is less than unity, and falls as the wage–rental ratio rises if it is less than unity. If the elasticity of substitution equals unity, one is in the Cobb–Douglas case where it is a constant.

Published data on the wearing apparel industry in Hong Kong indicate that θ [HK] was approximately 22.64 percent in 1987.[8] For Indonesia, the industry data suggest a θ[I] of approximately 12.55 percent in 1985.[9] Thus, the labor shares adjustment factor is around 1.80. The results of this adjustment are shown in Table 15.1, columns (7) and (8). This adjustment lowers the imputed license prices as expected; however, it goes too far—in 39 cases, (i.e., 83 percent of the sample), the imputed license price was lower than the actual license price! Setting negative imputed license prices to be zero, there were only seven cases (one–sixth of the sample) in which the imputed price exceeded the actual price.

These results are summarized pictorially in Figure 15.3. Table 15.3 presents the results from regressing the imputed license price with the labor share adjustment against the actual license price. This time, the hypotheses that the intercept is zero but the estimated slope coefficient is significantly below one cannot be rejected; and the joint test of the two conditions together is resoundingly rejected. The correlation coefficient between the imputed and actual Indonesian license prices in this case is 0.37, even lower than the figure of 0.42 in the standard case.[10]

B. Quality Differences

A plausible explanation for the inaccuracy of the imputation procedure is that the quality of Hong Kong apparel exports is vastly different from that of Indonesian apparel exports. After all, Hong Kong's textile and apparel industry is well established in the global market, whereas Indonesia's is relatively new, having grown mostly in the last decade. In fact, Hill 1992 declares that Indonesia's export quality is below that of its neighboring ASEAN countries, much less that of Hong Kong.

Following Swan 1970, quality can be considered in terms of the amount of services embodied in a piece of apparel. Assume services are a homogeneous good produced and sold at a constant marginal cost. Then higher quality items will cost more to produce and will sell for more than lower quality items.

---

8. The figures were taken from the 1989 *Hong Kong Annual Digest of Statistics.* The latest year for which access was available to published information was 1987. θ [HK] was calculated as: (Compensation of Employees) / (Purchases of Materials, Supplies and Industrial Work and Services + Other Expenses including rent + Compensation of Employees).

9. The figures were obtained from the 1987 *Statistik Indonesia.* The latest year for which published information was available was 1985. Note that the figures are for the combined textile, wearing apparel and leather industry. θ[I] was calculated as: (Labor Cost) / (Input Costs + Labor Cost), where Input Costs consists of the cost of raw materials, fuel electricity and gas, other materials, repairs and industrial services received, and non–industrial services received, as well as rent of building, machinery and equipment.

10. However, this may paint too dismal a picture since, as explained earlier, there are reasons to believe that the sample data may overstate the actual Indonesian license prices.

TABLE 15.3. Indonesia: Regression of Imputed License Price on Actual License Price (Labor Cost Share Adjustment)

Dependent variable = $\hat{L}_{it}^{I}$

Independent Variable	Coefficient	t–statistic
Constant	0.1125	1.0334
	(0.1089)	
L_{it}^{I}	0.3654	1.7103
	(0.2136)	

Number of observations = 41
$R^2 = 0.0698$
Standard errors are in parentheses beneath the parameter estimates.

Results of hypothesis testing:
F–statistic for joint test of intercept=0 and slope=1:
F = 979.8635; reject the null hypothesis at the 5 percent level.
t–statistic for test of slope=1:
t = -2.9709; reject the null hypothesis.

FIGURE 15.3. Indonesia: Imputed Versus Actual Indonesian License Prices (Allowing for Different Labor Shares)

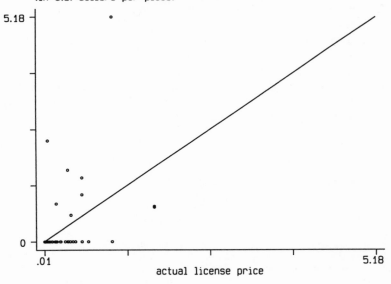

Imputed vs actual Indonesian license prices from Table 2
(in U.S. dollars per piece)

Furthermore, the relative quality of Hong Kong apparel vis–à–vis Indonesian apparel will be reflected in the price ratio of the respective products. If Hong Kong quality is higher than Indonesian quality, then the estimated Indonesian marginal costs should be adjusted downward to take into account the relative inferiority of the Indonesian goods compared to Hong Kong goods. This would have the effect of raising the estimated Indonesian license prices![11] Adjusting for quality differences, therefore, will only exacerbate the overestimation problem if Hong Kong quality is assumed to be better than Indonesian quality.

Although quality differences alone cannot account for the discrepancy between the actual and imputed license prices, it is worth considering whether quality differences together with the different labor shares assumption will accomplish the objective. Columns (9) and (10) in Table 15.1 present the results of the imputation procedure adjusted for differences in quality as well as labor cost shares. These results are shown in Figure 15.4. Clearly, the adjustment is insufficient to close the gap between the actual and imputed license prices, as 39 of the imputed license prices exceed the actual prices, and only seven of the imputed license prices are below the actual prices.

Regressing the imputed license prices from this procedure against the actual license prices in Indonesia yields results very similar to those in Table 15.2. Table 15.4 shows that the estimated intercept in this case is US\$ 0.74 and

TABLE 15.4. Indonesia: Regression of Imputed License Price on Actual License Price (Labor Cost Share Adjustment and Quality Differences)

Dependent variable = $\hat{L}_{it}^I$

Independent Variable	Coefficient	t–statistic
Constant	0.7409	4.6744[a]
	(0.1585)	
L_{it}^I	0.7581	2.4372[b]
	(0.3111)	

Number of observations = 41
$R^2 = 0.1322$
Standard errors are in parentheses beneath the parameter estimates.
[a] Significant at the 1 percent level.
[b] Significant at the 5 percent level.

Results of hypothesis testing:
F–statistic for joint test of intercept=0 and slope=1:
F = 15.4883; reject the null hypothesis at the 5 percent level.
t–statistic for test of slope=1:
t = -0.7775; do not reject the null hypothesis.

---

11. See Section V.D for a more formal derivation.

statistically significant although the estimated slope coefficient is not significantly different from one. The joint test of a zero intercept and slope coefficient of one is again rejected at the 5 percent level. The correlation coefficient between the imputed license price and the actual license price is 0.45, not very much higher than in the standard case.

C. Differences in Quota Allocation Systems

As described in Chapter Seven, there are vast differences in quota allocation systems across countries. If there are exogenous hidden costs in obtaining a license of any sort, then the license price would be less than the difference in the f.o.b. price and the costs of production. These hidden costs could be search costs involved in locating licenses, red tape transactions costs,[12] or simply bribery costs. If these costs were substantially greater in Indonesia, then the imputed license prices following the usual procedure would be overestimates of the license prices.[13]

The Hong Kong quota allocation procedure is well–documented. As mentioned in Part I of the Appendix, the official guidelines regulating this procedure are published by the Hong Kong Trade Department and made available to the public. Quotas are allocated to manufacturers on the basis of past performance, and they are transferable (either temporarily or permanently) to a large extent. The complete set of rules governing Hong Kong's quota allocation system is set out in the 1987 Hong Kong Trade Department publication, *Textiles Export Control System*; the quota holders' list is available annually through the Hong Kong Trade Department.

Considerably less information is available on the workings of the Indonesian quota allocation system. As described in Part III of the Appendix, the rules are vague and subject to constant change. Indeed, according to Hill 1992, p.73, "...the administration lacks transparency. The Department of Trade rarely publishes a complete list of quota holders, nor are its grounds for quota allocation clearly established..." The absence of published information on quotas serves to reinforce suspicion and mistrust in sections of the business community, and to force exporters to spend excessive amounts of time lobbying

---

12. For example, a careful reading of the 1990 decree concerning textile exports reveals that in order to receive a Textile and Textile Products Export Certificate, an Indonesian firm would have to submit no fewer than six documents: a copy of the Goods Export Notification giving loading approval by the customs authorities; a copy of the on–board original bill of lading or airway bill validated by the issuing transport company; the letter of credit or sales contract and invoice; a statement from the producer describing the goods and their value; a Notification of Textile and Textile Products form with the Goods Export Notification number and the date approved by a foreign exchange bank; and a receipt of payment for the cost of monitoring the export of quota textile and textile products.

13. See Section V.C for a fuller derivation.

key government officials. This suggests that hidden costs are indeed greater in Indonesia, and provides a credible explanation for the low actual license prices observed.

Unfortunately, no measure, or proxy, is readily available for hidden costs and thus, adjustments cannot be made for them in the data. However, if one thinks of these hidden costs as an addition to the unit costs of production, then they would be reflected in the intercept in a regression of the imputed license price against the actual license price. The regression results in Table 15.2 yield a positive and statistically significant intercept using the standard imputing procedure, and the regression results in Table 15.3 show that this positive and significant intercept persists even after adjusting for quality differentials and different labor shares.

D. Market Imperfections

The imputation procedure described in Section II is based on the assumption of perfect competition everywhere. There are two places where the competitive assumption is crucial. First, it is assumed that removing the Hong Kong license

FIGURE 15.4. Indonesia: Imputed Versus Actual Indonesian License Prices (Allowing for Different Labor Shares and Quality Differences)

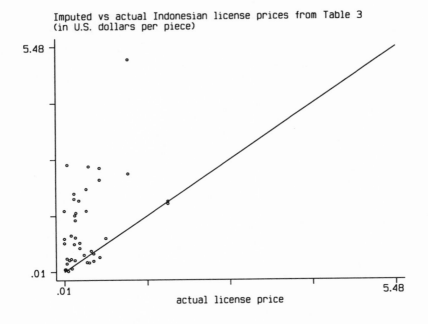

Imputed vs actual Indonesian license prices from Table 3 (in U.S. dollars per piece)

price from the f.o.b. price gives the supply price which equals the production cost in Hong Kong. This assumption requires that neither the sellers in Hong Kong nor the buyers in the importing country have market power. If this is not the case, then the license exclusive price in Hong Kong could exceed the cost of production.[14] For example, if there were a monopoly in Hong Kong, then costs would equal marginal revenue, which is less than price. Assuming the market in Indonesia is competitive, following the usual procedure in this instance would lead to an overestimate of Indonesian costs, and an underestimate of Indonesian license prices.

The second place where the competitive assumption is crucial is the estimation of Indonesian costs as the license–exclusive price of Indonesian apparel exports. If the Hong Kong market is competitive but the Indonesian market is not, then the cost estimates would be correct but the license–exclusive prices would exceed costs in Indonesia. In this case, the imputation procedure would indeed overestimate Indonesian license prices. However, given the large number of apparel suppliers, there may be little reason to expect imperfections of this kind to exist.

If both the Hong Kong and Indonesian markets are not competitive, then little can be said about the direction of the bias. The procedure would overestimate Indonesian costs but since price exceeds cost, it may over or underestimate the license exclusive price, and consequently under– or overestimate the license price in Indonesia.

It is worth noting that the imputation procedure would be valid as long as suppliers are competitive even if license markets are not, since the cost of production in Hong Kong would still be given by removing the license price from the f.o.b. price. As long as the product market in Indonesia is competitive, this approach would still give the correct estimate of Indonesian costs—the license price, even if it is artificially high, would still be added on to costs to arrive at the f.o.b. price.

V. A More General Model

Some of the considerations raised in Section IV can be incorporated into the model of Section II. This section sets up a general model incorporating productivity, quality and labor cost share considerations, well as hidden costs in Indonesia and Hong Kong, and, using the data on f.o.b. prices and license prices from the two countries, estimates the magnitudes of the parameters that would yield imputed license prices that accurately reflect the actual license prices in Indonesia.

---

14. See Chapter Three for a full explanation of rent sharing.

Let hidden costs in the quota allocation systems be represented by the variable α so that in Hong Kong, for example, we now have:

$$L^{HK} = P^{HK} - \hat{C}^{HK} - \alpha^{HK} \tag{9}$$

where carets indicate variables to be estimated.

The imputation procedure of Section II can be described in three steps:

1. First, the Hong Kong unit cost is calculated from equation (9):

$$\hat{C}^{HK} = P^{HK} - L^{HK} - \alpha^{HK}. \tag{10}$$

2. Then the Indonesian unit cost is calculated. For notational convenience, let:

ϕ = Productivity adjustment,
μ = The ratio of labor shares, and
δ = The quality adjustment factor (all else constant, the higher is the quality of Hong Kong apparel relative to Indonesian apparel, as reflected in the relative prices of the two products, the lower will be the estimated Indonesian unit cost).

Then:

$$\hat{C}^I = \frac{\mu}{\delta\phi}\hat{C}^{HK}$$

$$= \frac{\mu}{\delta\phi}[P^{HK} - L^{HK} - \alpha^{HK}] \tag{11}$$

where:

$$\mu = \frac{\theta^{HK}}{\theta^I}, \quad \phi = \frac{w^{HK}a_L^{HK}}{w^I a_L^I}, \quad \delta = \frac{P^{HK}}{P^I}. \tag{12}$$

The data indicate that $\phi > 1$, $\mu > 1$, and $\delta > 1$. No data exist for α^{HK} and α^I.

3. Finally, the Indonesian license price is imputed as follows:

$$\hat{L}^I = P^I - \hat{C}^I - \alpha^I$$

$$= P^I - \frac{\mu}{\delta\phi}[P^{HK} - L^{HK} - \alpha^{HK}] - \alpha^I. \tag{13}$$

A. $\alpha^{HK} = \alpha^I = 0$, $\mu = 1$, $\delta = 1$

The basic model of Section II assumes no hidden costs that is, $\alpha^{HK} = \alpha^I = 0$, equal labor cost shares, that is, $\mu = 1$, and no quality differences, that is, $\delta = 1$, to arrive at the formula:

$$\hat{L}^I = P^I - \frac{1}{\phi}[P^{HK} - L^{HK}]. \tag{14}$$

B. $\alpha^{HK} = \alpha^I = 0$, $\mu \neq 1$, $\delta = 1$

If there are different labor cost shares in the two countries but no hidden costs and no quality differences, then the estimated license price is:

$$\hat{L}^I = P^I - \frac{\mu}{\phi}[P^{HK} - L^{HK}]. \tag{15}$$

If $\mu > 1$, then the estimate of equation (15) will be smaller than that of equation (14), as established in Section IV.A where μ was estimated to be 1.80.

C. $\alpha^{HK} \neq \alpha^I$, $\mu = 1$, $\delta = 1$

If there are different degrees of hidden costs involved in the quota administration systems of the two countries but identical Cobb Douglas technologies and product qualities, then the estimated license price is:

$$\hat{L}^I = P^I - \frac{1}{\phi}[P^{HK} - L^{HK} - \alpha^{HK}] - \alpha^I. \tag{16}$$

Without any information on α^{HK} and α^I, it is not possible to compare equation (16) with equation (14). However, the Hong Kong quota allocation system is assumed to be smoothly functioning while the Indonesian system is not, that is, $\alpha^{HK} = 0$ and $\alpha^I > 0$, then the formula in equation (16) will yield smaller license price estimates than that in equation (14). Although there is no measure of hidden costs, it is very possible that they are an important reason why the actual license prices fall below the imputed license prices.

D. $\alpha^{HK} = \alpha^I = 0$, $\mu = 1$, $\delta \neq 1$

If there are differences in quality but identical labor cost shares and no hidden costs, then the estimated license price is:

$$\hat{L}^I = P^I - \frac{1}{\delta\phi}[P^{HK} - L^{HK}]. \tag{17}$$

If $\delta > 1$, as is expected to be the case, then the formula in equation (17) yields higher license price estimates than that in equation (14), so that introducing quality differences can only exacerbate the inaccuracy of the imputation process! Given that this is the case, the results of the imputation procedure adjusted for quality differences is not presented.

E. $\alpha^{HK} = \alpha^I = 0,\ \mu \neq 1,\ \delta \neq 1$

If there are also differences in labor cost shares (but no hidden costs), then the license price estimate is:

$$\hat{L}^I = P^I - \frac{\mu}{\delta\phi}[P^{HK} - L^{HK}]. \tag{18}$$

This formula yields a smaller license price estimate than equation (14) if $\delta < \mu$.

VI. Estimating the General Model

Using the model set up in Section V, the imputed license price can be represented generally by:

$$\hat{L}^I = P^I - \frac{\mu}{\delta\phi}(P^{HK} - L^{HK} - \alpha^{HK}) - \alpha^I. \tag{19}$$

In order for the imputed license price, $\hat{L}^I$, to equal the actual license price, L^I, one must have:

$$P^I = (\alpha^I - \frac{\mu}{\delta\phi}\alpha^{HK}) + L^I + \frac{\mu}{\delta\phi}(P^{HK} - L^{HK}). \tag{20}$$

Therefore, in a regression of P^I on a constant, L^I, and (P^{HK} -L^{HK}) the intercept would represent the difference in hidden costs, the coefficient on L^I should be unity, and the coefficient on (P^{HK}-L^{HK}) would represent the combined productivity, labor share and quality adjustment.

Table 15.5 presents the results of this regression. Note that the coefficient on L^I is indeed not significantly different from one. The estimated intercept is statistically significant at US$2.38. Although individual estimates of α^I and α^{HK} cannot be obtained, one can think of US$2.38 as representing an upper bound on Indonesian hidden costs in the event that no such costs exist in Hong Kong. Finally, the coefficient on (P^{HK}-L^{HK}) is statistically significant at 0.2944. Again, individual estimates of μ, δ and ϕ, could not be extracted, but this figure is quite consistent with the data. Using the estimate of $\mu = 1.80$ from Section IV.A, and the estimate of $\phi = 1/0.5742 = 1.7416$ from Section III, the regression coefficient of 0.2944 results in a δ estimate of 3.5 (that is, Hong Kong quality being three and a half times better than Indonesian quality).

TABLE 15.5. Indonesia: Regression Using General Model

Dependent variable = P_{it}^I

Independent Variable	Coefficient	t–statistic
Constant	2.3756	4.1475[a]
	(0.5728)	
L_{it}^I	1.0154	1.6322[b]
	(0.6221)	
$P_{it}^{HK} - L_{it}^{HK}$	0.2944	4.2012[a]
	(0.0701)	

Number of observations = 42

$R^2 = 0.3199$, Adjusted $R^2 = 0.2851$

Standard errors are in parentheses beneath the parameter estimates.

[a] Significant at the 1 percent level.

[b] Significant at the 10 percent level.

Results of hypothesis testing:

t–statistic for test of coefficient on $L_{it}^I = 1$:

$t = 0.0248$; do not reject the null hypothesis.

PART IV

Conclusion

CHAPTER SIXTEEN

Summary and Conclusion

This book had two broad objectives. The first objective was to look at the possibility that exporting countries that are subject to quotas under the MFA may be receiving less than all the potential quota rents despite the fact that the implementation of the quota itself and the allocation of quota licenses is left in their hands. The second objective was to examine and understand the consequences—both intentional and inadvertent—of the myriad quota implementation procedures used by different countries in the MFA.

The case studies and empirical analyses presented in this book reveal that many facets of the real world are inconsistent with the basic competitive model often used in studies of the MFA. The picture that emerges is one where details of quota implementation, market structure, and the institutional setup play a significant role. In many countries, such as India, Indonesia, and Pakistan, the quota implementation system is discretionary and nontransparent, forcing agents to operate with imperfect information. Implementation rules, such as the length of the quota period, license transferability, and free quota, also introduce complications in the valuation of quota licenses and rents. Even in Hong Kong, the one case most likely to satisfy the assumption of perfect competition, where licenses are relatively freely traded and the quota implementation process is transparent, the possibility of rent sharing between exporting firms and importers with market power cannot be ruled out.

What lessons are to be gleaned from the experiences of these countries in implementing the MFA quotas? Why did some countries, like Hong Kong, end up utilizing almost all their quota fairly early on, while others, like those in the Indian subcontinent, had difficulty exporting up to their quota limits? The various pieces of theoretical analyses and empirical evidence presented in this book point to a number of interesting conclusions.

1. First, it is quite apparent from studying the implementation of the MFA quotas that micromanagement does not work. All too often, the following pattern is evident in the country experiences: (i) initially, some implementation procedure is chosen; (ii) following this, disadvantages of the procedure become apparent; (iii) in an attempt to remove these perceived disadvantages, further layers of regulations are added; (iv) when loopholes are discovered in these regulations, additional regulations are added, and so on. The end result is a cumbersome, inefficient, nontransparent system that impedes exports and hinders the appropriation of rents by the exporting country. The implementation of free quota in

India is the classic example. One motivation for having open quota was to level the playing field between established firms that were allocated past performance quota, and new firms that were not eligible for such quota. However, as documented here, it was the established firms who often found ways to take advantage of the free quota despite attempts to plug the loopholes. In addition, the many layers of regulations often reflect conflicting objectives on the part of the authorities. In India, attempts to raise revenue by establishing a cutoff price to ration free quota conflicted with the objective of using free quota to allow entry and level the playing field between established and new firms: established firms were more easily able to skim their high value orders off to apply for open quota than were new entrants.

2. Second, the experiences of the different countries suggest that it is important to assign property rights in a way that does not undermine the bargaining power of exporters, make licenses tradable, and interfere as little as possible following that. Making quota allocation contingent on orders, as is commonly done in allocating free quota, is likely to raise the bargaining power of buyers and shift rents into their hands. Making licenses tradable is desirable for a number of reasons: (i) first, it puts exporters in a stronger position in terms of their bargaining power vis-à-vis importers and allows the exporting country to reap greater rents: buyers often permit quota license costs to be added to total costs during price negotiations if the licenses had to be purchased by the exporter, but not if they were owned by the exporter (e.g., allocated on the basis of past performance), especially if the licenses were nontransferable; (ii) second, transferability is welfare-maximizing if surplus and revenue are given equal weight in the welfare function; and (iii) third, as a mechanism that works through the price system, it has all the efficiency properties associated with that system. Abuses such as the exercise of monopoly power in the license market could be dealt with as in any other antitrust case.

3. Third, there does not seem to be much reason to worry about the abuse of market power in the license market. Hong Kong license prices seem to follow patterns predicted by market forces in conjunction with the rules in implementation. In Indonesia, there is no evidence of clubs of old exporters keeping out new ones. Markets seem to work well!

4. Fourth, there were real differences across countries in their ability to export under the MFA. Contrary to expectation, the low wage countries did not do as well as some of the more developed, higher wage, countries did. A large part of this is likely to be due to the difference in implementation procedures followed. Although it is difficult, if not impossible, to present incontrovertible proof, the case studies presented

here suggest that countries with transparent and simple implementation schemes tended to do better, while uncertainty and discretionary implementation tended to create costs and lead to difficulties in exporting.

Where does one go from here? There is certainly much scope for further study of some of the topics explored in this book. For example, one main thesis of this book is that there might be sharing of the quota rents between importers and exporters due to implementation practices and the existence of monopsony power. The evidence presented here calls into question the prevailing practice of assuming a perfectly competitive framework in empirical studies of the MFA. As the case studies for Hong Kong and Korea show, the standard competitive model, even after allowing for quality differences, does not generally fit the data. Current estimates of quota rents, based on the prices of quota licenses in Hong Kong, are as high as 25 percent of total export value, but the results in this book imply that even these figures may be too small, as some 65 percent of the rent may be retained in the United States. The implication is that the overall welfare cost imposed by the MFA on exporting countries may be even heavier than initially thought; besides the acknowledged reduction in trade volume, these countries may not even be receiving the full amount of the quota rent. However, the data and case studies used to reach this conclusion were by no means as complete as one would have liked, despite being the best obtainable. It is hoped that further research will be done in this area as more and better data become available.

Additionally, there are a number of important issues regarding the implementation of the MFA that are not touched upon here. For example, the role of governments in certifying quality and providing incentives for exporters to meet their obligations to importers is clearly an omitted area. One reason why importers choose not to place orders with firms in certain developing countries is often the uncertainty with regard to the quality of the product and the (non)availability of legal recourse in the event of contract violations.

It is important to point out that much of the work in applied economics these days does recognize the importance of implementation to a certain extent. For example, much attention has been focused on how antidumping law can be implemented in a manner that provides domestic protection. Nevertheless, in most cases, direct intervention, with its promise of direct rewards, seems to be the easy answer. (If the Japanese are not importing our goods, require them to do so directly! If the United States does not produce flat panel displays, subsidize local firms until they do! If the auto industry or steel industry is having trouble competing, implement a voluntary export restraint on its competitors!) Studying the implementation of the MFA suggests that direct intervention can easily become a nightmare and that at the very least, the details of implementation of such direct policies, including a timetable for their dismantling, must be a part of the policy discussion, rather than an unimportant side issue.

PART V

Appendices

Quota Implementation in Hong Kong

I. Introduction

Hong Kong prides itself on administering an efficient textile quota system. The quota year in Hong Kong runs from January to December. The initial quota allocation is historically based; past performance, transfers, and changes in the quota level guide the process by which this allocation changes in subsequent years.

II. Initial Quota Allocation

When a product category is newly brought under restraint, the quotas are allocated according to past performance.[1] Each company receives a quota amount corresponding to its share in total shipments of that particular category to the market concerned. Where the manufacturer and the exporter are not the same company, they each share the quota pertaining to a shipment on a 50–50 basis.[2] If the level of total shipments exceeds the restraint limit, the allocations are scaled down proportionately. If the quota is larger than total past shipments, then the balance remaining is put into a free quota pool, which is open to any firm registered with the Hong Kong Trade Department which has documentary proof of a current overseas order.

III. Quota Transfers

To a certain extent, unused quotas may be transferred between categories (under the swing provision) and between years (under the carry–over and carry–forward provisions). Quota holders are also allowed to transfer part of their quota to other firms. There are two types of quota transfers:

1. Permanent transfers, whereby the transferee obtains the use of the quota for the year in question and, based on its performance against the transferred amount, receives a quota allocation in the following year.

---

1. The reference period is usually the most recent twelve–month period for which shipment performance can be ascertained prior to the introduction of the restraint.

2. In the case of finished piece–goods, the exporter receives 40 percent of the quota and the finisher and weaver each receive 30 percent. In the case of finished fabrics manufactured using imported grey fabrics, quotas are allocated on a 50–50 basis to the exporter and the finisher.

2. Temporary transfers, whereby the transferee obtains the use of the quota for the year in question, but the performance against the transferred quantity is attributed to the transferor.

In order to allow sufficient time for the transferee to obtain the quota, transfer applications are not normally accepted after the middle of November. Free quotas are not transferable.

IV. Subsequent Quota Allocations

Quota entitlements in subsequent restraint periods are based on shipment performance in the preceding period. Quotas can only be allocated after this performance has been fully verified against shipping documents, a process which usually takes two to three months. In order to make a portion of the quotas available during the first few months of the year, the Trade Department makes preliminary quota allocations to companies. Final quota allocations are normally made in March and they supersede any preliminary allocations. Both the utilization rate and the amount of transfers are important factors in determining a firm's future quota allocation:

1. A firm which uses less than 95 percent of its quota holding will obtain an allocation in the subsequent year equal to the amount it used.
2. A firm which uses 95 percent or more of its quota holding will be given an allocation equal to 100 percent of its holding.
3. A firm which uses 95 percent or more of its quota holding and does not transfer out any of its quota (on either a temporary or permanent basis) will be awarded an additional amount equivalent to the growth factor for that category provided for in the restraint agreement.

In addition, a firm which transfers out 50 percent or more of its quota holdings on a temporary basis in a year is liable to have its quota allocation reduced in the following year.[3] A firm which transfers in 35 percent or more of its quota holdings on a temporary basis during the year is eligible for a bonus allocation in the following year.

Finally, a firm which obtains a free quota and utilizes 95 percent or more of it qualifies for a quota allocation in the subsequent year. A firm which fails to utilize at least 95 percent of its free quota may be barred from future participation in free quota schemes for a period of time.

---

3. This amount was reduced to 35 percent in June 1985, but was changed back to 50 percent in July of the following year.

V. Export Licenses

All textile and apparel exports from Hong Kong have to be covered by valid export licenses issued by the Director of Trade—valid export licenses are required for shipments to be brought on board. Export licenses are only issued to firms which are able to present quota to cover the consignment in question. An export license is normally valid for 28 days from the date of issue. The consignment must be shipped within this period. The final licensing date is the first day of December. All licenses covering shipments applied for against quotas held by a company must be acquired not later than this date. However, shipments may be effected up to the last day of the year.

Further details of Hong Kong's textile quota system can be found in the Hong Kong Trade Department publication, *Textiles Export Control System*. A good description of the system is also contained in Morkre 1979, 1984.

Quota Implementation in Korea

I. Introduction

Several agencies are involved in the administration of MFA quotas in Korea. The allocation of quota licenses is managed by two export organizations—the Korea Garment and Knitwear Export Association and the Korea Export Association of Textiles—which are also responsible for issuing visas (commercial invoices) and regulating quota transfers. In addition, the Korea Federation of Textile Industries, together with the Korean Association of High Fashion make recommendations as to which companies should receive licenses, and the Korea Foreign Trade Association compiles the relevant statistics and performs the necessary computations used in determining license allocation.

Quota implementation policies in Korea appear to aim at encouraging full quota utilization, and transfers are encouraged only to the extent that they aid this goal.

II. Basic Quota and Open Quota

Every quota is divided into a basic quota and an open quota. The basic quota, which represents about 85 percent of the total quota, is distributed on the basis of past export quantities of the restricted product. The open quota is allocated according to three different criteria:

1. Past export performance to an unrestricted country.
2. Average unit price of the restricted product.
3. Recent investment in production facilities.

Thus, the Korean concept of the open quota is very different from the free quota in Hong Kong and India, which is allocated simply to companies with evidence of an overseas order on a first come first served basis.

All firms with proven production capabilities are eligible for the open quota. The main consideration for awarding the open quota is export performance in non–restricted countries: 60 percent of the open quota is allocated to firms according to their share of total exports to non–quota areas in the previous year. Additionally, in order to encourage investment in production facilities, 25 percent of the open quota is allocated to firms on the basis of such investment in the previous three years. Finally, to stimulate the growth of high–priced high fashion exports, 15 percent of the open quota is allocated only to those companies that exported the quota item at a price higher than the average unit price in the previous year. The quota is distributed among these firms according to their export shares.

III. Initial Quota Allocation

When a product is newly brought under restraint, the basic quota is allocated to firms in proportion to their export share in the first twelve months for which trade in that product took place. The rationale for using the original export shares rather than the export shares in the most recent twelve–month period is to avoid over–exporting by firms anxious to establish a favorable record just before the restraint is imposed. The total allocated basic quota may not exceed 85 percent of the restraint limit. If total exports in the first twelve months of trade in that product exceed 85 percent of the quota level, the basic allocations are scaled down proportionately. The remaining amount (at least 15 percent of the restraint limit) forms the open quota which is then distributed, on the basis of the three criteria mentioned earlier, among the new companies that did not receive a basic allocation.

IV. Subsequent Quota Allocations

In subsequent restraint periods, the key factor determining each firm's basic quota allocation is its quota utilization rate. At the beginning of the quota year, each firm is awarded a basic quota equal to its total shipments in the previous year less a penalty for the total unused licenses which the firm returned to the regulating authorities for redistribution during that year. If the return was made within seven months of the last date of allocation (i.e., before the end of the previous July), the company's basic quota allocation in the following year is reduced by 50 percent of the surrendered licenses. The penalty increases to 60 percent of the unused licenses if they were returned the previous August; 70 percent of the unused licenses if they were returned the previous September; 80 percent of the unused licenses if they were returned the previous October; and 100 percent of the unused licenses if they were returned the previous November or December.[1] The penalty amounts are added to the open quota. These rules governing the return of unused quota are extremely severe compared with the system in Hong Kong, where instead of penalties for late surrender of unused quota, there are incentives for early surrender.

V. Quota Transfers and Exchanges

Basic quota licenses may be transferred between companies. However, they may not be freely bought or sold, unlike the case in Hong Kong. In Korea, quota

---

1. For example, suppose a firm is allocated 200 licenses but utilizes only 100 licenses. If it returns the unused licenses before July, it will receive a basic quota allocation of 50 (i.e., 100 less 50 percent of the 100 unused licenses) the following year. If it returns the 100 licenses in September, it will receive a basic quota allocation of only 30 (i.e., 100 less 70 percent of the 100 unused licenses) the following year. If it returns the 100 licenses after November 1, it will not be allocated any licenses (i.e., 100 less 100 percent of the unused licenses) the following year.

transfers are regulated by the export associations which allocate the quotas. The regulatory authorities have the power to confiscate quotas from companies engaging in unfair transfers. Such unfair transfers arise when, for example, the receiver of the allocated basic quota and the transferor of the quota are not the same entity,[2] or when the transferor does not have any production facilities. Hence the quota brokers which are ubiquitous in Hong Kong are technically illegal in Korea. In practice, however, it seems that some market trading does occur.

As in Hong Kong, there are two types of quota transfers in Korea: temporary transfers, and permanent transfers. In a temporary transfer, the transferor retains renewal rights whereas in a permanent transfer, the transferee obtains the renewal rights. A firm may not transfer more than 80 percent of its basic allocation for two consecutive years; for example, a firm which has transferred 90 percent of its quota may transfer a maximum of 80 percent of its quota in the following year. The basic quota may not be transferred more than once in the same year, except under certain conditions. If, for example, the transferee is unable to fully utilize the quota received, he may return the unused portion to the transferor who is then free to transfer it to another company. For permanent transfers occurring after November 1, the transferee must return any unused quota to the transferor, even if it incurs a penalty for the latter in the following year. This is to prevent firms that are unable to fill their quotas from transferring them permanently to other firms so as to avoid any penalties.[3] Open quotas are not subject to transfer.

Depending on market conditions, companies may be granted permission to exchange quota licenses in one category for licenses in another category, or quota licenses to one destination for licenses to another destination. To a certain extent, unused quotas may be transferred between categories (under the swing provision) and between years (under the carry–over and carry–forward provisions). Quotas to be carried forward to the following year are allocated as open quotas.

VI. Export Licenses

All textile and apparel exports from Korea must be covered by valid export licenses, or visas, issued by the relevant export association. The visas are usually issued for the duration of the quota, although occasionally, they may be issued for the following year up to January 10 in anticipation of an exporter having excess sales during the end of the year.

---

2. If Firm A transfers 100 licenses to Firm B, Firm B may not transfer the same licenses to Firm C, although it may return them to Firm A.

3. For example, a company that was allocated 300 licenses but only managed to utilize 200 of them by the end of October would have the incentive to transfer its unused licenses permanently to another firm—in that way, it would be assured of a basic allocation of 200 licenses the following year, whereas if it returned the unused licenses to the authorities, it would only receive 100 licenses (i.e., 200 minus the 100 unused licenses) the following year. Note that this ruling is redundant for temporary transfers since the transferee's utilization counts against the transferor's performance in this case.

Quota Implementation in Indonesia[1]

I. Introduction

Indonesia's quota allocation system is fraught with uncertainty as the regulations are changed practically every year.[2] Rather than recount the detailed evolution of the system, this appendix lays out the basics and discusses some themes within the changing regulations so as to give the reader a flavor of how the Indonesian system differs from that in other countries, such as Hong Kong.

Quota administration and allocation in Indonesia come under the purview of the Directorate of the Export of Industrial and Mining Products. MFA quota licenses are distributed through the regional offices of the Ministry of Trade during each quota period, which extends from July 1 to June 30 for exports to the United States.

II. Eligibility Requirements

In order to apply for an MFA license, a potential exporter must be a Registered Textile and Textile Products Exporter (ETTPT). Both producers as well as non–producers are eligible for licensing. Prior to 1988, in order to be eligible, a producing ETTPT had to have a valid business license and own (or be supported by) at least 100 primary or main machines, while a non–producing ETTPT had to have a cooperation contract with a producer that met these requirements.

In 1988, the 100 machines requirement was dropped. Instead, the applicant had to submit a statement of readiness to export non–quota textile and textile products[3] with a free on board (f.o.b.) value of at least US$100,000 within six months.[4] Upon approval of the application, the exporter would be granted a status of provisional ETTPT.[5] In order to become a permanent ETTPT, an exporter would have to realize non–quota textile and clothing exports worth at least US$400,000 f.o.b. within two years. The two–year time limit was eliminated in 1990, at which time a new rule was introduced requiring permanent ETTPTs to realize, in each quota period, non–quota exports worth at least US$200,000 f.o.b. and not less than the previous period's realization. The rationale behind the non–quota export requirement was to increase

---

1. Written with Elaine McCormick Watt.

2. Pangestu 1987 provides a comprehensive description of the quota allocation system and its modifications up to 1987, but in 1990, the system underwent another overhaul.

3. These include exports of textiles and clothing to non–quota countries as well as exports of textile and clothing not under restriction to quota countries.

4. This requirement was dropped in 1990.

5. However, if he did not meet his commitment of US$100,000 worth of non–quota exports within six months, his status of provisional ETTPT would be revoked.

Indonesia's textile and textile products exports and to weed out potential bogus applicants. However, the requirement also limited the number of small exporters who could apply for quota.

III. Quota Categories

There are essentially three types of quota:

1. Permanent quota.
2. Provisional quota.
3. Loan quota.

Permanent quota is allocated mainly on the basis of past performance and may be reallocated to the same ETTPT in the following quota period.

Provisional quota, which was first introduced in 1990, is similar to the free quota offered in Hong Kong. Provisional quota is allocated only for the current quota period—there is a lengthy set of rules determining when provisional quota may be allocated, to whom, and for how long. In summary, an ETTPT that receives provisional quota is required to use it within four months, or else the quota will be canceled and deducted from the firm's next permanent allocation and the firm will be barred from applying for more provisional quota in that category for the rest of that quota period.

The swing, carry–over, and carry–forward provisions found in most MFA exporting countries are also available in Indonesia. A permanent ETTPT may make use of the carry-forward option to borrow quota from its allocation for the following year, as long as it has sufficient permanent quota to pay it back. Such quota is termed loan quota. If the ETTPT does not use all of its borrowed quota, its next permanent allocation will be reduced by the unused amount.

IV. Initial Quota Allocation

The first time a new category comes under quota, the licenses are divided between exporters with past performance and new exporters, with the former receiving the largest share of the quota although special preference is given to exporters from economically weak groups[6] and to cooperatives. Prior to 1988, the allocation rules also favored export–only producers and exporters achieving high sales values. The division of quota among the various groups during different years is shown in Table A3.1: there appears to have been an ongoing

---

6. These are defined to be companies with capital of not over Rp 100 million, of which at least 50 percent is owned by members of an indigenous group *(pribumi)*; in addition, the majority of the board of directors of the company have to be *pribumi*.

political tug–of–war between the groups, especially between the exporters with past experience and the economically weak groups and cooperatives.[7]

V. Subsequent Quota Allocations

In subsequent quota periods, licenses are basically allocated such that exporters receive 100 percent of their previous year's utilization. Prior to 1988, some attempt was made to commit quota recipients to target rates of growth in their

TABLE A3.1. Indonesia: Distribution of First–Time Quotas Among Firms

Date Regulation Went into Effect	Exporters with Past Performance	New Exporters	Economically Weak Groups and Cooperatives	Export–only Producers
January 1984	90 percent	10 percent (5 percent equally[a])	(2.5 percent additional[a])	(2.5 percent additional[a])
January 1988	80 percent	15 percent	5 percent	
July 1988	80 percent	10 percent	10 percent	
September 1990[b]	70 percent	12.5 percent	17.5 percent	
July 1991[b]	94 percent		6 percent	

[a]Of the 10 percent allocated to newcomers, 5 percent is distributed equally among all newcomers, with an additional 2.5 percent to producers from economically weak or cooperative groups, and an additional 2.5 percent to producers whose production is only intended for export.
[b]Allocation in the second quota period. The initial quota allocation is provisional only. All exporters with valid contracts with importers are invited to a consultation on the allocation of the quota. Any remaining quota is proportionately allocated to firms that have exported the product in the twelve months prior to the date of the call.

non–quota exports, although it is not clear if these conditions were ever enforced. In 1988, the allocation criteria were expanded to include not just the firms' quota and non–quota export performance in the previous period, but also their success in exporting higher priced items; however, the relative weights of the various criteria were not specified. In 1991, a new regulation was introduced whereby 6 percent of the permanent quota allocation was to be set aside for exporters from economically weak groups and cooperatives.

Any excess quota, such as that originating from the annual quota growth rate, penalties and returned quotas, is allocated as permanent quota among new exporters, economically weak groups and cooperatives, and exporters who

---

7. For example, the May 1986 issue of *Textile Asia* p. 116 reports on a complaint by KPB, a knitwear cooperative of 87 small producers, that it had applied unsuccessfully for quota three times while some brand new firms with no experience of exports and very little production had already obtained some.

produced only for export. Table A3.2 shows the percentages that each group received during different years.

One frequent criticism of the quota allocation process in Indonesia is that it is inordinately slow. According to Hill 1992, p.72, "[quotas generally are not allocated until after the commencement of the quota year ... in some cases the delay can be as much as three to four months. Without a quota allocation, exporters often miss out on lucrative contracts at the beginning of the year, when much business is transacted." In 1988, the authorities tried to alleviate this problem by allowing permanent ETTPTs to use temporary quota up to 40 percent of their previous period's export realization pending their official allocation. This amount was later increased to 75 percent, and 100 percent by 1990.

It is clear that the authorities are also aiming for fuller utilization of quotas by introducing increasingly strict penalties for non–utilization. Before 1988, exporters that did not use their entire allocation by the end of the quota period had their quota for the following period reduced by the unused amount, unless they transferred or returned it. After January 1988, the penalty was doubled.

TABLE A3.2. Indonesia: Distribution of Growth–Rate Quotas Among Firms

Date Regulation went into Effect	New exporters	Economically Weak Groups and Cooperatives	Export–only
January 1984	50 percent	25 percent	25 percent
January 1988	50 percent	50 percent	
September 1990	40 percent	60 percent	

In 1990, timing restrictions were also introduced, possibly in an attempt to smooth the volume of exports over the quota period. A permanent quota recipient is now required to realize 30 percent of his quota by the first six months of the quota period, and 60 percent by the first nine months. If he does not meet these conditions, the balance (i.e. the difference between the percentage required and the percentage used) will be canceled and his next allocation will be reduced by 50 percent of the canceled amount.

VI. Quota Transfers

Before 1987, an exporter could transfer all or part of his permanent quota to another exporter only with approval from the Ministry of Trade. In July 1987, a Textile Quota Exchange (TQE) was established in the Indonesian Commodity Exchange, whereby unused quotas could be transferred through an auction system. The workings of the TQE are described further in Chapter Twelve.

Unlike the Hong Kong system where both permanent and temporary transfers are allowed, all transfers in the Indonesian system carry a penalty for the transferor and a reward for the transferee.[8] As with all the other aspects of the Indonesian quota allocation system, this penalty/reward scheme for quota transfers has seen many changes over the years. The regulations are summarized in Appendix Tables A3.3 and A3.4. These regulations, of course, only cover legal transfers. According to Pangestu 1987, there is also an illegal quota market called the *Bursa Pasar Pagi*, where it is estimated that 50 percent of all quota transfers were undertaken in 1987. Quotas transferred in this illegal market generally count fully toward the transferor's performance as long as the transfer is not recorded, of course.[9]

VII. Climate of Uncertainty

The constantly changing requirements with regard to non–quota exports are an example of how the Indonesian quota allocation system creates a great deal of uncertainty for the exporters. Between 1984 and 1987, exporters were required to increase their non–quota export value at very specific rates according to their export performance in non–quota items relative to quota items. However, Pangestu 1987, p. 15 notes that "in practice this requirement was never enforced according to regulations."

In 1988, the requirements were over–simplified to such a degree that no mention was made as to how the firms' non–quota export performance would be weighted relative to other criteria for the allocation of quota. Presumably, the decision was left to the discretion of the allocating official, and this created further uncertainty for the exporters.

In 1990, the non–quota export requirement was set at an f.o.b. value of US$200,000 per quota period and not lower than the ETTPT's non–quota export the previous quota period, creating a disincentive for the ETTPT to export more than US$200,000 worth of non–quota goods. Then, in March 1991, the "not lower than the ETTPT's non–quota export the previous quota period" clause was removed and permanent ETTPT of weak economic groups and of cooperatives were only required to export f.o.b. US$100,000 worth of non–quota goods.

Vacillation such as that regarding non–quota exports is also apparent in the policy toward returning quotas. Between 1984 and 1987, exporters were allowed to return all or part of their quota to the Director of Export of Industrial

---

8. Provisional quota may not be transferred.

9. Hill 1992, p. 72 also mentions that quotas for profitable items such as jeans are sold "generally illegally" as "a sale through the largely moribund bourse entails a cut in the quota holder's entitlement the following year..." The 1988 regulations state that exporters who transfer quota outside of the TQE would have their quota allocations reduced the following year by the transferred amount, but that, of course, only applied if they were caught and punished.

TABLE A3.3. Indonesia: Regulations Concerning Quota Transfer

Date Regulation Went into Effect	If Transfer Conducted in:	Transferor's Penalty / Transferee's Reward in Following Period's Allocation:
January 1984	1st 4 months	25 percent of transferred amount
	2nd 4 months	50 percent of transferred amount
	3rd 4 months	75 percent of transferred amount
January 1988		20 percent of transferred amount
September 1990		100 percent of transferred amount

TABLE A3.4. Indonesia: Penalties for Non–Utilization of Transferred Quota

Date Regulation Went into Effect	Transferee's Penalty in Following Period's Allocation:
January 1984	100 percent of unused amount
January 1988	200 percent of unused amount
September 1990	100 percent of unused amount

and Mining Products, although the returned amount would be deducted from their next quota allocation. In 1988, returns were not allowed once the exporter had made a written acceptance of their quota allocation. In 1990, the policy was changed so that returns were allowed: firms could return their quota without penalty within the first six months, but returns made after that time involved a reduction in their following period's allocation. In 1991, returns were once again disallowed.

There were also multiple changes in other regulations. Although the rule changes are published in the *Indonesian State Gazette*, exporters not located in Jakarta or on Java are at a disadvantage when it comes to anticipating and keeping track of the changes. In particular, smaller firms suffer due to the relatively costly need to constantly monitor and make allowances for the changes. Also, the regulation changes create a high degree of uncertainty that makes it difficult for firms to plan ahead.

VIII. Restrictions on Non–Producing Exporters

According to Hill 1992, p. 73, it is suspected that "there are many 'bogus' quota holders who possess little, if any, productive capacity and operate simply by 'subcontracting' quotas while exporting under their own name." Several attempts have been made to restrict the number of non–producing quota holders and the amount of quota for which they were eligible.

For example, the 1988 regulations stipulated that applicants for non–producing ETTPT licenses had to attach at least three years' worth of marketing cooperation contracts with producers of textiles and textile products instead of just one contract. After 1990, their ETTPT applications and marketing cooperation contracts had also to be validated by the head of the local trade office or other designated authorities.

Also, after 1990, the first–time quota was distributed only to new exporters and permanent ETTPTs from economically weak groups and cooperatives. The non–quota requirements for becoming a permanent ETTPT may have deterred some of the potential bogus quota holders, though they could still have set up dummy organizations.

Limits were also placed on who could receive growth rate quota, specifically barring ETTPTs that had transferred quota for the category concerned in the current or previous quota period. However, though this regulation would cut down on the number of non–producing exporters who transferred their quotas legally, through the Textile Quota Exchange, of course, those who subcontracted their quotas while keeping their names on the papers were still eligible for the quota.

IX. Paperwork

As the regulations became more complex, the required paperwork also grew. As from September 1990, in order to get a Textile and Textile Products Export Certificate, an ETTPT would have to submit:

1. A copy of the Goods Export Notification giving loading approval by the customs authorities.
2. A copy of the on–board original Bill of Lading or Airway Bill validated by the issuing transport company.
3. The letter of credit or sales contract and invoice.
4. A statement from the producer describing the goods and their value.
5. A Notification of Textile and Textile Products form with the Goods Export Notification number and the date approved by a foreign exchange bank.
6. A receipt of payment for the cost of monitoring the export of quota Textile and Textile products.

In March 1991, yet another layer of paperwork was added, requiring that ETTPTs intending to hand in the forms after the date of shipment submit a written statement of their readiness to do so within 21 days.

Despite the increases in paperwork, Hill 1998, p. 77 reports that "the problem of over–shipment due to poor record–keeping appears to be becoming more—not less—serious over time. In 1990, for example, embargoes were imposed on Indonesian exports by both Canada and the United States in response to alleged over–shipment."

With each additional form, the potential for corruption also increased. Pangestu 1987, p. 10 notes that in 1987, "all the documents relating to the export of quota goods [were] approved at the [local Department of Trade office]. The signature of one official at the [Department of Trade was] registered at the respective customs office in the importing country and only that signature [was] accepted." Clearly, that official had quite a bit of power.

As well, facilitating costs are involved along the entire process of obtaining the quota allocation, acquiring the right signatures, and having the forms processed. Such costs are a drain for smaller companies in particular. For example, Pangestu 1987, p. 13 mentions that "one company, which had sales of US$5.5 million estimated his facilitating costs to be US$300,000 or 5 percent of sales."

Quota Implementation in India

I. Introduction

MFA quotas in India are administered by the Apparel Export Promotion Council (AEPC), a quasi–governmental body under the Ministry of Commerce, managed by elected representatives of registered apparel exporters.[1] The system—like the one in Indonesia—is fraught with rules and regulations which are highly complex and frequently changing. A detailed exposition of the intricacies of the system can be found in Khanna 1991. The following discussion, which draws heavily on Khanna 1991, focuses only on the main elements of the system.

Three key features in India's quota allocation system are:

1. Floor prices.
2. Open and closed quota allocations.
3. Sub–categorization.

II. Floor Prices

Floor prices are specified for each MFA textile/apparel category to be exported to a given destination. These floor prices are set annually by the AEPC on the basis of current labor and materials costs, and represent the minimum cost of production of a particular textile/apparel category, allowing for a normal rate of return. Exports below these floor prices are not permitted. The rationale for imposing floor prices appears to be: to increase foreign exchange export earnings by discouraging price undercutting; to reduce incentives to under–invoice exports; and to induce higher unit value exports, thus contributing to quality upgrading which would both improve the image of Indian exports and raise foreign exchange.

According to Khanna 1991, p. 53, "Indian authorities are raising floor prices from year to year. A rough method used to fix floor prices in the current year is the 'mean' price of all exports in a given country/category during the past year. The floor price is generally on the lower side of this mean price."

III. Closed Quotas and Open Quotas

Under the Indian system, quotas are subdivided into open and closed sections. The open quotas are allocated on a first–come–first–served basis, hence they are

---

1. Quotas for woolen and certain acrylic garments are administered by the Wool and Woolens Export Promotion Council.

similar to the free quotas in Hong Kong and provisional quotas in Indonesia; however, notwithstanding the similar terminology, they are very different from the open quotas in Korea. The closed quotas are allocated according to different criteria, reflected in the following subdivisions:

1. Past performance entitlement (PPE): allocated to firms on the basis of their past export performance in the country/category concerned.
2. Manufacturer–exporters entitlement (MEE): allocated to manufacturers based on their production capacities.
3. Non–quota exporters entitlement (NQE): allocated to firms based on their export performance to non–quota countries and export performance in non–quota items to quota countries.
4. Public sector entitlement (PSE): allocated to central and state government corporations.

The following subsections describe, in further detail, how quotas are allocated under the various systems.

A. Allocation of closed quotas

1. Past Performance Entitlement (PPE) System

PPEs for a particular category/destination are allocated to firms which have previously exported in that category/destination. Prior to 1991, firms that had exported at any time within the previous two and a half years—the base period—were eligible for PPEs. Since the number of applicants usually exceeded the available PPE quota, allocations were made on a pro rata basis, with each applicant receiving a share equal to the ratio of its volume of exports in the base period (in the particular category/destination) to the total volume of exports of all applicants:

$$Allocation \ of \ firm \ i \ = \left(\frac{X_i}{\sum_i X_i} \right) V$$

where:

X_i = quantity shipped by firm i
V = quota level.

According to Kumar and Khanna 1990, PPEs are freely transferable and an active secondary market exists in which these quotas are bought and sold. There is little mention of penalties for non–utilization of allotted PPEs; indications are that such penalties are not severe, unlike the case in Korea, for example.

The PPE allocation rules changed in 1991. The base period now excludes the immediately preceding year. For example, to be eligible for a PPE in 1991, a firm must have exported in that category/destination during 1988 and/or 1989. Furthermore, PPE allocations are now proportional to the firms' realized value of exports, subject to a ceiling equal to the exporter's value realization divided by the average value realization of all applicants:

$$Allocation \ of \ firm \ i \ = \ min\left[\left(\frac{P_i X_i}{\sum_i P_i X_i} \right) V, \ \left(\frac{P_i X_i}{\sum_i P_i X_i} \right) \sum X_i \right]$$

where:

P_i = *price of firm i's exports.*

Recent official documentation of the quota allocation system indicates that PPEs, once allocated, may be transferred any time during the year up to September 30. However, only permanent transfers are allowed. Shipments against transferred quota will be counted towards the export performance of the transferee; re–transfers are not permitted. Rules have also been instituted to encourage full utilization of PPEs. A PPE recipient must utilize at least 50 percent of his allotment between January 1 and May 31 (the first period), and the balance between June 1 and September 30 (the second period).[2] Any unutilized quota at the end of each period is automatically surrendered to the authorities to be distributed as open quota.

2. Manufacturer–exporters Entitlement (MEE) System

According to Majmudar 1990, manufacturer–exporters are trading firms which receive export orders, organize production for export, and monitor the quality of the exports. These firms are required to conform to labor and factory laws, and form part of the organized garment sector.

Approximately 10–20 percent of the total quota is allocated to manufacturer–exporters deemed eligible by the Textile Commissioner on the basis of their past performance and production capacity. The most recent official documentation of the quota allocation policy (AEPC, 1992) states that MEEs are not transferable, and are subject to the same utilization rules as PPEs. The actual production of apparel for export is mostly sub–contracted to numerous fabricators who hire seasonal labor for this purpose. These fabricators represent the decentralized garment sector, and are not eligible for MEEs.

---

2. Under certain conditions, the second period may be extended up to December 31.

3. Non–quota Exporters Entitlement (NQE) System

Beginning in 1987, a portion of the total quota for a category/destination has been allocated to firms which exported that category to non–restricted countries (or exported a non–restricted category to that destination) during the base period.

4. Public Sector Entitlement (PSE) System

A special allocation representing 2–5 percent of the total quota for a category/destination is made to central and state government corporations. Prior to 1986, no strict manufacturing requirements were placed on these corporations, and as a result, PSEs were often sold to private sector exporters in the secondary market. Since 1987, however, applicants for PSEs have been required to own manufacturing facilities and to be registered with the AEPC. Moreover, PSEs are now nontransferable.

B. Allocation of Open Quotas

Prior to 1992, a fraction of the total quota for a category/destination was reserved as open quota, to be distributed on a first–come–first–served basis. In addition, any closed quota entitlement that becomes available (e.g., by surrender) is placed in the open quota pool.[3] The rationale for this category is to enable new entrants to the industry or new entrants to the category/destination to obtain free quota allocations. Open quotas, once allocated, must be utilized within 60 days, and may not be transferred.

1. Eligibility

Applicants for open quotas have to present firm contracts backed by valid, operative and irrevocable letters of credit.[4] Prior to 1992, only firms that had been in operation for two to two and a half years were eligible for open quotas. The rationale for this restriction was to limit the proliferation of paper firms, as PPE holders seeking additional quota allocations had the incentive to set up shadow companies to apply for open allocations. Of course, PPE holders could circumvent the restriction, at a cost, by either waiting for the paper firms to become eligible or by acquiring firms which were old enough to meet the requirement; such practices are documented in Khanna 1991, p. 58. The time

---

3. No open segment was set aside in 1992, only quantities that became available from flexibilities or surrenders were used as open quotas and allocated on a first–come–first–served basis.
4. Khanna 1991, p. 56.

limit was relaxed in 1992 when applicants were required only to have registered with the AEPC one week in advance in order to be eligible.

Before 1983, firms holding PPEs were not eligible for open quotas. However, since then, PPE holders have been allowed to apply for open quotas once they have utilized more than 50 percent of their entitlement.

2. Allocation Periods

The open segment is subdivided into three parts and distributed at different points during the year. For example, in 1986 and 1987, 25 percent of the total quota was designated as open and subdivided in the following way:

1. 15 percent was distributed in the first period, between January and April.
2. 7 percent was distributed in the second period, between May and August.
3. The remaining 3 percent was distributed between September and December.[5]

Although the justification for this procedure was to ensure that exports were spread throughout the year, it is clear that subdividing the quota year in this way could lead to quota underutilization in conjunction with a binding constraint. As India exports primarily cotton apparel, the demand for which is highly seasonal, some open quotas could be left unutilized during the winter months even though many applicants could have been unsuccessful (i.e., the quota could have been binding) in early summer, when demand was high.

3. Cut–off Price

In the event that demand for open quota exceeds the availability of such quota on a given day, allocations are made on the basis of the cut–off price: all applicant export prices are arranged in descending order and the cut–off price is determined as the price above which the total quantity demanded by applications exactly equals the availability of open quota on that day. Only applications above the cut–off price receive an allocation; unsuccessful applicants have no choice but to wait for the release of the next period's open quota, or to purchase quota from a PPE holder. Often, open quotas are exhausted on the first day of their release.

4. Superfast Categories

A new FCFS quota distribution system was implemented beginning in 1988. Under this new system, about 15 percent of the FCFS quotas for certain

---

5. For certain items such as knitwear, there were only two periods, with 85 percent of the open quota distributed during the first period and the balance during the second period.

superfast country/categories are allocated by auction, under the so–called Open Tender System. Superfast categories are those for which exports have exceeded 91 percent of the restraint limit for the past three years. According to Khanna 1991, p. 160, "these categories represent quotas which bear the highest levels of quota rents. Auction of quotas is designed to allocate a part of quota rents for objects of public policy. The Government of India is not using this device to generate public revenue, rather it has set up an industry development fund to be used for apparel export promotion objects."

5. Do Open Quotas Really Help New Entrants?

Although the open quota was designed to allow new entrants to acquire quota rights over time, the presence of the cut–off price mechanism actually leads to a built–in bias against such firms: older firms with many orders can easily shut out new entrants by applying for open quota for their highest–priced orders and using their closed quota entitlements to fill their lower–priced orders. In addition, the strict eligibility requirements prior to 1992 also served to penalize genuine new entrants to the export market.

Table A4.1 shows how the total quota is distributed among the open section and the four component closed sections: PPE, MEE, NQE and PSE. The share of closed quota relative to open quota has increased steadily, from 45 percent in 1981 to 75 percent in 1987, finally reaching 100 percent in 1992. This means that it has become almost impossible for new firms entering the industry to obtain a quota free of charge. Khanna 1991, p. 54 attributes this bias against new entrants to the fact that "[t]he AEPC, whose views influence the government's policy formulations, is dominated by old and established exporters" who were seeking to increase their share of the total quota allocation over the years.

IV. Subcategorization

Subcategorization is a running theme throughout all sections of the Indian quota allocation system. For example, the closed segment is divided into four different systems of entitlement, of which three do not allow transfers. Penalties for

TABLE A4.1. India: Percentage Distribution of Total Quota

	1981	1982[a]	1983	1984	1985	1986	1987	1991	1992
Open Quota	55	45	35	35	30	25	25	10	0
Closed Quota	45	50	65	65	70	75	75	90	100
PPE	40	45	50	50	55	65	65	60	60
MEE	0	0	10	10	10	7	7	18	20
NQE	0	0	0	0	0	0	1	10	18
PSE	5	5	5	5	5	3	2	2	2

[a] Figures obtained from Khanna 1991 do not add up to 100 percent.
Sources: Khanna 1991, p. 58; APEC 1992.

non–utilization seem to be minimal, aside from the rule that half of every PPE holder's allocation has to be surrendered to the AEPC if it is not utilized by the end of May.[6] This effectively reduces the total amount of quota available for use. The open allocations are also subcategorized—albeit in a different way—by having portions available at different times over the year. As mentioned earlier, subdividing the quota year in this way can easily result in under-utilization despite a binding quota.

Furthermore, even though the MFA categories for export to the United States are quite detailed (by fabric and garment type), the Indian authorities further split them into subcategories (e.g., knitted, handloomed and mill–made/powerloomed garments), with the entitlements calculated separately. For example, special quantities are reserved for garments made of 100 percent cotton handloom fabrics, to be allocated on the open system as well as to the public sector (PSE). Portions of the total quota are also set aside for woolen and acrylic garments and knitwear, even when the United States imposes no specific limits for these categories—one clause in the *Garment Export Entitlement Policy 1991–1993* p. 22 states that: "The Textile Commissioner may reserve quantities for knitwear, children's wear, woolen garments or any other segment and may announce separate floor prices for such quantities..."

---

6. For example, bank guarantees and earnest money deposits are not required for the allocation of PPEs, MEEs, PSEs and NQEs; they are only required for the purpose of extending the validity of these entitlements. Of course, firms which transfer out a portion of their PPEs should receive a reduced allocation in the following year since the transferred quota counts towards the export performance of the transferee; however, the secondary black market in quota licenses is active and temporary transfers are commonplace.

Quota Implementation in Pakistan[1]

I. Introduction

The management of MFA quotas in Pakistan is the responsibility of the Export Promotion Bureau (EPB), which designs its rules ostensibly to meet the following objectives:

1. The fulfillment of Pakistan's obligation under bilateral textile agreements with importing countries.
2. Maximization of foreign exchange earnings through improvement in quality.
3. Encouragement of value addition.
4. Promotion of ethical business practices.
5. Prevention of misuse of quota allocations.[2]

However, control over the actual allocation of the quotas has swung between the EPB and the numerous trade associations involved in textile and apparel manufacture and export. In 1983, the EPB assumed sole responsibility for the MFA quota administration. Prior to that, quota allocation had been the domain of certain trade associations, namely the All Pakistan Textile Mills Association, the Towel Manufacturers' Association, and the Hosiery Manufacturers' Association, each of which was responsible for handling a few categories, with the remaining work carried out by the EPB.

II. Management by the EPB

The basic guidelines set out by the EPB in 1983 stipulated that 90 percent of the total quota in each category was to be allocated on the basis of the previous year's performance, with the remaining 10 percent of the quota reserved for newcomers, defined according to four criteria:

1. New firms established in 1982 and later.
2. Registered export houses.
3. Exporters of the same item to non–quota countries.
4. Exporters having contracts with non–exporting manufacturers.

However, the actual implementation of the MFA quotas by the EPB became the source of much dissatisfaction. For example, established exporters complained that they did not receive allocations amounting to 100 percent of their past performance. In fact, the allocation of the 10 percent newcomers' quota was made at their expense so that their performance quotas were reduced

---

1. Written with Kishwar Ahmed and Kerstin Berglöf.
2. Ministry of Commerce 1987, p. 1.

by 10–15 percent yearly. Moreover, it was frequently alleged that the newcomers' quotas were never actually allocated on the basis announced by the EPB, which instead preferred to use its discretion. According to one disgruntled trader: "Every exporter came with a contract with a new manufacturer asking for quota, and EPB officials could accept or reject the application at their own convenience" in return for political favors.[3] Available accounts of the system at that time suggest that the quotas were freely transferable. Penalties for infractions of the rules were never clearly stated, as much was left to official discretion.

III. Management by the Trade Associations

In 1985, in response to mounting criticism by the trade associations (who felt that their job had been usurped by the EPB) and an imminent lawsuit from an exporter who had been denied quota, the Ministry of Commerce decided to withdraw the administration of textile quotas from the EPB and return it to the trade associations. Since 1986, therefore, the quota management policy has been administered by approximately sixteen textile associations,[4] each responsible for a set of MFA categories. Only associations whose members had at least 15 percent export performance in a particular category in the previous year are qualified to manage quotas in that category, and it is possible for any given MFA category to come under the purview of more than one association.

At the beginning of the year, the EPB gives the bulk of the quotas for each MFA category[5] to the relevant export associations. It is then up to the associations to distribute the quotas among their members. Usually the allocation criterion is the export performance of the firm in the relevant category/destination in the preceding twelve months. Recently, however, the EPB, in an effort to encourage the export of higher value products and the inflow of foreign exchange, has included in its judgment of performance a value factor, (i.e., the amount of foreign exchange earned per unit). The basis for entitlement for the years 1988–1991 is shown in Table A5.1 Quotas are freely transferable, but the transfers are always permanent.

Any growth in the quota levels is generally earmarked for newcomers and economically weak areas (e.g., Baluchistan and the Federally Administered Tribal Areas). According to the most recent administrative notification, the growth rate in quotas is allocated in the following manner: 80 percent of the

---

3. *Textile Asia,* April 1985, p. 115.

4. Ministry of Commerce 1987 lists the sixteen associations and the MFA categories they manage.

5. The general pattern of allocation (i.e., 90 percent on a performance basis, and 10 percent for newcomers) remained unchanged in 1986 and 1987. However, in 1988, the system was amended so that the EPB now allocates to each association all the quota that it received in the preceding year for the categories for which the association is responsible, adjusted for any changes due to growth.

growth amount is set aside for new manufacturing units, and the remaining 20 percent is allocated to those exporters realizing the highest net foreign exchange earnings for non–quota items for each category. In both cases, allocation to eligible firms is made through open auction to the highest bidder, and these quota licenses are not transferable. The EPB is responsible for ensuring that quota allocated under this arrangement does not result in the concentration of quota into a few hands.

Security deposits, calculated as a percentage of the average free on board (f.o.b.) price of the relevant category in the preceding year, are required from both performance holders and newcomers. The reason for these security deposits seems to be to encourage firms to use up their quota as early in the year as possible, since the rate increases every three months. The Pakistani government is always in need of foreign exchange and encourages the speedy transfer of funds into the country. In fact, exporters bringing in the most foreign exchange (in U.S. dollars per unit) are eligible to receive a reward of an extra

TABLE A5.1. Pakistan: Distribution of Performance Quota

Year	On a Value Basis:	On a Quantity Basis:
1988	25 percent	75 percent
1989	35 percent	65 percent
1990	50 percent	50 percent
1991	60 percent	40 percent

Source: Ministry of Commerce 1987.

5 percent allocation of quota in the following year over and above their normal entitlement.

As is the case with most MFA exporting countries, there is a certain amount of flexibility in the MFA restraint limits, in the form of the swing and carry–over/carry–forward provisions. Over–shipments from Pakistan are usually denied entry into the United States. If they are permitted to enter, they are charged to the applicable limit in the following year. In addition, MFA categories for which the quota utilization is far below the quota ceiling may have some of their quota reallocated to other classes of exporters at the discretion of the EPB.

IV. Mismanagement and Under-utilization

As quota administrators, the trade associations do not seem to have fared much better than the EPB. Accounts of infighting between their various factions and the distribution of lucrative quotas by their leaders have left a bad general impression.[6] Moreover, there have been widespread reports of cheating: when large quantities of quotas remained unutilized at the end of each year, certain exporters presented fake shipping documents to the EPB, thus boosting their performance so that they could claim larger quotas in the following year. Also, the ruling that newcomers submit a valid letter of credit with their quota application is easily surmounted as established exporters have no difficulty setting up dummy corporations with letters of credit obtained from their overseas offices. In their defense, the association leaders claim that the government has been inefficient in monitoring the quota utilization and slow to establish the rules under which the quota is to be distributed to them. These problems were so severe in 1987 that a substantial quantity of quota rights were not released until the middle of October. The resulting confusion left the quota system in such disarray that quotas were finally distributed on December 31, for immediate shipment! The problems extended into the following year, when some 50 percent of the quota in several categories remained unutilized by early November.

---

6. *Textile Asia*, April 1987, p. 120.

Quota Implementation in Bangladesh[1]

I. Introduction

Bangladesh first exported apparel in any considerable quantity in 1977. In 1983, there were 93 factories producing garments for export. By 1984, this number had soared to an astounding 455. Most of these new firms produced garments that were easy to make, such as cotton shirts. The major destination for the exports was the United States. By December 1984, made–in–Bangladesh cotton shirts and jackets represented 2–3 percent of U.S. imports. The extreme concentration of exports in a few items triggered calls to MFA negotiations, and in early 1985, formal quota restraints were imposed by the United States on twelve categories of Bangladesh–made apparel.[2] In the years immediately following the imposition of quotas, the growth of establishments slowed significantly, although signs of renewed growth have been seen in the last several years.

II. Background

By most accounts, the authorities had not foreseen the imposition of quotas in 1985. After the initial MFA agreement with the United States was signed, fully four months passed before a quota allocation system was drawn up. The initial set of rules divided quotas into three parts: performance quota, allocated to manufacturers/exporters with past performance in that category; free quota, distributed to firms with no export performance before the start of the quota year; and reserved quota, set aside for clothing exports by state trading organizations.

New rules introduced in 1989 called for 10 percent of the total available quota to be set aside for firms using 100 percent domestic fabrics in their apparel production[3] and 2 percent of the free quota to be reserved for allocation to the Trading Corporation of Bangladesh. Furthermore, in order to ensure maximum quota utilization, firms were required to have exported 50 percent of their allotted quota by the end of the fifth month of the quota year, and 75 percent by the end of the seventh month, with all shipments to have been completed by the tenth month.

---

1. Written with Kerstin Berglöf.
2. In 1987, the number of restricted categories rose to eighteen.
3. At least half the domestic fabrics quota was to go to firms with past performance, the remainder to new users of domestic fabrics. At the same time, domestic fabric users would be entitled to import fabrics up to 20 percent of their performance in the previous year.

Despite the institution of these fairly elaborate regulations, the conventional practice in the first five years of MFA restrictions appears to have been for quotas to be allocated on a simple first–come–first–served basis, with no official records of individual quota holdings of garment exporters.[4]

III. Quota Allocation Rules

In 1991, a revised set of rules was delivered, the details of which are described below:

The quota year for Bangladesh MFA exports runs from February 1 to January 31. An Allocation Committee, comprising representatives of the Ministries or Divisions dealing with commerce or textiles and the Export Promotion Bureau, holds the responsibility for allocating quota among the exporting firms.

To avoid under–fulfillment of the quota, the actual quota made available for allocation is the quota negotiated with the United States plus an additional 20 percent, to allow for any possible slack such as over–shipment (subtracted) or carry–over (added). All exports must be completed before the end of the quota year.

Quotas are divided into three groups:

1. Performance quota—allocated to firms based on their previous export performance in that category.
2. Free quota—allocated to firms with no previous export performance.
3. Local fabrics quota—reserved for firms which make use of domestically produced textiles.

Different allocation rules apply for each of these groups.

Performance quota represents the lion's share of the total allocation. Usually, over 80 percent of the total available quota is distributed to firms which exported the relevant category of clothing or textiles in the previous year. The general rule states that an exporter's actual sales in the previous quota year convert directly into the number of quota licenses to be received for the following year.[5] As long as a manufacturer exports 95 percent or more of his quota holding, he is considered to have performed adequately, and stands to receive quota for the following year based on a performance of 100 percent. In order to enable exporters to maintain a smooth flow of shipments, advance allocations may be made of up to 75 percent of their performance quotas. The

---

4. This information was obtained during an interview with a representative of the Bangladesh Garment Manufacturers and Exporters Association (BGMEA) in June 1992.

5. There is no particular reason for firms to return unused licenses to the authorities as they are not rewarded for early surrender of these licenses (as they are in Hong Kong), nor are they penalized for late surrender (as in Korea).

free quota is allocated equally to eligible manufacturers that have no export performance in the previous quota year. A manufacturer may apply for free quota in as many as eight MFA categories in one quota year. However, if he fails to utilize the free quota by the end of the quota year, he will be barred from applying for free quota in the following year. A manufacturer or exporter with performance quota may apply for free quota upon surrendering his claim for performance quota. His share of performance quota would then be automatically transferred to the available free quota.[6] This provision allows existing exporters to choose to be treated like new entrants. Of the free quota, 5 percent is reserved for the Trading Corporation of Bangladesh.

The local fabrics quota, which constitutes 10 percent of the total available quota, is an explicit attempt to encourage the use of domestically–produced fabrics. At present, almost all of the apparel exporters meet the demands for fabrics from abroad—Draper 1992 estimates the costs for intermediate inputs to be as high as 74 percent of the total export earnings. An application for local fabrics quota must be accompanied by a letter of credit from the fabric supplier. At least 40 percent of this quota is allocated to manufacturers with past performance in the use of local fabrics. The remaining 60 percent is distributed equally among new users of local fabrics.

IV. Initial Allocation

When a product category is first brought under restraint, past performance is not used as the leading criterion. Instead, the new quotas are first distributed on a proportional basis to exporters with distress cargo, (i.e., apparel products already manufactured and awaiting shipment).[7] Any remaining quota after the release of distress cargo is then allocated as performance quota (on a pro rata basis to firms with export performance in the twelve months preceding the imposition of the quota), free quota, and domestic fabrics quota. In subsequent years of the quota's existence, increasing emphasis is placed on past performance, at the expense of free quota, as outlined in Table A6.1.

V. Eligibility and Documentation

According to the 1991 quota allocation rules, a manufacturer becomes eligible to apply for quota by registering with the Export Promotion Bureau and paying a fee of 1000 taka (approximately US$36). All exporters must bemanufacturers. Non–manufacturers are not eligible for quota. The registration must be renewed each year at a fee of 500 taka.

---

6. It is conceivable, for example, during the course of the quota year, for an exporter to be in receipt of an order larger than the remainder of his performance quota holding. In this event, if the free quota amount were large enough, he could opt to apply for free quota.

7. Exports of distressed cargo under this provision are not, however, reckoned as past performance for the following year.

Bureaucratic procedures involved in the next step—applying for quota—are more onerous, as the number of required accompanying documents is quite staggering, including, among others:[8]

1. manufacturer registration certificate,
2. export registration certificate,
3. warehouse license,
4. tax records, and
5. certificate of membership in the Bangladesh Garment Manufacturers and Exporters Association (BGMEA).

TABLE A6.1. Bangladesh: Distribution of Total Available Quota

	Length of Time for Which Quota Is in Existence:				
	1 year	2 years	3 years	4 years	5 years[a]
Past	80	95	100	100	105
Local Fabrics Quota	10	10	10	10	10
Free Quota	30	15	10	10	5
Total	120	120	120	120	120

[a] The Year 5 distribution applies for the sixth and subsequent years.

Source: Government of the People's Republic of Bangladesh, Ministry of Commerce 1991.

In a developing country like Bangladesh, such procedures may well work in favor of larger agents who may be in a better position to meet the fixed cost elements introduced by this red tape, hence it would not be surprising to find a resulting increased concentration in license holding as well as directly unproductive rent–seeking activities.

VI. Transferability

Under normal circumstances, a manufacturer–exporter is allowed to transfer part of his quota holdings to other firms. However, allocations under the local fabrics quota are not transferable.[9] The BGMEA estimates that in recent years, about 10 percent of quotas, mostly free quotas, have been traded.[10] All transfers of quotas are considered permanent transfers, which means that the performance is credited to the transferee.

---

8. According to a 1987 report, "as many as 57 formalities have to be completed by exporters after receipt of an order." *Textile Asia*, April 1987, p.127.

9. Allocations made in the year a new product category is first brought under restraint are also not transferable.

10. Information conveyed by facsimile on September 24, 1992.

References

Anderson, J. E. 1987. "Quotas as Options: Optimality and Quota License Pricing under Uncertainty." *Journal of International Economics* 23: 21–39.

Apparel Export Promotion Council. 1992. *Garment Export Entitlement Policy (1991–1993).* New Delhi: AEPC.

Armington, P. 1969. "A Theory of Demand for Products Distinguished by Place of Production," *IMF Staff Papers* 61:159–178.

Bannister, G. J. and P. Low. 1992. "Textiles and Apparel in NAFTA: A Case of Constrained Liberalization." World Bank Working Paper No. 994. Washington, D.C.

———. 1994. "Rent Sharing in the Multi-fibre Arrangement: The Case of Mexico," *Weltwirtscchaftliches Archiv* 130: 800–827.

Bhagwati, J. 1965. "On the Equivalence of Tariffs and Quotas," in R.E. Baldwin, et al. *Trade, Growth and the Balance of Payments.* Chicago: Rand McNally & Co.

Biro, Pusat Statistik. 1988. *Statistik Indonesia 1987.* Jakarta, Indonesia.

Brajard, N. 1991. "A Study of Garments Industry in Bangladesh—Its Role as a Factor of Economic Development." Manuscript. Dhaka: Banque Indosuez.

Choi, Y. P., H. S. Chung and N. Marian. 1985. *The Multi Fibre Arrangement in Theory and Practice.* London: Frances Pinter.

Corden, W. M. 1971. *The Theory of Protection.* Oxford: Clarendon Press.

Dasgupta, P. S. and G. M. Heal. 1979. *Economic Theory and Exhaustible Resources.* Cambridge, England: Cambridge University Press.

Draper, C. 1992. *Bangladesh Clothing Industry.* Chapter VI: Domestic and Export Markets. Manuscript.

Eldor, R. and A. J. Marcus. 1988. "Quotas as Options: Valuation and Equilibrium Implications." *Journal of International Economics* 24: 255–274.

Faini, R., J. de Melo and W. Takacs. 1992. "A Primer on the MFA Maze." Brussels: European Centre for Advanced Research in Economics. Xerox.

Fomby, T. B., R. C. Hill and S. R. Johnson. 1984. *Advanced Econometric Methods.* New York: Springer-Verlag.

GATT. 1974. *Arrangement Regarding International Trade in Textiles.* Geneva: GATT.

Goto, J. 1989. "The Multi-Fibre Arrangement and its Effects on Developing Countries," *The World Bank Research Observer* 4:203–227.

Government of the People's Republic of Bangladesh, Ministry of Commerce. 1991. *Notification: The Textile Trade and Quota Administration Rules.* Dhaka. March 12.

Hamilton, C. 1984. "ASEAN Systems for Allocation of Export Licenses under VERs" in C. Findlay and R. Garnaut (eds.) 1986. *The Political Economy of Manufacturing Protection: Experiences of ASEAN and Australia.* Sydney: Allen and Unwin.

———. 1986. "An Assessment of Voluntary Restraints on Hong Kong Exports to Europe and the USA," *Economica* 53:339–350.

———. 1986a. "ASEAN Systems for Allocation of Export Licenses under VERs," in C. Findlay and R. Garnaut, eds. *The Political Economy of Manufacturing Protection: Experiences of ASEAN and Australia.* Sydney: Allen and Unwin.

———. 1988. "Restrictiveness and International Transmission of the `New' Protectionism," in R. Baldwin, C. Hamilton and A. Sapir, eds. *Issues in US-EC Trade Relations.* Chicago: University of Chicago Press.

————, ed. 1990. *Textiles Trade and the Developing Countries*. Washington, D.C.: The World Bank.

Hamilton, C. and C. Kim. 1990. "Republic of Korea: Rapid Growth in spite of Protectionism Abroad," in C. Hamilton, ed. *Textiles Trade and the Developing Countries*. Washington, D.C.: The World Bank.

Hill, H. 1992. *Indonesia's Textile and Garment Industries: Developments in an Asian Perspective*. ISEAS Occasional Paper No. 87, Institute of Southeast Asian Studies. Singapore.

Hirschleifer, J. And J. G. Riley. 1992. *The Analytics of Uncertainty and Information*. Cambridge Surveys of Economic Literature. Cambridge University Press.

Hong Kong Census and Statistics Department. Various years. *Hong Kong Monthly Digest of Statistics*. Hong Kong: Government Printer.

————. 1990. *Hong Kong Annual Digest of Statistics 1989*. Hong Kong.

Hong Kong Trade Department. 1987. *Textiles Export Control System*. Hong Kong: Government Printer.

Hotelling, H. 1931. "The Economics of Exhaustible Resources." *Journal of Political Economy* 39: 137–175.

Johnston, J. 1985. *Econometric Methods*, New York: McGraw-Hill Book Company.

Keesing, D. B. and M. Wolf. 1980. *Textile Quotas against Developing Countries*. London: Trade Policy Research Centre, Thames Essay No. 23.

Khanna, S. R. 1991. *International Trade in Textiles: MFA Quotas and a Developing Exporting Country*. New Delhi: Sage Publications.

Kim, C. 1986. "Effects of Neo-Protectionism on Korean Exports." Seoul: Korean Institute for Economics and Technology. Xerox.

Krishna, K. 1987. "Tariffs and Quotas with Endogenous Quality," *Journal of International Economics* 23:97-122.

————. 1990. "The Case of the Vanishing Revenues: Auction Quotas with Monopoly." *American Economic Review* 80: 828–836.

————. 1991. "Making Altruism Pay in Quota Auctions," in E. Helpman and A. Razin, et al. *International Trade and Trade Policy*. Cambridge: MIT Press.

————. 1992. "Auction Quotas with Imperfect Competition," in Robert S. McNamara Fellowship Program, Tenth Anniversary Publication, 1982–1992. Economic Development Institute of the World Bank: 151–174.

————. 1993. "Theoretical Implications of Imperfect Competition on Quota License Prices and Auctions." *The World Bank Economic Review* 7: 113–136.

Krishna, K., R. Erzan and L. H. Tan. 1994. "Rent Sharing in the Multi-Fibre Arrangement: Theory and Evidence from U.S. Apparel Imports from Hong Kong." *Review of International Economics* 2: 62–73.

Krishna, K. and L. H. Tan. 1990. "Oligopsony and Quota Rents." Xerox.

————. 1994. "On the Importance and Extent of Rent Sharing in the Multi-Fibre Arrangement," in R. Stern and A. Deardorff (eds.) *Analytical and Negotiating Issues in the Global Trading System*. Ann Arbor: University of Michigan Press.

————. 1996a. "Transferable Licenses vs. Nontransferable Licenses: What is the Difference?" NBER Working Paper 5484. Forthcoming in *International Economic Review*.

————. 1996b. "The Dynamic Behavior of License Price Paths," *Journal of Development Economics* 48: 301–321.

————. 1997a. "Notes on India's MFA Quota Allocation System: The Effect of Rules on Outcomes," *Annales d'Economie et de Statistique and Review of International Economics*. Forthcoming.

————."The Multifibre Arrangement: Challenging the Competitive Framework." in D. Robertson (ed.) *East Asian Trade after the Uruguay* Australian National University. Forthcoming.

Krishna, K., and A. Krueger. "Implementing Free Trade Areas: Rules of Origin and Hidden Protection." *New Directions in Trade Theory.* J. Levinsohn, A. Deardorf, and R. Stern, eds. Ann Arbor: The University of Michigan Press, 1995. To be reprinted in J. Bhagwati and A. Panagaria, Eds.

Krishna, K., W. Martin and L. H. Tan. 1997. "Imputing License Prices: Limitations of a Cost-Based Approach." *Journal of Development Economics*. Forthcoming.

Krishna, K., and J. Morgan. "Implementing Results-Oriented Trade Policies: The Case of the U.S.-Japanese Auto Parts Dispute." Forthcoming in the *European Economic Review.*

Krishna, K., and A. Ozyildirim. "Transferability vs. Nontransferability with Endogenous Investment Choice." 1998. Working paper.

Krishna, K., M. Thursby and S. Roy. "Implementing Market Access." Forthcoming in the *Review of International Economics.*

Krugman, P. and E. Helpman. 1989. *Trade Policy and Market Structure.* Cambridge, Massachusetts: MIT Press.

Kumar, R. and S. R. Khanna. 1990. "India, The Multi-Fibre Arrangement and the Uruguay Round," in C.B. Hamilton (ed.) *Textiles Trade and the Developing Countries.* Washington, D.C.: The World Bank.

Lott, J. R. 1987. "Licensing and Non transferable Rents." *American Economic Review* 77: 453–455.

Maddala, G. S. 1992. *Introduction to Econometrics.* New York: Macmillan.

Majmudar, Madhavi. 1990. "Indian Garment Exports to the USA, 1980–8: Market Access or Supply-Side Response?" *Development Policy Review* 8: 131–153.

Ministry of Commerce. 1987. *The Gazette of Pakistan, Statutory Notifications.* Pakistan.

Morkre, M. E. 1979. "Rent Seeking and Hong Kong's Textile Quota System." *The Developing Economies* 18: 110–118.

————. 1984. "Import Quotas on Textiles: The Welfare Effects of United States Restrictions on Hong Kong," *Bureau of Economics Staff Report to the Federal Trade Commission*, Washington, D.C.: U.S. Government Printing Office.

Pangestu, M. 1987. *The Allocation of Textile Quotas in Indonesia.* Memorandum.

Pindyck, R. S. 1980. "Uncertainty and Exhaustible Resource Markets." *Journal of Political Economy* 88: 1203–1225.

Rodriguez, C. A. 1979. "The Quality of Imports and the Differential Welfare Effects of Tariffs, Quotas and Quality Controls as Protective Devices," *Canadian Journal of Economics* 12: 439–449.

Rothschild, M. and J. E. Stiglitz. 1970. "Increasing Risk: 1. A Definition." *Journal of Economic Theory* 2: 225–243.

Rottenberg, S. 1985. "The Allocation of Textile and Apparel Export Quotas." The World Bank. Mimeo.

Shibata, H. 1968. "A Note on the Equivalence of Tariffs and Quotas." *American Economic Review* 64: 291–303.

Solow, R. M. 1974. "The Economics of Resources or the Resources of Economics." *American Economic Review* 64: 1–14.

Spencer, B. J. 1996 "Quota Licences for Imported Capital Equipment: Could Bureaucrats Ever Do Better Than the Market?" *Journal of International Economics*, forthcoming.

Sung, Y. W. 1989. "The Political Economy of `Voluntary' Export Restraints in Hong Kong." Department of Economics, Chinese University of Hong Kong. Xerox.

Swan, P. L. 1970. "Durability of Consumption Goods," *American Economic Review* 60: 884–894.

Takacs, W. 1987. *Auctioning Import Quota Licenses: An Economic Analysis.* Institute for International Economic Studies, University of Stockholm Seminar Paper No. 390. September.

Tarr, D. and M. Morkre. 1984. *Aggregate Cost to the United States of Tariffs and Quotas on Imports.* Washington, D.C.: Federal Trade Commission.

Textile Asia, various issues.

Trela, I. and J. Whalley. 1990. "Global Effects of Developed Country Trade Restrictions on Textiles and Apparel." *Economic Journal* 100: 1190–1205.

———. 1995. "Internal Quota Allocation Schemes and the Costs of the MFA." *Review of International Economics* 3: 284–306.

UNIDO. 1991. *Handbook of Industrial Statistics 1990.* New York.

United States International Trade Commission. 1991. "The Likely Impact on the United States of a Free Trade Agreement with Mexico," Report to the Committee on Ways and Means of the United States House of Representatives, Washington, D.C. Publication No. 2353.

Van Wijnbergen, S. 1985. "Trade Reform, Aggregate Investment and Capital Flight." *Economics Letters* 19 :369–372.

White, H. 1984. *Asymptotic Theory for Econometricians*, Florida: Academic Press Inc.

Index

STUDIES IN INTERNATIONAL TRADE POLICY

Studies in International Trade Policy includes works dealing with the theory, empirical analysis, political, economic, legal relations, and evaluations of international trade policies and institutions.

General Editor: Robert M. Stern

J